Bishops and Prophets in a Black City

MARTIN WEST

BISHOPS AND PROPHETS
IN A BLACK CITY

African Independent Churches in Soweto
Johannesburg

DAVID PHILIP / CAPE TOWN / 1975

WITH REX COLLINGS / LONDON

First published in 1975 by David Philip, Publisher, 3 Scott Road,
Claremont, Cape Province, South Africa, and Rex Collings Ltd.,
69 Marylebone High Street, London
© text and illustrations Martin West 1975
ISBN 0 949968 45 5 (David Philip, Cape Town)
SBN 90172093 3 (Rex Collings, London)
Printed by Printpak (Cape) Ltd., Dacres Avenue, Epping, Cape,
South Africa

Contents

Appendixes

Illustrations fall between pages 98 & 99

Foreword

BY PROFESSOR MONICA WILSON

African independent churches have been proliferating in South
Africa for ninety years: they continue to increase in number and
membership, and now include about 3 000 organisations. For the
most part they are small, close-knit groups, which provide emotional
support for those living in the urban jungle of Soweto and other
African towns in the Republic and, very often, a link between town
and country where members have relatives. For many of the churches,
Soweto is the headquarters of an organisation which, though number-
ing no more than about 600 members (Wilson and Thompson II,
1971: 81), has branches in various parts of South Africa. In a per-
cipient account of one category of independent church, the Zionists,
in Kwa Mashu, Natal, Dr J. P. Kiernan (1924: 79–90) describes how
they 'close off the outside world' in their ritual. The creation of an
in-group is typical also of many of the churches other than Zionist.

Independent churches have been of great interest to anthropolo-
gists as one of the new social forms in Africa, which can be studied
like the lineages of earlier societies: they are of immediate concern
also to Christians, who ask themselves how clearly the independent
churches reflect the Christian gospel. It is no accident that the first
books on independent churches in South Africa were by missionaries
(Lea 1926; Sundkler 1948). On the one hand these churches have
been characterised as 'schismatic' and 'syncretist', and on the other
as an expression of the working of the Spirit, with small groups of
believers holding close to one another, led by a 'tent-making'
ministry, reflecting the pattern of early Christians. They are recognised as a growing-point of indigenisation in ritual, and are preoccu-
pied with healing, which bulks so large in the New Testament. Is
the explicit recognition of the 'shades', the ancestors, and of witchcraft, in the rituals of some independent churches, to be seen as
'syncretist' or 'indigenisation'? Views on this differ, among both
black and white Christians.

With certain conspicuous exceptions, such as the Presbyterian
Church of Africa (Mzimba's), the leadership in independent churches

has been without much schooling (some leaders have been barely literate) and has felt itself looked down upon by the better-educated black ministers of historic churches (West 1974: 122).

One of the things mentioned again and again as an aim of certain independent churches has been a theological college for the training of its ministry. A 'Joint Council Representing Native Churches' formed in 1922 stated this as an aim and so did one church in Langa in 1962 (West 1974: 122; Wilson and Mafeje 1963: 97). Finance presented a major hurdle, and this was the point at which the Christian Institute of South Africa, led by the Revd Beyers Naudé, with overseas support, sought to provide help. An African Independent Churches Association (AICA) was formed in 1965 and reached a membership of about 400; its 'major aim' was 'to provide theological education for AICA ministers, by establishing theological refresher courses, a theological college, and a theological correspondence course'. (West 1974: 122.)

This aim was achieved, but a struggle for leadership among AICA members developed, and the organisation fragmented. Dr West gives an account of its growth and splitting, based on an intimate knowledge of the leaders concerned and attendance at AICA conferences. The difficulties of large-scale organisation and administration of funds are made clear: without some large-scale co-operation theological training could not be provided. One of the interesting threads is the evidence of the greater success of the Women's Association of the African Independent Churches in maintaining co-operation and conserving funds. WAAIC continues to function. A further point of theoretical and practical interest is that, though independent churches continually split, they sought co-operation with other like groups, both for ordinations and for special services of healing, worship, and evangelisation.

Dr West worked for six months in the Christian Institute as an AICA 'advisor' and then began fieldwork in Soweto. He rightly saw the need to make a systematic investigation of independent churches in a demarcated area, rather than to pursue colourful groups picked at random. Two surveys were made, one of 58 churches and one of 194. Of the 58, 13 were selected for more intensive investigation.

By and large, recruitment of independent churches is from the poor: Zionists recruit from the very poor and illiterate, and from outside their group rather than among the children of Zionists (Kiernan 1974: 86). Dr West found that the independent churches he studied attracted members primarily because they provided healing for those physically and mentally sick. The identity, character, and function of 'prophets' and lesser 'healers' is examined in depth: three prophets even kept diaries of cases for Dr West, and I know at first hand that his rapport with them was excellent. In Soweto (though not among the Zionists Dr Kiernan reports on in Kwa Mashu [1974: 88]) women were important as 'healers' and 'prophets', men as 'bishops' or 'presidents', and in most of the churches examined there was a double hierarchy: that of administrative authority headed by an 'archbishop', 'bishop' or 'president'; and that of 'prophet', 'healer' and 'prayer-woman'. The first consisted almost exclusively of men, the second mostly of women.

Fieldwork in an African city of the Republic of South Africa in 1969–71 was very difficult, whether carried out by a black or a white anthropologist, because, for diverse reasons, many people were suspicious of any sort of investigation. Dr West avoided the very real hazards of being excluded from Soweto by the authorities; cold-shouldered by the people he wanted to study; or attacked in a township where life is very insecure. He had already gained experience as a fieldworker in the *Divided Community* of Port Nolloth (West 1971), and this stood him in good stead. To that should be added the 'shadow' (*isithunzi*) of Dr Beyers Naudé, whose spiritual power subdues even his opponents in South Africa.

I commend this book both as an addition to our knowledge of the dynamics of a contemporary society, and as a means of extending understanding and sympathy in the midst of revolution.

Hogsback, Cape Province

Acknowledgements

It would be impossible to acknowledge all the people who have contributed to this study over the last six years, but certain names must be mentioned. I am very conscious of the privilege of having been able to work with Professor Monica Wilson and Dr Beyers Naudé. Monica Wilson supervised my fieldwork, spent long hours reading and discussing my material, and then devoted the same meticulous attention to the thesis that followed. I owe her much. Beyers Naudé was instrumental in getting the project started, and I learned from him in many ways. As a very small tribute, this book is dedicated to these two exceptional South Africans.

During two years in Soweto I was assisted by many people, in particular the Revd Danie van Zyl, whose wide knowledge of the independent churches was made freely available, and Archbishop M. P Radebe, who acted as a research assistant for part of the time. Of the many citizens of Soweto who befriended me I must single out Archbishop and Mrs M. P. Radebe, Bishop J. E. Makgalemele, President and Mrs A. Nakeli, and President W. B. Macheke. To these and all the others my thanks and my hope that they will not be disappointed by this book.

During the period of writing I was helped by discussions with many people both in South Africa and in Europe. I learned much from seminars at the Universities of Cape Town and the Witwatersrand, and from discussions with Professor Bengt Sundkler, Dr M. L. Daneel and Dr H. J. Becken. The final manuscript has also profited from the response to a number of classes and talks given about the independent churches.

Fieldwork was made possible by generous grants from the Christian Institute of Southern Africa and from the Free University of Amsterdam, and publication has been sponsored by the University of Cape Town and the Algemeen Diakonaal Bureau of the Gereformeerde Kerken in the Netherlands.

I am also most grateful for technical assistance. My father, W. B. West, and the publishers, were most valuable editors. Mr K. A. Behr

of the Department of Geography of the University of Cape Town
drew the map, and Mr Robin Palmer of the School of African
Studies of the same University was responsible for two drawings.

TO MONICA WILSON AND BEYERS NAUDÉ

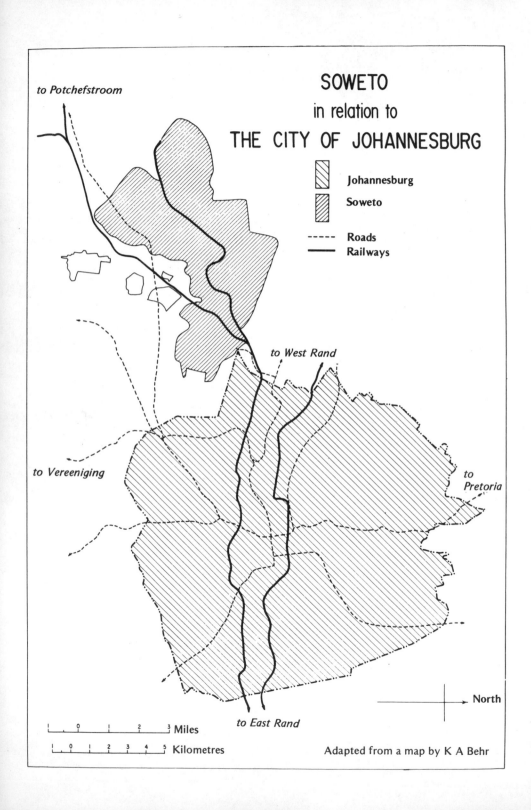

SOWETO
in relation to
THE CITY OF JOHANNESBURG

to Potchefstroom

Johannesburg
Soweto

Roads
Railways

to West Rand

to Vereeniging

to Pretoria

to East Rand

North

0 1 2 3 Miles

0 1 2 3 4 5 Kilometres

Adapted from a map by K A Behr

CHAPTER 1 Introduction

African independent churches described in this book are autonomous groups with an all-African membership and leadership. The African independent church movement as a whole arose from a number of breakaways from white-controlled mission churches, and most churches today have no contacts with any white groups. Most African independent churches are small, and they include a wide variety of types: some have remained very close to the mission bodies from which they originally came, whereas others have combined Christianity with certain traditional beliefs to produce a synthesis very different from their parent bodies. Reaction to these African independent churches has not always been favourable, and they have been criticised by black and white: they have been accused of being purely politically motivated and also of being not sufficiently political; they have been judged as not being Christian at all but bridges back to paganism; they have been looked down on by the educated as uneducated, and by the 'sophisticated' as being 'primitive'.

This sort of criticism is not helped by the fact that most independent churches present a rather narrow and exclusive image to the outsider. Non-members are likely to be misinformed about their beliefs and activities, and sometimes puzzled by their external appearance. Within Soweto the bright colours, sticks, robes and symbols of some of the churches are well known, but in the white city they are relatively unusual and certainly unexplained. Religious and class differences within African society hinder understanding of the African independent churches, and the South African colour-bar ensures that nearly all whites have little or no knowledge of the movement.

Despite criticism and opposition in some quarters, African independent churches have proliferated. Although it is impossible to obtain accurate figures, it was estimated in 1967 that there were approximately 6 000 independent churches on the African continent (Barrett 1968: 38). One of the most interesting features of the distribution of these churches was that half of them were to be found at the tip of the continent, in the Republic of South Africa. This imbalance needs to be explained.

The growth of the African independent church movement in South Africa has been spectacular. From its beginnings in the late nineteenth century a handful of churches grew to include by 1970 approximately 3 000 churches:[1]

Year	Number of churches
1913	30
1939	600
1955	1 286
1960	2 200
1970	3 000

According to census reports in 1960, 21,2 per cent of the total African population in South Africa belonged to independent churches (Population Census, 1960, vol. 3) and in 1967 Barrett (1968: 69) calculated that approximately 3 million people belonged to the movement.[2] The estimated African population in mid-1974 was 17,7 million, so that even if the independent church share of the population has not increased — which is unlikely — their total membership would be about 3,7 million people. In the light of all available information it seems reasonable to estimate that there are about 3 000 African independent churches in South Africa with a total membership of nearly a quarter of the African population — about 4 million people. It is therefore a religious force to be reckoned with.

At this point I should distinguish between what I call 'independent churches' and what I call 'mission churches'. The terminology is

1. Figures from van Zyl (1968), Barrett (1968) and personal communication with the Bantu Administration Department. Barrett (1968: 69) gives 3 000 churches as an extrapolation from the 1960 census figures. He appears not to have considered that there may be a saturation point for the total number of independent churches in South Africa, and that at some stage the growth rate might even out. Most of his figures are taken from official reports or from estimates by social scientists, and there can be no way of checking exact numbers in an ever-changing and often ephemeral movement. However, these figures are the best available.

2. Unfortunately the results of the 1970 census are not yet available. A sample tabulation made available to the author in 1975 suggested that 2,7 million people belonged to the independent churches in 1970 — only 18,4 per cent of the population. If correct this would mean that the churches were losing support. However, the category 'Other Christian' in the census has risen markedly to 1,4 million (9,2 per cent). There is reason to believe that many independent churches are enumerated under this heading, and that consequently the figure for independent churches cannot be accepted as reliable. Based on 1975 population figures, an estimate of 4 million members of the independent churches would still not be excessive. What the census figures do suggest, however, is that the proportion of independent church membership has remained fairly static in the last ten years, at between 20 and 25 per cent of the total African population.

important, to avoid misunderstanding. The churches in Soweto may be categorised according to a wide variety of criteria, both social and theological, and different churches fall into different groupings as the criteria are changed. To take a simple example, churches classified according to the languages used in services would produce very different groupings from those that would arise through a classification based, say, on baptismal practices. In Soweto, however, there is one important, initial criterion on which churches can be divided and that is whether or not a church is entirely under African control.[3] Those churches that are entirely under African control, and which have no links with churches that have any white members, we call African independent churches.

This is not an ideal term, as in some cases 'independent' is taken as having a negative connotation – meaning 'independent from whites' rather than stressing the positive connotation, the African nature of the churches. More importantly, it has been observed that very few of the independent churches use the word 'independent' when describing themselves in an African language. There the terms used would be, in Zulu, *amabandla amaAfrika*, or in Sotho, *dikereke tsa ma-Afrika*, both meaning 'African' churches. However, the term 'independent churches' has become so rooted in the wealth of literature on the subject, that it will be used here to avoid further confusion. The use of the term is not intended to convey any negative connotation whatsoever.

The term 'church' is used in preference to 'sect', 'cult' or 'movement'. The latter terms are generally used by people who do not belong to the groups they describe, and often give the impression that the independent churches are not 'proper' churches, and are in some way inferior; 'separatist' and 'syncretist' also have negative connotations when applied to these churches, and are consequently not used.

A similar problem of terminology exists with those churches that are not independent: they are variously called 'mission churches', 'historical churches', 'white churches', 'established churches', etc., although none of the terms is entirely accurate or suitable. To call them 'historical' or 'established' is to suggest inaccurately that these

3. Dubb (1961) preferred to classify churches according to various degrees of 'European control' rather than adopt a simple mission-church/independent-church dichotomy. While this was useful in terms of the particular church examined in that study, from an independent church point of view the crucial factor is whether a church is under *entirely* African control. Thus many independent churches in Soweto do not regard the African Methodist Episcopal Church as truly independent because, although it has no contact with mission churches in South Africa, it still has strong links with the American church – despite the fact that the American church has a predominantly black membership.

are not attributes of independent churches; to call them 'white churches' is inaccurate in view of the number of multiracial churches in South Africa. The term 'mission church' is thus used here, as in many respects this is the way they are viewed by members of the independent churches. Mission churches, then, are those churches that have white participation at any level of their structure. The scope of this study does not include mission churches, however, so we now turn to the independent churches as represented in Soweto.

In South Africa the greatest concentration of independent churches is found in the urban complexes round the cities of Johannesburg and Pretoria in the Southern Transvaal (Van Zyl 1968: 4). We deal here with the largest complex of townships in this area, known as Soweto. Soweto, described in the next chapter, is an urban sprawl covering some seventy square kilometres with a population of a million people. It is estimated that there are some 900 independent churches represented in Soweto itself, and this study is based on two years of intensive fieldwork among these churches, subject to the restrictions placed on any white fieldworker in an African township (see Appendix 1).

The size and importance of the African independent church movement in South Africa is now being realised in many quarters, but in the early days interest was shown mainly by missionaries — notably those of the Church of Scotland, which suffered a secession in 1898 when the Revd P. J. Mzimba, who had been a minister in the church for twenty-two years, left to form the Presbyterian Church of Africa. The Mzimba secession was discussed in a series of articles in the *Christian Express* in 1899,[4] and mentioned again by a number of writers on missionary affairs (Young 1902: 150f; Wells 1908: 294f; Taylor 1928: 78–9; Shepherd 1942: 245f). African independent churches had been the object of government attention since before the turn of the century (Sundkler 1961: 65), and particularly after the part some church members had played in the Zulu Rebellion of 1906 became known (Sundkler 1961: 69; Marks 1970: 64, 178); but the movement only came to national prominence following the Bulhoek incident of 1921 when over 150 followers of the Israelite leader, Enoch Mgijima, were killed by government forces as a result of their refusal to move off state-owned land.[5] A commission of

4. *Christian Express*, February, March, April and September, 1899. The same journal also published some of the earliest articles on the independent churches. See for example the issues of April 1897, May 1898, and July 1898.

5. The Israelite confrontation with authority is documented in the Report of the Native Affairs Commission relative to 'Israelites' at Bulhoek (A. 4—1921) and in the Report on Native Churches Commission (U.G. 39—1925). See also Sundkler 1961: 72–3. The official report of the Commissioner of Police gives the toll as 163 killed, 129 wounded and a further 95 arrested. As far as be

inquiry following the incident published a report in 1925 which dealt also with the movement as a whole.

The publication of the report led to another early attempt to view the whole independent church movement — that published by the Revd Allen Lea, a missionary, in 1926. In the same year C. T. Loram, one of the members of the Native Churches Commission, published a summary and analysis of the commission's report (1926: 481), and prophesied that 'in spite of the obvious weakness of the separatist churches . . . the desire of the Natives for autonomy in religious matters is undeniable, and there is no doubt that the separatist movement will grow'.

As has been shown, the movement did indeed continue to grow at a rapid rate, but for some time literature concerning the independent churches did not keep pace with their growth. In 1928 an interesting article appeared written by the Revd L. N. Mzimba, a descendant of the founder of the Presbyterian Church of Africa, in which he discussed the rise of independent churches (in Taylor 1928: 86f), but in 1946 a more notable event was an article in *African Studies* by L. Mqotsi and N. Mkele which dealt with the *Ibandla lika-Krestu*. The authors mentioned that despite 'the phenomenal growth in the number of African separatist churches . . . unfortunately no thorough study has hitherto been made'. (Mqotsi and Mkele 1946: 106.) Such a study came in 1948 with the publication of Professor Sundkler's classic *Bantu Prophets in South Africa*. Although it dealt almost exclusively with rural Zulu independent churches, it brought the whole subject of independency to the attention of social scientists.

Following Sundkler's pioneering work, there have been many publications on the subject by missionaries, theologians, historians and social scientists (Barrett 1968: 38). These include a variety of approaches, ranging from theological assessments to historical studies and sociological investigations, and deal with independent churches in many parts of the world.[6]

The broad framework of this study was in fact provided by a suggestion in Sundkler's *Bantu Prophets in South Africa*. His work dealt almost exclusively with rural Zulu independent churches, but pointed out (1961: 80) that:

a study of the influence of urbanization of the South African Bantu on

---

ascertained from the report, only one policeman was wounded. The Israelite Church still exists in Queenstown, and holds an annual service at the graves of those members who were shot. (Vincent Master, personal communication.)

6. A select bibliography on independent churches in South Africa showing the variety of approach would include: Lea, 1926; Mqotsi & Mkele, 1946; Sundkler (1948) 1961; Sundkler, 1960; Schlosser 1948 and 1958; Pauw, 1960; Brandel-Syrier, 1962; Martin, 1964; Missiological Institute, 1965; Oosthuizen, 1967 and 1968.

their church life in general and on the emergence and development of
independent churches in particular, would be very much worthwhile . . .
this important subject still waits to be treated in all its implications and in
its sociological setting.

This suggestion was made over twenty years ago, and since then the
rapid growth of independent churches in urban areas has made the
need for a study of this sort more pressing. The material presented
here attempts to fill the gap in some measure by dealing with a
number of independent churches in a specific urban area, and seeks
to discuss them in relation to their particular environment.

But there is a danger in doing this, as there is in any anthropological study based on intensive fieldwork in a small area. The problem
of explanation has to be faced on both a general and a specific level.
Clearly the fact that there are so many African independent churches
in Soweto suggests that some aspects of Soweto may in fact stimulate
their growth. But there are also a great many similar churches in the
rest of South Africa, so any explanation should come to terms with
this. Extending the argument, there are a great many independent
churches in the rest of Africa which show similarities to South African
ones (see, for example, Daneel 1971; Hayward 1963; Welbourn 1961;
Welbourn & Ogot 1966; Wishlade 1965). So any explanation should
not be peculiarly South African, but take in the whole continent as
Barrett (1968) has tried to do.

A further danger is in seeing the African independent church
movement as entirely an African phenomenon. This view is of course
facilitated by the uniquely African aspects of the movement. Non-
Africans, particularly, see this in the vernacular languages used, in
the borrowings from African belief and ritual, in the colourful
uniforms and emotional services, in faith-healing and immersion in
rivers. In isolation it is easy to see in this something peculiar to
Africa, and for those who look down on the movement to relate it
to a particular people in time and space. However, if one looks at
other areas and other times important parallels are apparent which
help to place the movement in a better perspective.

One need go no further than Knox's great study of the history of
Christian enthusiasm. Knox (1950) starts with the first Epistle of
Paul to the Corinthians, where at that early date in the history of
Christianity the Christians at Corinth were divided into parties, and
had to be warned by Paul against fraternisation with heathens and
against too free a use of spiritual gifts; he argues convincingly that
here in first-century Corinth was an enthusiastic movement. From
there he roams the centuries in search of enthusiastic movements,
and some striking parallels with contemporary African independent
churches are found. The Familists of the seventeenth century carried

staves, as do many independent church members today; James Nay-
ler in England and Jemima Wilkinson in America showed messianic
tendencies to match anything Sundkler could produce in Zululand;
the description of the preaching and propheting of the French Cami-
sard prophets in the seventeenth century, with shivering, foaming at
the mouth and falling, far exceeds anything observed of a prophet's
behaviour in Soweto; and similar parallels could be drawn in the
healing by convulsions in the Saint-Médard cemetery, the Wesleyan
paroxysms, and the devotional dances of the Shakers. These are but
a few examples of the many that could be drawn from the history
of Christianity.

If we move to the present day we can find further parallels on
other continents. Perhaps the most obvious comparison is to be made
between African independent churches and the 'store-front' churches
of the United States of America. These small, predominantly black
churches with their emotional services, their charismatic leaders and
their appeal to the poor and ill-educated, have much in common
with their African counterparts, and show as much variety (Fauset
1944). Similar, too, are many of the numerous other Christian sects
in America (Clark 1949), and important parallels can be drawn with
the burgeoning pentecostal movements in various parts of the world
today (Hollenweger 1972).

It is important to bear these parallels in mind for a balanced view
of the African independent church movement. They will be dealt
with again in the final chapter. But before explanations and comparisons can be made it is necessary to present some detailed information on the independent churches in Soweto and on the environment in which they find themselves. In the following chapter we
shall look at what is known about Soweto and the condition of the
people that live in it and then turn to the various types of church
found in the area — mission and independent. The variety of churches
within the independent church movement is discussed and various
broad types are presented in terms of their most important attributes.

With the large number of independent churches in Soweto it was
decided to do a general survey of as many churches as possible before
studying one or two in greater detail. A preliminary general survey
eventually included 252 churches, and with this background three
churches were selected for detailed study, as fairly representative of
the different types of church in Soweto (see Appendix 1). In chapter
3 they are described at some length and comparisons are made
between them and the churches covered in the general survey.

The role of charismatic leadership within the independent churches
and their importance in affording opportunities of leadership has
been stressed by a number of writers, and chapter 4 offers an analysis

of leadership and leadership patterns, succession to office, various
types of hierarchy, and the status and functions of church leaders.
Sundkler (1961: 106) distinguished between independent church
leaders who were bureaucratic and those who were prophetic leaders,
depending on the type of church. An interesting development in
Soweto was the existence of both sorts of leader within the same
church, in the persons of the bishop and the prophet.

While leadership is analysed in one or other way in much of the
literature on independent churches, insufficient attention has been
paid to the followers who form the bulk of church membership. In
chapter 5 there is an analysis and description of followers of the
three selected churches, as well as discussion about congregations
and the role of men and women members. Independent church
followers emerge from this as middle-aged people of little education
and largely rural background with, in the main, unskilled jobs providing low salaries. A particularly interesting finding was the fact
that the congregations of nearly all the churches visited cut across
ethnic and linguistic ties, with members coming from different tribal
groups and speaking different languages in the same church.

A striking aspect of some of the congregations studied was the
very high proportion of members who said that they had joined
their church because they had been healed in it. As fieldwork progressed the importance of faith-healing in a large section of the
independent church movement became clear, and a considerable
amount of time was devoted to it. In chapter 6 healing practices
are examined in detail: the various types of healing, the various
sorts of healers and particularly the prophets, and the great variety
of complaints that are treated by them. Some life histories of prophets are given, as well as information taken from the diaries of two
healers. The chapter also compares independent church healing with
western techniques, and explains the attraction of the former for
many independent church members.

The independent church movement is often portrayed as being
divided against itself, plagued with leadership disputes and highly
fissile. While these attributes are present to some degree it became
clear during fieldwork that there was considerable co-operation
among and within churches. Chapter 7 examines, firstly, networks
of co-operation within individual churches and, secondly, between
different churches. Reasons for the extent of inter-church contact
are advanced. Chapter 7 deals with what has been called informal
church contacts, and chapter 8 continues with more formal contacts
as embodied in formal associations of independent churches. Associations of independent churches exist throughout South Africa, and a
number operate in Soweto. They allow considerable autonomy to

individual churches on the one hand, and on the other allow member churches to combine and co-operate for various purposes. Most of this chapter deals with the largest of these associations, the African Independent Churches' Association, and examines in depth its aims, objects and problems. Two smaller associations are compared, and the wider role of these movements is considered.

Opinions have varied over the degree of syncretism in the beliefs of the African independent churches, and this question is discussed in chapter 9. The role of traditional African beliefs and rituals is examined in independent church ritual, with special attention being paid to the shades, animal offerings, spirit possession and the parallels between independent church prophets and traditional diviners. Independent church ritual is discussed as a positive synthesis of western and African elements, and not as a nativistic phenomenon.

The final chapter seeks to sum up the attraction of the independent churches in Soweto for their members and to place the whole movement in perspective. The general appeal of the movement is examined as well as its specific relation to the urban situation. The relationship between church structure and social structure is explored in relation to the process of urbanisation, and on this basis the future of the African independent churches is considered.

CHAPTER 2 Soweto and Its Churches

There are approximately 900 African independent churches in Soweto. This is the largest single concentration of these churches in South Africa, and one of the questions to be pursued is the reason for this. Before describing the churches, however, it is necessary to know something about Soweto itself, its people and their condition.

Soweto (the name is derived from the first letters of South-Western Townships) officially comprises twenty-one townships coverir ; some 70 square kilometres south-west of the city of Johannesburg. Its nearest point is about 13 kilometres from the centre of the city, and its farthest more than 30 kilometres away. This area, the official Soweto, was under the control of the Johannesburg City Council until it was taken over by the West Rand Bantu Affairs Board in July 1973. However, when speaking of Soweto, its inhabitants generally include two large townships on its borders, Diepkloof and Meadowlands, which were under the control of the central government's Bantu Resettlement Board.[1] These areas, together with the adjacent Dobsonville, a township attached to the suburb of Roode-poort, form the largest African urban area in South Africa with a population of nearly one million people.

Despite Soweto's size and importance, outsiders know little about it. Few South African whites have ever visited it (special permits being needed for such visits), and to many Africans in different parts of the country it is an almost mythical place, typifying *eGoli*, the City of Gold, with its teeming population, its danger and excitement. In fact Soweto is too large and diverse to be described accurately — it is simply the largest and most cosmopolitan African city in South Africa.

1. Following the Bantu Resettlement Act of 1954, thousands of Africans have been moved from areas around Johannesburg to the Soweto area. The moves have been compulsory, with many people losing freehold rights in the process. By the end of 1968 the Bantu Resettlement Board had moved 22 516 families and 6 494 single people (Hellmann 1971: 3). There are a number of differences between those areas controlled by the Board and those under the jurisdiction of the Johannesburg City Council (Hellmann 1971: 3-4).

There have been a number of phases in the development of Soweto (P. Lewis 1966; Maud 1938), starting with the proclamation of the goldfields of the Witwatersrand in 1886, when the first African labourers started working on the mines. Up to 1917 civic authorities accepted no responsibility for the welfare of the African population in the area until high mortality rates following an influenza epidemic in 1918 resulted in the start of the first housing scheme. In 1927 a Native Affairs Department was created and building began in what was to become Soweto.

In 1939 thousands of Africans moved to town following the outbreak of war and the demands created by the commercial and industrial expansion as a result of the war effort. The supply of housing was totally inadequate and squatter camps and shantytowns emerged (Hellmann 1948). After the war it was estimated that about 50 000 African families were living in bad slum conditions, but the supply of new housing was slow, partly through high building costs and partly through official hesitance (P. Lewis 1966: 6–7). But the 1951 Bantu Building Workers Act made it legal to train African workers in the building trades provided they worked only in proclaimed African townships, and the wages paid to these men, lower than those of their white counterparts, enabled more houses to be built than with white labour. The introduction of the Bantu Services levy in 1953 also assisted. Whereas in 1953 fewer than 18 000 houses had been built, by 1970 there were 70 000 houses and 9 hostels accommodating 15 000 men.

The population of Soweto has grown proportionately. According to a Department of Statistics report the 1970 population of Soweto, including Meadowlands and Diepkloof, was just under 600 000 people. However, no accurate assessment of the true population is available. With the policy of the South African Government in endorsing out all 'superfluous' Africans to rural areas, there is an understandable reluctance to take part in census enumerations, particularly as it is believed that there are a great many Africans living in Soweto illegally. The problem of estimating Soweto's population has been indicated by Hellmann, who says: 'Estimates of the African population in the Soweto complex by people closely concerned with its administration vary from 750 000 to one million.' (Hellmann 1971: 28n.)

In this period of rapid development, the Soweto complex has become not only the largest, but also the most cosmopolitan African city in South Africa. Although Zulu- and Sotho-speaking people predominate, citizens of Soweto belong to virtually all South African tribes. While Zulu is narrowly the most-spoken language, people also speak Xhosa, Swazi, Pedi, Tswana, Sotho, Ndebele, Venda and

Tsonga. As would be expected in any city of this size, the population is heterogeneous with people of different languages, backgrounds, religions, levels of education, occupations, and attitudes to urban life. As Hellman says (1971: 7):

> The first thing that must be stressed in talking about the people of Soweto is their variety. They range from unskilled labourers to highly-trained professional men and women, sophisticated businessmen and executives in personnel departments. There are washerwomen and models, artisans and artists, but mostly there are ordinary working people.

There are relatively few opportunities for employment in Soweto[2] apart from the approximately 1 500 small businesses in the area, so most working people commute daily to the city. Nearly a quarter of a million people commute at peak hours by train alone, and many more use buses and private transport. Soweto, therefore, is largely a dormitory suburb.

Soweto is a dormitory suburb by decree of the South African Government, and government policy regarding urban Africans has a pervasive effect on the whole community. Thus much of life in Soweto is externally determined, with the most important determinants being what Mitchell (1966: 50) has called 'administrative and political limitations'. Soweto was administered until 1973 by the Non-European Affairs Department of the Johannesburg City Council within a framework of legislation laid down by the central government and enforced by various government departments and officials. P. Lewis (1966) cites ninety Acts of Parliament passed between 1945 and 1966 which affect the administration of Soweto and other African townships, and which lay down rules and regulations pertaining to most aspects of life, including among other things mobility, education, land tenure, housing, transport, witchcraft, building, trespassing, brewing of beer, marriage, and settlement of labour disputes.

The citizen of Soweto has no say in the numerous laws and regulations that materially affect him. They are made by the Parliament of the Republic without consultation with Africans. Representation in Soweto itself is restricted to an Urban Bantu Council, which has no executive power, and may act only in an advisory capacity to the white authorities. As a largely powerless body, Soweto's Urban Bantu Council does not enjoy widespread support, and has a history of low polls and refused recommendations (Horrell 1970: 155; 1971: 174). Soweto is administered through a system of eleven

---

2. Hellmann 1971: 1: 'As [Soweto] is not permitted to develop any industries of its own, the work opportunities within its area are very limited.' In the 1967 edition of the same work, Hellmann estimated that there were only approximately 6 000 employment opportunities for Africans in Soweto.

administrative offices throughout the area, each in the charge of a
white superintendent. Superintendents wield considerable power,
including the right to have residents removed and sent to rural areas.

Within the severe limitations laid down by the central government
the Johannesburg City Council provided Soweto with more recrea-
tional and welfare facilities than any other African urban area in
South Africa. To do this it subsidised Soweto from general rates,
the estimated subsidy for the period 1970–1 being R1 250 000
(Hellmann 1971: 5). Services thus provided included a variety of
sports fields, a sheltered-employment workshop, schemes for assisting the aged, disabled and destitute, and a comprehensive health
service including seven general clinics as well as tuberculosis, dental
and child health clinics. In addition various welfare organisations
operate, among other services, a school-feeding scheme and a number
of crèches for children of working mothers.

As mentioned, the central government introduced a system of
Bantu Affairs Boards to take over from local authorities. The purpose
was to provide for a more efficient administration of African areas,
and to allow greater mobility of African workers (Horrell 1972:
132–41). Under Government policy, however, all areas have to be
financially 'self-balancing', and it was feared that the take-over by
the Boards would mean that in Soweto's case more than R1 000 000
worth of essential services would be lost (Hellman 1971: 5).

Despite the services which then existed, however, Soweto was
beset with a variety of problems over which the population in most
cases had no control. Soweto's African newspaper *World* listed some
of the most urgent problems as: the very high crime rate, families
being split by legislation, overcrowded schools, and a general lack
of facilities (*World*, 13/10/69). Soweto is a dangerous place to live
in. A market research survey in 1969 revealed that 30 per cent of
those interviewed had been attacked on the street at one time or
another, and that 22 per cent had been robbed on the street, that
15 per cent had been robbed on trains and that 14 per cent had had
their homes burgled. More recent figures showed that in the first six
months of 1973 there were 255 reported murders, 3 652 cases of
assault, 1 944 cases of theft and 366 cases of rape and attempted
rape. Over the twelve-year period 1962–73 just over 15 000 serious
crimes were investigated (Horrell 1975: 88). The murder rate in
Soweto is one of the highest in the country, and Baragwanath
Hospital adjoining Soweto has one of the largest paraplegic units
in the world, which deals with the results of stabbing cases.

In addition to the high incidence of crime, numerous laws and
regulatìons add to insecurity. As Hellmann points out (1971: 14):
'The Bantu (Urban Areas) Consolidation Act of 1945, with the 21

amending Acts passed in subsequent years, is the main instrument governing the lives of urban Africans.' The right of Africans to remain in 'prescribed areas' — and all towns fall in this category — is governed by Section 10 of the Act. People are qualified to live in town under Section 10 if they can prove 10 years' continuous employment with one employer or 15 years' continuous residence, but such qualifications do not provide immunity from being 'endorsed out' of the urban area by administrative action. This can be done for a number of reasons.

While Section 10 at present provides certain limited safeguards, there has been talk in Government circles of abolishing it completely. The pass laws are intimately related to influx control, and regular raids and inspections are carried out in Soweto to detect illegal residents. Raids on houses are usually conducted in the early hours. Two police forces operate in Soweto — the national police and a municipal police force.

Citizens of Soweto have no freehold rights, nor the right to choose the area in which they would prefer to live.[3] In 1968 a government directive prohibited Africans from building their own homes in Soweto on 30-year leasehold plots as some had been doing; a further regulation prohibited those who had already built homes from bequeathing their properties to their heirs, and required them to sell to the local authorities (Hellmann 1971: 6). Other regulations have prevented certain categories of women from obtaining houses, and made it very difficult for widows to retain possession of their houses after the death of their husbands (Hellmann 1971).

Residents in Soweto are faced also with the problem of poverty. A survey by the Non-European Affairs Department in 1967 found that 68 per cent of the families living in Soweto earned below the estimated minimum monthly income necessary for a family of five, which at that time was approximately R53. With the rising cost of living, a survey in 1971 placed the Effective Minimum Level of income for a family of five at approximately R74 per month, and in 1973 the figure was between R110 and R120 (Horrell 1974: 199). Most families cannot survive unless the women go out to work, and this adds to the burden of the women in Soweto, who, as we shall see later, are saddled with the problems of household budgets and

3. Ethnic grouping in urban townships became obligatory in 1955. By that time a number of Soweto's townships were inextricably mixed. All townships have now been zoned, and when a house is vacated it can be rented only to an occupant of the right group. However, zoning itself is imprecise: 'Nguni' townships may include Zulu, Xhosa, Swazi and Ndebele, for example. In 1971 there were 13 townships with more-or-less effective zoning, and 12 which were mixed. At the end of 1970 more than 13 000 families were on the official waiting list for houses.

educating children as well as having to earn in jobs which are usually a long way from home. All in all, Dr Hellmann (1971: 9) has summed up the situation of the average family: 'It still remains abundantly clear that for urban Africans, the majority clinging precariously to the breadline, resources cannot meet basic needs.'

All these factors create a feeling of deep insecurity in most of Soweto's population. They may not own land, they may not elect where to live, their sources of employment are limited by administrative decree, and their continued residence in town is subject to the decision of white administrators. It has been made clear by the government that all Africans are in urban areas in a 'casual capacity' irrespective of where they were born.[4]

The citizen of Soweto is therefore, to use the *World*'s phrase, 'poor and voiceless'. He lives insecurely in a large and uniform complex of townships with row after row of uniform houses (usually called 'matchboxes' by the locals because of their shape and size) with inadequate facilities. Schools in Soweto are badly overcrowded (in 1970 at least 5 000 children were turned away) and he is likely to have difficulty in educating his children. He lives in an area where crime is rife, and where a variety of complex laws and regulations affect him directly, although he has no say in them.

Soweto itself is a strange mixture of uniformity and diversity. Most of its citizens share the lot of all Africans in South Africa: their lack of political power and their unequal share of resources.[5] Most, as Dr Hellmann says, are ordinary working people, struggling to make ends meet. But Soweto shows also a diversity of people of different languages and backgrounds and attitudes. Soweto mirrors many of the changes taking place in African society; its citizens include people of conservative, rural background and highly sophisticated urban-dwellers and there is a growing differentiation, in socio-economic terms, among its population. It is also the scene of a fast-growing black consciousness movement among the young and better-educated. These factors are magnified, in comparison with other African urban areas, by Soweto's greater size, and in turn they highlight the situation of the poorer, less-educated, conservative Sowetan — the sort of person, in fact, who belongs to the African

4. This statement, by the Minister of Bantu Administration and Development, made in Parliament in 1971, is typical: 'Section 10 of the Urban Areas Act does not confer rights of citizenship . . . but only grants general exemption from influx control. . . . I say that the Bantu are here in a casual capacity, i.e. they do not have the comparable entrenched claims, rights and privileges which the Whites have in the White area. The Bantu have them in their Bantu homelands.' (Hansard, 15, 19.5.71:7196.)

5. See, for example, Horrell (1973) for figures on economic inequalities (p. 47–9) and differences in education (p. 69–82) and health (p. 83–7). See also Randall (1971) and the whole series of Spro-Cas reports.

independent churches.

The social situation in Soweto has indeed played an important part in the rise of African independent churches in the area. In later chapters we show how these churches are able to provide important outlets for the poorer and less-educated people in Soweto, and how in some respects they are able to satisfy needs which have arisen out of their specific urban situation. But first it is necessary to know something about the churches in Soweto.

THE CHURCHES

Most Christian denominations in South Africa are represented in Soweto, and have church buildings there. Edelstein (1971: 85) states that 'Soweto has 154 churches, 70 recognised denominations and 900 sects', although the last figure is an approximation. No accurate, up-to-date information is available regarding church adherence. One source is a market research project among Soweto housewives who were interviewed in 1962 and 1967. In that period African independent church membership had risen from 14 per cent to 28 per cent and mission church affiliation had dropped from 72 per cent to 65 per cent (Market Research Africa 1968: 21). Although the figures are open to question on a number of grounds, they give a broad impression of the relative strengths of the independent churches and the mission churches, and indicate how the independent churches have been gaining ground.

In discussing the independent churches in Soweto in any detail, there is again a problem of terminology, as various attempts have been made to classify different types of independent church. The first and most durable classification has been that of Sundkler (1961: 38–59), who distinguished between 'Ethiopian' and 'Zionist' independent churches. Ethiopian churches were those that had broken from mission churches or their offshoots, on broadly political grounds, and which remained patterned on their parent churches. They are typified by such churches as the Presbyterian Church of Africa, which retains the mission-church constitution, hymnbook, doctrine, and form of service, but which refuses to have anything to do with the mission church.

The Zionists, on the other hand, were a pentecostal, apostolic movement, stressing the influence of the Holy Spirit and of divine healing, and combining both African and European cultural elements. The elementary Ethiopian–Zionist classification is still used by some people, but it has been modified in different ways by certain authors. For example Martin (1964) was instrumental in adding the category 'messianic', which had been suggested first by Sundkler.[6]

6. Messianism has attracted a lot of interest, particularly from theologians

Turner introduced the term 'Aladura' as an alternative for 'Zionist', and later incorporated Sundkler's categories in a more detailed typology (Hayward 1963: 13). Other authors have attempted to classify according to different criteria using different terminology — for example Oosthuizen (1968) suggested distinctions between 'churches', 'sects' and 'nativistic movements', with various subdivisions, and Pauw (1960) produced yet another typology.

It must be questioned whether the various typologies have in fact added significantly to our knowledge of the independent church movement: too often they are like Leach's butterfly-collecting, where information is pigeon-holed and the terms of reference are inadequately explained (Leach 1961: 2–5). To take a simple example, some independent churches are Sabbatarian. But to create a category of independent church called 'Sabbatarian' and place all Sabbatarian churches in it may be misleading, in that Sabbatarianism may not be the most important feature of the church. Even if it is, however, the new category has not increased our knowledge of the churches themselves.

Consequently there will be no attempt in this study to produce a new typology of independent churches. In describing the variety of churches in Soweto, I shall go no further than the categories — which are not clear-cut — recognised by the churches themselves.

The first broad division of independent churches in Soweto corresponds roughly to Sundkler's Ethiopian–Zionist dichotomy. A general distinction is made between churches that have remained close to protestant mission churches in structure, doctrine, and dress — for example the Presbyterian Church of Africa, the Zulu Congregational Church, or the Bantu Methodist Church — and those churches of apostolic or pentecostal background with an emphasis on the working of the Holy Spirit and a form that combines both African and western attributes. Churches in the former category, while recognising that they belong to one sort of independent church, do not have a name for themselves. The term 'Ethiopian' (*amaTopia*) is generally used only by people who do not belong to that type of church, or by members of churches that have 'Ethiopian' specifically in their title — for example the Ethiopian Church of South Africa, or the Ethiopian Catholic Church. In the absence of any suitable term, however, it seems best to refer to this

(Martin, 1964), following Sundkler's new emphasis on the subject in the second edition of his standard work (1961: 302, 323–337). Sundkler emphasised the 'strictly limited' number of messianic groups, and has himself encountered only five (personal communication, 1972). No messianic groups were found in the research conducted in Soweto. The concept itself has not been sufficiently rigorously defined, at least sociologically, and we conclude therefore that messianism has received attention disproportionate to its sociological importance.

sort of church as being 'Ethiopian-type'.

In contrast to Ethiopian-type churches are those that are 'Zionist-type', where the term Zionist (*amaZiyoni*) is most often used by members, although some people prefer to call themselves Apostolics. The difference between Zionists and Apostolics will be discussed below, but for the moment they can be taken as one group. The distinction between the two types of church is perhaps clearest from the Zionist side — for example there is often a distinction made between what are called in Sotho *dikereke tsa Moya*, churches of the Spirit, and *dikereke tsa molau*, churches of the law. Zionists see a basic division between those churches in which the Holy Spirit is believed to work through dreams, faith-healing and spirit possession, and those churches where this is not a factor.

A more visible distinction between the two types is in church dress. The Ethiopian-type churches will often use black in their uniforms, and are sometimes referred to as *amabandla ezingubo ezimnyama*, churches with black clothes. For Zionist-type churches black is the colour of death and disease, and is ordinarily never worn — their uniforms are basically white, symbolic of cleanliness and purity, with a number of other symbolic colours such as blue, green, red and yellow. This difference is occasionally seen in the derogatory terms used by members of the different groups. Zionists sometimes refer to *izimvu* or *izimbuzi ezimnyama*, black sheep or goats (the latter being more insulting), and in turn are referred to as *amalanda*, (white) tick-birds.

While Zionist-type churches may be viewed from outside as one homogeneous group, in fact they display many differences. The range of differences usually defies neat classification, and the only division of any importance appears to be that between Apostolics and Zionists. This is largely a qualitative distinction which is often unclear, although it is important to some churches. Broadly speaking, while Apostolics and Zionists have basically the same type of church, Apostolics would claim to be less 'traditional' than Zionists, and although still fundamentalist, would place more emphasis on education and theological training for ministers. For example, a minister in an Apostolic church explained in the following way why he had left a Zionist church: 'I left the Zionist church because there was a difference. Because I liked the teaching of the Bible and they spent more time propheting. We that have a bit of education like to learn more about the Bible. . . .' It also appears that some churches — even though they may have 'Zion' in their title — prefer to be called Apostolic as they feel that Zionists are often regarded as rather 'primitive' by mission church members as well as other townspeople.

It should not be assumed that the Zionist-type/Ethiopian-type division in Soweto is clear cut. This becomes obvious if one tries to isolate, for example, distinctive features of Zionist-type churches. A long list of such features could be drawn up, and would include among the more important: faith-healing, the presence of prophets, use of drums, dancing and spirit possession during services, insistence on river baptism by immersion, holy communion services at night only, and wearing of special uniforms. These specific features have been mentioned because their presence in a church is not a matter of debate — as for example would be the degree to which traditional customs have been integrated into a church's ritual, which is another very important aspect of many Zionist churches.

Taking the first six features mentioned — healing, prophets, drums, dancing, night communion and river baptism — it is quite clear that in Soweto any church that exhibits all six would be regarded as Zionist-type; and conversely, any church that had none of these features would definitely fall into the Ethiopian-type category. Table 1 below gives the incidence of these six features for a survey of 194 independent churches in Soweto (survey B, see Appendix 1). and shows that while healing was common to all, the other features varied. Thus healing was a feature of *all* the churches surveyed, including some Ethiopian-type churches, although it is generally regarded as a feature of only Zionist-type churches. At the same time, another general Zionist feature — the use of drums — was found in far fewer Zionist-type churches than might have been expected.

TABLE 1 : FEATURES OF 194 INDEPENDENT CHURCHES

Feature	*Incidence*	*Per cent*
Healing	194	100
River baptism	180	93
Dancing	175	90
Prophets	170	88
Night communion	154	79
Drums	121	62

The lack of a clear-cut division may also be viewed in another way, still using the same six features. Table 2 below gives the incidence of the features for four offshoots of the Church of Christ Mission (CCM). (The first three churches in this table have the same name: the Church of Christ Mission. The fourth is called the Bantu Church of Christ Mission.)

TABLE 2 : CHURCH OF CHRIST MISSION

	Prophets	Drums	Night Communion	Dancing	River Baptism	Healing
CCM-1	No	No	No	No	Yes	Yes
CCM-2	No	No	Yes	Yes	Yes	Yes
CCM-3	Yes	Yes	No	Yes	Yes	Yes
CCM-4	Yes	Yes	Yes	Yes	Yes	Yes

The original Church of Christ Mission, from which the churches in Table 2 split, exhibits none of the six features, and the four offshoots mentioned here could be placed on different points of a continuum between ideal-type Zionist and ideal-type Ethiopian.

This is broadly the position for all the independent churches in Soweto: a continuum exists, with perhaps most churches falling towards one end or the other — but any simple division would not be entirely accurate, as the variety of churches found within the independent church movement precludes easy classification. Thus the Zionist-type/Ethiopian-type distinction offered here is strictly an oversimplification although it corresponds broadly to the situation in Soweto.

Arguments against an external classification in any more detailed form have been mentioned above. Classifications used by members of the churches themselves are of more interest in this study, but again they vary according to the classifier, and the same problem of frame of reference applies. Since Zionist-type churches are the major focus of this study, their classification is of most interest, and reference has already been made to the 'church of the law'/'church of the Spirit' dichotomy, as well as to the distinction between Apostolics and Zionists.

FIG. i

	Spirit	*No Spirit*
Black control	Zionists Apostolics	Ethiopian-type
White control	Some pentecostal mission churches	Most mission churches

From the Zionist point of view there appear to be two major factors in classifying churches in Soweto: whether a church is entirely under black control or not, and whether or not it emphasises the work of the Spirit. These two factors can be brought together in a simple diagram, as in Fig. i.

It is not possible to say categorically that one factor is more important than another — thus on a theological level the Spirit factor is most important, whereas on a socio-political level the question of black control is dominant. This can be seen, for example, in the fact that Zionist-type churches will co-operate with Ethiopian-type churches in certain associations, but not with white apostolic missions.

CHAPTER **3 Three Churches**

Some of the problems of attempting to classify independent churches in Soweto were pointed out in the previous chapter. In any movement of 3 000 individual churches, with limited contact, there must be considerable variety, and this variety is to be found in the 900 independent churches in Soweto. It is therefore impossible to describe independent churches in Soweto in any comprehensive sense. But it has been suggested that certain broad divisions do exist within the movement, and in this chapter we shall examine three churches in Soweto in some detail — the first two being broadly Zionist-type, and the third, for purposes of comparison, Ethiopian-type.

This detailed description gives some idea of what some, perhaps most, of the independent churches are like in Soweto, without claiming that they are archetypal. The churches described here, for example, are relatively well established with a bureaucratic organisation and no messianic tendencies. Doubtless in Soweto there are ephemeral prophet bands, and there may be one or two budding messiahs, but two years of fieldwork involving contacts with nearly 300 churches suggests that the majority fall into the categories of the churches described here.

The three churches were selected for detailed study after a preliminary survey of 58 churches and before a second survey of 194 churches (surveys A and B, see Appendix 1). The second part of this chapter compares important aspects of the selected churches with information collected from the churches in the two surveys, thus giving a somewhat broader view of the movement in Soweto. The surveys do not include very large churches, such as the Zion Christian Church which is reputed to have well over 200 000 members; firstly because there are very few such churches, and secondly because their size makes them worthy of study on their own. As will be seen, the churches described here are 'average' in terms of the total number contacted.

THE BANTU BETHLEHEM CHRISTIAN APOSTOLIC CHURCH OF SOUTH AFRICA (BBCAC)
This church, which has its headquarters in Central Western Jabavu,

Soweto, was founded in Johannesburg on 28 November 1938 by the
Revd Gilbert Radebe. He had broken away from the Apostolic Faith
Mission to which his parents belonged, and in which he had been
brought up. After eight years as leader the founder died in 1946, but
before his death he nominated his younger brother, M. P. Radebe,
to succeed him, provided that he was married before taking over the
church leadership.[1]

M. P. Radebe succeeded his brother four months after his death
in 1946, and by 1972 he had been leader of the church for over
twenty-five years. He was born in the Orange Free State and joined
his brother's church when he came to Johannesburg in 1941. As a
young man of 24 when he assumed the leadership he had only the
title 'Reverend', but in 1952 he was named President, and was finally
consecrated Archbishop in 1962, sixteen years after first becoming
leader. He has a standard-four education, and has taken a number of
short correspondence Bible-study courses.

In common with most other independent churches, the BBCAC
has an elaborate leadership hierarchy. At the time of the study, the
church had an Archbishop, a Vice-Bishop, a President, and a number
of ministers, deacons, evangelists, preachers and sidesmen.[2] In addition there were two secretaries, one of whom was also a minister,
and a church treasurer. The Conference of the church, held annually
and usually in July, elects all office-bearers. The climax of the Conference is the final service when ordinations and installations take
place.

As will be shown in detail in chapter 4, the various office-bearers
in the independent churches have specifically defined roles. To take
one example, the Archbishop or Vice-Bishop would ordain ministers,
who would in turn be allowed to ordain evangelists, and so on. It is
also customary for office-bearers to be promoted from time to time
until their particular ceiling is reached — for most the rank of Minister. But the BBCAC, in common with a number of other churches,
had a senior category — that of President — for those promoted
above the rank of Minister. People holding this title would usually

1. It became clear during this study that a general requirement exists in
nearly all independent churches that men holding the rank of minister or above
should be married. It is felt that unmarried men would not have the confidence
of their congregation, as they are not fully adult. Two specific cases arose during
the research period: one of a man who was not ordained as a minister because
his wife was ill and could not attend, and the second of a man who was expelled
from his church, although he was a successful minister, because it was found
that he was unmarried.

2. A sidesman is usually called *umgosa* in the independent churches, a term
meaning elder or deacon in mission churches. The *umgosa* in the independent
churches fulfils the role of doorman and usher. The term is sometimes translated by church leaders as 'porter' or 'steward'.

have some regional responsibility and rank third equal in the hierarchy after the Archbishop and Vice-Bishop. The importance of this office as the church expanded and drew in senior members was shown by the fact that in 1973 the church had not one but five Presidents (which included the original President, appointed on grounds of age and seniority in the church, three men with responsibilities for Carletonville, the Transkei and Durban, and the newly promoted General Secretary).

As is usual in most independent churches, the women have their own hierarchy. In this church it consists of women who hold office by virtue of the position of their husbands, as well as some elected members. The leader of the women is the Lady Bishop, wife of the Archbishop, who is assisted by a deputy, *mongamedikazi*. The most important elected position is that of Chairlady, who presides at meetings but not services. The chairlady, too, has an assistant. The next position in the hierarchy, the Organiser, is also elected, as are the Secretary and Treasurer. The rest of the hierarchy hold position by virtue of their husbands: wives of ministers (*abefundisikazi*), deacons, evangelists, preachers and sidesmen.

Women's services — known as *manyano* (Brandel-Syrier 1962) — are held every Thursday afternoon. Full uniform is worn, and only *manyano* women are present. At these services there is often emotionalism and public confession. The women's *manyano* of the BBCAC is in many respects the backbone of the church, and its members are much respected.

As in all churches of this type, prophets are extremely important. Very often they stand outside the established hierarchy, although their actual authority may be considerable. In the BBCAC the major prophet is the Lady Bishop, and there are a number of lesser prophets, most of whom are women.

The BBCAC, like the majority of independent churches, has never been an officially recognised church. Prior to the early 1960s a church could receive certain benefits — for example travel concessions for ministers and building sites for churches — only if it was registered by the government (Sundkler 1961: 73–9). With the great rise in the number of independent churches it was impossible for the authorities to check applications for registration, and the whole system was finally abandoned in favour of one where local authorities are given power to grant concessions based on the merits of individual applications.[3] Despite this new provision, the BBCAC enjoys no concessions — it has no church building sites, nor ministers who are marriage

3. The Bantu Administration Department in Pretoria keeps files on every church which writes to them, and in 1970 they had over 3 000 such files. Each

offi... f the state, and officials do not qualify for railway con-
cess...

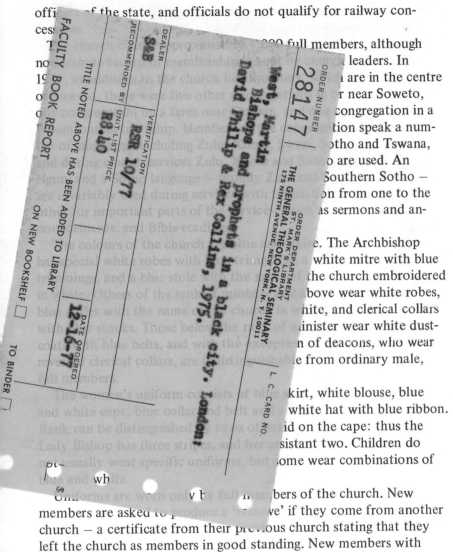

...full members, although
no... ...ye... membership... ...leaders. In
19... ...in addition... the church ha... ...are in the centre
o... ...there were five other... ...r near Soweto,
... congregation in a
...ship. Member... ...tion speak a num-
...including Zulu... ...tho and Tswana,
...services Zulu... ...are used. An
Nguni... ...language... ...Zulu... Southern Sotho —
are... ...during serv... ...on from one to the
other... important parts of the service... as sermons and an-
...ments, and Bible-read... ...e. The Archbishop
ha... special white robes with... ...white mitre with blue
tr... ...ings, and a blue stole... the church embroidered
in white. Others of the rank... ...above wear white robes,
blu... ...es with the name of... chief in white, and clerical collars
with... stocks. Those below the r... of minister wear white dust-
co... ...blue belts, and with the exception of deacons, who wear
rev... clerical collars, are distinguishable from ordinary male,
full members.

The women's uniform consists of b... skirt, white blouse, blue
and white cape, blue collar and belt and... white hat with blue ribbon.
Rank can be distinguished... rows of... id on the cape: thus the
Lady Bishop has three stripes, and her assistant two. Children do
not usually wear specific uniforms, but some wear combinations of
blue and white.

Uniforms are worn only by full members of the church. New
members are asked to produce a 'remove' if they come from another
church — a certificate from their previous church stating that they
left the church as members in good standing. New members with
removes are usually on probation for three months before becoming
full members; prospective members without removes are usually on
trial for about six months.

The BBCAC — again in common with most independent churches

file has a reference number, which has perpetuated the idea among many independent church leaders that registration still takes place. A letter to the Department applying for registration will result in a reply instructing the applicant to
contact his local authorities. The file number quoted on these letters is often
taken as evidence of registration, and is then displayed on all church documents.
Thus the BBCAC quotes 'Pretoria reg. no. P 120/4/1323' on all official documents, although this is not a registration number.

— is not a wealthy church. Full members pay R1,80 per annum in quarterly instalments of 45c. This money is used for salaries, uniforms, books, candles and other articles used in the church — such as wine and wafers for communion services. Money is also set aside for emergencies — for example to assist members of the congregation with funeral expenses. Although small salaries are paid to some officials, these are insufficient to support them, and the church consequently has no full-time officials: all, including the Archbishop, are either in full- or part-time employment.

Annual dues are usually paid by members at important services, where much of the money is spent immediately on the costs of the services, which may include feeding all the church members for a couple of days, and hiring a hall or classroom. A small amount of extra money is obtained in collections, but the most important source is in fund-raising services, which are held regularly in combination with other churches. At these services — often held on Saturday nights — first one church and then another will alternate in taking the combined proceeds.

The major goal of most independent churches is to save enough money to be able to build a church, and the BBCAC is no exception. Despite this, the church is only able to make ends meet, and has no cash reserves. The church draws its membership from the poorer section of the community, and very often any cash surplus will be spent on needy members of the congregation, particularly in case of sickness or death. The church keeps money in a building society savings account, which is administered by the Archbishop, the Vice-Bishop and one ordinary member. Many independent churches have suffered breakaways through financial disputes, and the presence of the ordinary member is designed to allay any fears the congregation might have about the use of church money.

Independent church congregations tend to be small for a number of reasons. As most meet in private houses or in classrooms in schools, space is often at a premium. In addition transport is difficult and expensive in Soweto, and churches tend to decentralise and have a number of small congregations. The average observed attendance at the BBCAC headquarters over the fieldwork period was 20 to 25 people, except for important occasions when people came from the different congregations in the area. Ordinary services, held at 11 a.m. on Sundays, are informal and consist of hymns, to the accompaniment of two drums, and prayers and sermons. It is usual to have more than one address at a service, and many members of the congregation are able to testify should they wish to. The senior leaders sit behind a table at the top of the small garage in which the church meets, the women sit down one side and the men down the other,

in order of rank. Children sit in front in the centre, and the rest of
the congregation — usually those without office — sit behind the
children.

The emphasis in these services is on participation, and the order
of service is flexible. Most hymns are sung by heart, as the church
possesses few hymnbooks. The leaders use the Bible, and a Methodist prayerbook, and some members of the congregation bring
Bibles with them. Most of the sermons delivered in the church are
based on biblical texts, but none of the church leaders uses any book
to assist in preparation of sermons. In keeping with the informal
approach allowing group participation, individual members are
allowed to make public confessions during services. Every Sunday
service ends with a healing ritual in the church, where the prophet
and her prayer-women assistants come forward to the Holy Place
of the church and treat those who are sick. Healers and patients,
having removed their shoes, stand in the centre over the holy place,
and most of the rest of the congregation dance round in a circle.
Dancing is believed to call the Holy Spirit down on to the congregation, thereby assisting the healers.

The Holy Place of the church is a painted circle, as shown in
fig. ii, in the centre of the floor of the church. The shape and symbols of this Holy Place were revealed to the Senior Prophet of the
church in dreams. Her interpretation of the symbols is that the cross
symbolises Christianity, and the star, suns and moons are symbolic
of heaven and the power which is believed to come from heaven.
The Holy Place is usually covered by an animal skin when not in
use, and people are only allowed to walk on it when they have
removed their shoes.

FIG. ii : BBCAC HOLY PLACE

In addition to ordinary services, there are a number of occasions for which special services are held, and also a number of important days for the church — particularly Good Friday and New Year's Day.[4] Usually many church members from different parts come together on those days, and the opportunity is taken to combine a number of important rites, from ordinations to baptism.

While the BBCAC will bless young children, baptism may not take place while a member is under sixteen years of age. A person below that age is not regarded as old enough to make a serious decision about baptism. Baptism is by immersion in a river. (The BBCAC does not regard a person as baptised who has not been fully immersed. New members who have been baptised by sprinkling are rebaptised, but any form of baptism involving immersion is recognised as valid.) In the normal form the Bishop questions candidates and if satisfied blesses them. Candidates then enter the water, where they are immersed three times — in the name of the Father, Son and Holy Spirit — by another leader, usually a minister, deacon or evangelist. After immersion candidates are blessed, and a thanksgiving is said. Often at the same service people are immersed to heal or purify them — in this instance there are links with traditional purification ceremonies. Some observers have confused this with rebaptism, but the churches themselves are very clear on the distinction between baptism and healing and purification rites.

No formal confirmation of members exists in the BBCAC, but there is a ceremony for admitting new full members, at which they are given their uniforms. Full members are the only ones allowed to take communion, and communion services are held quarterly. The communion service broadly follows the pattern of the Last Supper, with foot-washing being obligatory beforehand. The service is held at night only, and only the Archbishop or ministers given authority by him may administer communion, which consists of bread and wine.

The BBCAC has a few rules which are obligatory for members: keeping the ten commandments; no drinking; no smoking; and monogamy. The church marriage rule is that members should have a civil ceremony — as no minister in the church is a marriage officer — and then come to the church to go through a wedding ceremony,

---

4. In most churches Good Friday and the Easter weekend is the most important time of year: often church Conferences are held, as well as communion services and ordinations. Christmas is not the time for large services in Soweto. The reasons advanced for this are (a) that the township is too dangerous at that time, with a lot of drinking, violence and merrymaking, and (b) that many church members are domestic servants who cannot get time off over Christmas to go to church. New Year is alleged to be quieter and more convenient for employees, and the main services are held then.

which is taken from the Methodist service. Although monogamy is the rule, a man with two wives who wishes to join the church will be accepted, although he will never be allowed to hold any office.

The BBCAC accepts the widespread custom that when she marries a woman will join the church of her husband, and no attempt is made to keep young women in the church when they marry. This is still the case when a young woman leaves to join a non-Spirit church, but church leaders believe that a person who has been a member of a Spirit church will eventually return to one.

The BBCAC has therefore many attributes of a Zionist-type church: it emphasises faith-healing, it has drums and dancing as well as baptism by immersion, it has prophets and spirit possession,[5] it has communion services at night only, and its members wear uniforms characteristic of the movement. The leader of the church characterises it as Apostolic and not Zionist: in his view Zionists are people with sticks (Sundkler 1961: 214–5) who have little learning and use no books. Also, in contrast to some Zionist churches, the position of the ancestors is not explicit, and the church does not make offerings. The church leadership regards the question of the shades as a personal matter for individuals, and of no importance to the church.

The leader of the BBCAC has many contacts with other independent churches, both through active membership of the African Independent Churches' Association (AICA) and through his personal prestige as a bishop. As will be described later (chapter 7), independent churches are often joined in a variety of networks of co-operation. The BBCAC combines for fund-raising purposes with other churches, and its leader is often asked to take part in consecration services of other bishops.

In 1970 these contacts led a small Ethiopian-type church to apply to amalgamate with the BBCAC to form a new church. The reason given by the leader of the applicants was that his members 'wanted the Spirit', and since they had no prophets in the church, they had looked around for a suitable church to join up with, where the Spirit was strong. This case, and others, is discussed in more detail later during discussion of networks linking churches.

The attractions of the independent churches are many, but it is

5. Spirit possession occurs most frequently among women, particularly during dancing, or during emotional services. The Holy Spirit is believed to enter the person, who is caused to stagger and palpitate and sometimes to cry out. Possession is approved by the church, as it is believed that it helps the one possessed as well as showing the effectiveness of the church. The phenomenon here is possession and not mediumship (v. Beattie and Middleton, 1969: x) in that no messages, visions or interpretations result from the state of possession (see article by Lee, 1969: 128ff).

clear that in the BBCAC the importance of healing practices is para-
mount. In this church the Lady Bishop is a prominent healer who
attracts patients from a wide area and from numerous denominations. In many cases patients who have been successfully treated
will join the church, although there is no compulsion to do so. Thus
in a survey of most of the active BBCAC members of the headquarters branch, 84 per cent stated that they had joined the church
because they had been healed.

THE APOSTOLIC FULL GOSPEL MISSION OF SOUTH AFRICA (FULL GOSPEL)

This church was founded in Vereeniging, Transvaal, in 1932 by
the Revd A. Maleke, who had broken away from the Apostolic
Faith Mission, and was later succeeded by his younger brother, N.
Maleke. The present leader, Bishop J. E. Makgalemele, was born in
the Orange Free State and was a member of the N. G. Kerk in Afrika
until he came to Johannesburg in 1937. He joined the Full Gospel
Church in 1938 and became a Preacher. He was promoted to Evangelist in 1940 and became a Minister in 1944. In 1965 he was made
Vice-Bishop, and in 1968 he was consecrated Bishop of the church.
The former leader, N. Maleke, retired in that year, and was promoted
to Archbishop. He no longer exercises any authority in the church,
and lives quietly in retirement.

The present leader has a standard-six education and has attended
some short theological refresher courses run by the African Independent Churches' Association. Since 1941 he has had a trading licence,
and runs a dry-cleaning and tailoring business. In addition to the
Archbishop and himself, his hierarchy consists of ministers, deacons,
evangelists, preachers and a secretary and treasurer, the last two of
whom are laymen. Officers of the church are elected at the annual
Conference, which is held in Soweto in February. The Full Gospel
hierarchy is unusual in that it contains two classes of minister: the
pastor, and the elder minister. The pastor is an ordained minister
who is judged to be sufficiently well educated, and who has had
some form of theological education — usually elementary Bible-
study courses by correspondence. Elder ministers are those who
have been ordained — although they are not considered sufficiently
well educated — because of long service in the church, their age, and
the respect in which they are held. Both classes have the same duties
and privileges, although pastors are of slightly higher status.

The Full Gospel church also has a women's *manyano*, which is
presided over by the Lady Bishop. Other office bearers take their
titles from the positions held by their husbands. As with all *manyano*, special meetings are held on Thursday afternoons. In addition

to church services, the women concern themselves with fund-raising
and visiting the sick.

An interesting feature of this church is that the most important
woman in the church is not the Lady Bishop, but the Senior Prophet,
who lives in a township eighty kilometres from Soweto. An indication
of her importance is that, although she holds no formal office in the
hierarchy, she is the only church member besides the Bishop who is
allowed to wear the church badge on her uniform. In addition to the
Senior Prophet, the church has a number of lesser prophets. It should
be noted that the Lady Bishop is not a prophet.

The church is not recognised by any local authority and has never
enjoyed government recognition, consequently its members enjoy
no privileges or concessions. The church has no fixed property, and
its most valuable assets are a number of musical instruments which
form a brass band. These are played by young men — the object of
the band is to keep young people 'off the street' — who perform at
important ceremonies and services.

The Full Gospel uniform is derived from a passage in the Bible —
Revelation 6:1–7. This passage refers to four horses of different
colours — white, black, red and pale — and these colours are the basis
of the church uniform. As has been mentioned previously, black is
not used in churches of this type, and so blue has been substituted.
The pale horse of the biblical passage has been interpreted as a
mustard-yellow colour. Church members wear white as the basic
colour, with yellow belts. The women wear blue capes and white
hats with yellow ribbons. The other two colours are worn on the
belt in the form of small squares of blue and red felt pinned together.
The Bishop and the Senior Prophet are the only two to wear a silver
badge with a crown and the initials of the church, and this is pinned
on top of the two squares of felt.

The church claims a membership of about 600 full members,
although no accurate records are kept by the leadership. In addition
to the headquarters in Soweto, there are a number of other congregations, or 'circuits', as they are known. The church has circuits in
two other parts of Soweto, and in three nearby areas in the Transvaal.
There are two congregations in the Orange Free State at Frankfort
and Bloemfontein, and two in Natal at Durban and Pietermaritzburg.
There is also a small group of members in a village in Lesotho.

As is usual in Soweto, members of the congregation speak a number of languages including Sotho, Tswana, Xhosa and Zulu. Sotho
and Zulu are most often used in services, and interpreters are used
for the important parts. A small amount of Afrikaans and English
is used in services, mainly in singing hymns.

The Full Gospel is not a rich church, although its church dues are higher than many other independent churches. Full members are required to pay R1 per head three times a year. The money is used mainly for the expenses of the major festivals, and for articles used in the church. Money is kept in a bank in Soweto, with the Bishop and secretary being signatories to the account. Ministers and other officials are not paid, and the church has no financial reserves.

The Full Gospel church has no church buildings, and to make up for this the present Bishop has utilised a small piece of land next to his house and shop. This is known in the church as the Holy Place, and is a rectangular area which is kept clean and regularly dung-smeared in African style. A small wire fence runs round the peri-meter to keep people away, and people are requested to remove their shoes (Exodus 3:5) when they enter. In the centre of this area, as shown in fig. iii, is a circle with an opening on one side in the shape of a kraal. The Bishop chose this shape as one that would be familiar to his congregation, and he views the circle in the centre as an altar such as one would find in an Anglican or Catholic church.

The Holy Place thus shows the same structural characteristics as, say, an Anglican church. The wired-off area parallels the body of a church building where the congregation is placed. The circle in the centre with a cross in the middle parallels the altar, where only the priest and other officials normally enter.

Outside the centre circle, near the opening, are two small symbolic structures. The first is a small tent, about 30 cm high, made of con-crete. This miniature tent symbolises the tents of the Israelites, still wandering in the desert in search of salvation. Next to the tent are some small whitewashed rocks, near which animals are occasionally slaughtered for feasts. Authority for this is taken from Deuteronomy 27: 2–7 ('. . . that thou shalt set thee up great stones, and plaister them with plaister. . . . Thou shalt build the altar of the Lord thy God of

FIG. iii : FULL GOSPEL HOLY PLACE

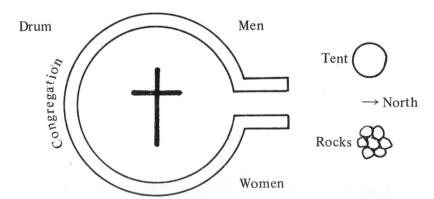

whole stones and thou shalt offer burnt offerings thereon unto the Lord thy God. . . .') but no burnt offerings are made. Occasionally a small offering of food is placed inside the tent, in the nature of a libation. When the parallel with an offering to ancestors was suggested the Bishop answered sharply: 'No, this is God's work, not *madlozi* (ancestors') work.'

In 1973 an addition was made to the Holy Place in the form of what the Bishop called a tabernacle. This was erected over the cross in the centre of the circle, and was a small blue-painted structure of brick consisting of a square base from which jutted a flat, triangular rock. Round this were seven small holders for candles. This was the holiest part of the Holy Place, kept covered when not in use, where holy water was placed during healing, and to which only the Bishop had access. A small red reflector was placed on the covering so that at night people could see where it was and avoid it.

The church meets indoors, either in the Bishop's house or occasionally for special services in a nearby church, which is loaned for the purpose. The Holy Place is used for healing services, blessing, offerings, feet-washing, dancing, and the climax of the Harvest Festival, which will be described below. During these services only the Bishop is allowed to stand in the centre of the Holy Place, except during the Harvest Festival, when a prophet is allowed to enter, and during healing services, when the patient is placed in the middle of the Holy Place.

Ordinary services of the Full Gospel church follow the pattern described for the BBCAC, and are held on Sunday mornings. The church has three major festival services: the February Conference, the Good Friday and Easter services (also known as the Passover), and the Harvest Festival, which is held in August. At these services church members attend from a number of different circuits, and the form of service follows a basic pattern. A detailed description of the 1970 Harvest Festival will give an idea of the sort of service that takes place.

In 1970 church leaders fixed the date of the Harvest Festival for 22–23 August. The authority for the service is taken from Deuteronomy 26:1–4. Preparations for the service included the writing of letters by the General Secretary to all circuits to remind them of the date of the service, and various other final arrangements including ordering an ox for slaughter, buying sufficient bread and wine for the communion service, cleaning uniforms, booking a church for part of the service, and ordering food.

On the Saturday afternoon the ox was delivered, and after prayers and a blessing accompanied by sprinkling with holy water, it was slaughtered at the Holy Place near the rocks. At the same time women members were preparing the food and getting the uniforms ready. Earlier in the week the Holy Place had been swept and re-painted. Towards the end of the afternoon and into the evening members from other circuits arrived at the headquarters. As groups arrived they were greeted with a hymn and a prayer at the Bishop's house. While women among the newcomers assisted the other women with the final preparations, the men congregated in the shop next to the house, where circuit leaders paid the usual R1 per member. Pay-ments were entered in a ledger by the General Secretary.

At about 10 p.m. members started putting on their uniforms, and at 10.30 p.m. the service started as the congregation assembled out-side the house at the Holy Place. After a prayer and a hymn, the foot-washing ceremony began with the text from John 13:4–17, and an explanation from the Bishop that this part of the service was 'to show the love of God'. While the Bishop led the singing and exhorted members to come forward to have their feet washed so that they would be purified, two evangelists did the washing.

After this ceremony the congregation moved to the Holy Place for the opening devotions, which consisted of prayers asking God to bless their endeavours, and singing and dancing. Dancing took place round the perimeter of the Holy Place, and one or two cases of spirit possession occurred. After the opening devotions, the con-gregation moved off in procession to the nearby Lutheran church, where they arrived at about 11.45 p.m. The service commenced with hymns and prayer.

The first part of the service in the church consisted of receiving new members into the church. The Bishop greeted the new members with the text, 'Ye are the salt of the earth' from Matthew 5:13, and blessed them individually by laying hands on them and pressing them with his stick. After this he informed them of the church regulations and shook hands with them. Church uniforms were then given to members who had completed their trial period – preceded by the reading of Revelation 6:1–7 – and they, too, were blessed by the Bishop.

The major part of the service, the Holy Communion, then fol-lowed. This began with a prayer and a hymn and the reading of I Corinthians 11:23–33, which recounts the story of the Last Sup-per. Communicants came up to a long table covered in a red cloth with a cross of white material. There were twelve candles on the table. The Bishop blessed the bread and wine and then administered it to the communicants, twelve at a time. The communicants were hidden from the rest of the congregation by a long white cloth with a blue material cross on it which was held by two men in front of the altar. Communicants were given a wafer of bread and then drank from a small glass. After the glasses had been removed the Bishop blessed each communicant.

When all full members had taken communion there was joyful singing and dancing in the aisles of the church. After the communion there was a sermon from the Bishop, followed by another hymn, and then a presentation of gifts to the Bishop in recognition of his services during the year (as mentioned previously, no church official draws any salary from the church). Gifts were of clothing and money — usually socks, handkerchiefs, or small amounts of cash up to R1. Nearly every member contributed something. After final prayers and a hymn the service closed, and the congregation returned to headquarters at about 6.50 a.m. to rest.

At 11 a.m. the morning service started, and the congregation assembled at the Holy Place. The service started with singing and prayer, and the singing continued while a Senior Prophet stood at the entrance to the Holy Place and accepted wallets, purses, knotted handkerchiefs with money in them and Bibles, placing them all on the cross in the centre of the Holy Place. Later a pot of water, a cup, a plate and two bags of seed were also placed in the centre.

There then followed a lengthy period of dancing round the Holy Place to the accompaniment of singing and drumming. There were numerous cases of spirit possession, and the Bishop led the congregation in the dancing, sometimes preaching or praying as he danced, asking the Holy Spirit to come down on the congregation. After about half an hour the dancing stopped and, while the congregation sang, the Bishop, two ministers, the Lady Bishop and the Senior Prophet entered the Holy Place and encircled the articles in the centre. Each pointed a stick at the articles and blessed them, praying for a good increase and harvest for the church. They then withdrew, and two evangelists removed some money which had been left as an offering. Individual members were then allowed to collect their possessions from the circle.

The Harvest Festival was thus concluded, and the final rite was the blessing of children. The Bishop donned a white stole and picked up each child in turn, laid hands on it, and said: 'N. I bless you in the name of the Son Jesus Christ, and the Father and the Holy Spirit under the Apostolic Full Gospel Mission of South Africa. Grow up under the word of God, be a good child, obey the family and attend Sunday School. Amen.' He then kissed the child and returned it to its parents. After this, the Bishop blessed the mothers of the children, one of whom became possessed.

While the congregation sang, the senior men went off in procession to bless the food for the final feast. They returned for the final blessing when the Bishop, ministers, evangelists, and the Lady Bishop and

Senior Prophet encircled the Holy Place, and the rest of the congregation passed in procession in front of them to be blessed. Finally the leaders all passed in front of the Bishop to be blessed, and the service ended at about 1.30 p.m. with a choral amen. The feast followed. Men and women ate separately, and a vast meal of meat, rice, potatoes, bread, pumpkin, several salads, jelly and custard, cake and home-made ginger-beer was consumed. In the afternoon the congregation dispersed, leaving a few women to clean up. In all about one hundred people attended the various parts of the festival.

The service outlined above follows the general pattern of festival services: a number of different features, including communion and admission of new members, over a period of about 18 hours. Variations would include, for example, ordinations at the conference, and a vigil at night on Good Friday.

The blessing of small children has already been mentioned. This rite takes the place of infant baptism as practised by most of the mission churches; the Full Gospel only baptises people who are at least fifteen years old. Only baptism by immersion is recognised, and people who have been baptised by sprinkling have to be rebaptised. The Bishop and ministers are allowed to baptise, and baptism is by triple immersion, after which members are blessed by the senior person present. As with the BBCAC, healing and purification rites are often held concurrently.

The Full Gospel church has no formal confirmation of members other than the short rite outlined in the description of the harvest festival. Full members wear the church uniform and are allowed to take part in communion services, which are held quarterly at night.

The main rules of the church are monogamy (with the same proviso that applies to the BBCAC), no drinking, smoking, fighting or gossiping, and a requirement that members should attend church regularly. The church marriage rules are similar to those of other independent churches: couples are required to marry in a civil ceremony and then to attend a church service. If members are found to be living together without a formal marriage ceremony they are not immediately suspended from membership as they would be in some churches, as long as they undertake to marry legally as soon as possible.

If we were to place the BBCAC and the Full Gospel church on a continuum between ideal-type Ethiopian and ideal-type Zionist, the Full Gospel church would be closer to the Zionist end of the spectrum than the BBCAC. Like the BBCAC it has many of the attributes of Zionism: dancing, drumming, faith-healing, spirit possession, communion services at night, and the characteristic uniforms. In addition, unlike the BBCAC it sacrifices animals, and believes in the

power of ancestors to aid the church. While the BBCAC leadership
was neutral on the question of ancestors, believing them to be a
personal matter for individuals that did not affect the church, the
Full Gospel leadership maintains that the shades are still interested
in the church and are able to assist it. The church remembers certain
shades by lighting candles and 'talking' to them: it was stressed that
whereas the shades were 'talked' to, it was God alone who was
'prayed' to. (For a full discussion, see chapter 9.)

While the BBCAC leader distinguished between Zionists and
Apostolics, and regarded his church as Apostolic, the Full Gospel
leader said there was no basic difference between Zionists and
Apostolics, and that he would accept either title. The attractions
of the Full Gospel church are similar to those of the other churches
of this type, and will be discussed fully in subsequent chapters, but
it is again clear that faith-healing is of particular importance. Like
the BBCAC the Full Gospel church has a prominent faith-healer as
a Senior Prophet in the church, and this undoubtedly adds to the
church's prestige, because although the prophet's patients are drawn
from members of many different churches, their cures come to be
associated with the Full Gospel church itself. Thus, for example, a
survey of active members of the main Full Gospel congregation
showed that 86 per cent had joined the church initially because
they had been healed.

THE HOLY UNITED METHODIST CHURCH OF SOUTH AFRICA (HOLY UNITED)

This church was founded in Johannesburg in 1963 by the present
leader, President W. B. Macheke, and traces its lineage back to the
Methodist Church of South Africa, although it is four generations
removed from it. The Bantu Methodist Church broke from the
Methodist Church of South Africa, and in turn the Free Bantu
Methodist Church broke from it. The Free United Methodist Church
broke from the Free Bantu Methodist Church. The Revd Macheke
became a minister of the Free United Methodist Church in 1958,
and was promoted to Vice-President in 1963. In the same year he
broke from the church to form his own Holy United Methodist
Church, and took the title of President.

The ostensible cause of the split between the Free United and the
Holy United was one that is very common in the independent churches: a dispute over finances. The Vice-President, the Revd Macheke,
was dissatisfied with an account given by the President of the Free
United about what had happened to certain amounts of money that
had been collected to buy church badges. As the money could not
be accounted for satisfactorily, the Revd Macheke left and formed

his own church. However, it is doubtful whether this was the sole reason for the split, as it was clear that the Revd Macheke had certain followers in the Free United church who had been urging him to form his own church for some time. Thus the dispute over finances may have been a convenient issue on which to split.

The Revd Macheke became leader of his own church at the age of 44, with a standard-two education, plus certificates from two Bible correspondence colleges. He came to Johannesburg in 1938 and, after a number of manual-labour jobs, became foreman of an electro-plating firm in Johannesburg. Born in Potgietersrus in the Northern Transvaal, he is Tsonga-speaking, and lives in the Tsonga/ Venda area of Soweto. His wife, the Lady President, is Sotho-speaking and comes from Lesotho.

When the church was founded the leader took the title of President — which is the one usually used by leaders of Ethiopian-type churches. The rest of the hierarchy consisted of ministers, deacons, evangelists and preachers, all of whom are elected at the annual conference which is held in November at various centres in rotation. An interesting aspect of the Holy United church was that the leader said that he would take the title Bishop when he considered that his church had grown sufficiently, and was well established.[6]

The Holy United church has an established women's *manyano,* under the leadership of the Lady President, with its own hierarchy, and the usual special services on Thursday afternoon. The church used to have a Sunday School for children, but this lapsed as there were no teachers available. The only other specific groups within the church are the two choirs, senior and junior, which are composed of girls and young women. The choirs have their own uniforms, red for the seniors and white for the juniors, and are very popular. They take a leading part in singing in church services and provide special entertainment on important occasions.

The Holy United church has never been officially recognised, and its ministers enjoy no special privileges. This church is another that has no property, and services are usually held in a school classroom, which is hired for the purpose. Other church gatherings are held in private homes. In common with most other independent churches, the Holy United is not rich, and no church leaders draw any salary: all are in full-time employment. Members pay 20c quarterly — known as the 'quarterly ticket' — and R1 on Good Friday.

The church claims approximately 400 members, although again

6. An indication of the co-operation still existing between the Free and Holy United Methodist churches, was that the Holy United leader said that he would ask the Free United leader to consecrate him as bishop. The Holy United leader became a bishop finally towards the end of 1971.

no accurate records are kept. The headquarters of the church are in Soweto, where the bulk of the members have come from the Free United church's districts formerly under the control of the Revd Macheke, when he was Vice-President of that church. There are also small branches of the church in Potgietersrus (the birthplace of the present leader, where he has relatives), in Lesotho (where his wife has relatives), in Vrede in the Orange Free State, and near Pretoria, where the leader has more relatives. Again like most other independent churches, members of the Holy United church speak a number of languages, including Tsonga, Southern Sotho, Zulu, Xhosa, Swazi and Venda. Tsonga and Sotho are the most-spoken languages, and these — in addition to Zulu — are the languages generally used during church services. An interpreter is used during most parts of normal services, usually translating Tsonga into Zulu or Sotho.

The Holy United church uniform is very different from that of the Zionist-type churches. Ministers wear black robes with clerical collars, and the President is distinguished from his ministers only in that he wears a black biretta. Lesser male officials and ordinary full members wear ordinary clothing with a red sash with white edging over one shoulder. They wear the church badge also, which is a modified version of the Methodist Church of South Africa's youth badge. Women full members wear the same uniform as most other Methodist churches, both mission and independent: a red blouse with black skirt, stockings and shoes and a white hat. As previously mentioned, the senior choir wears red dresses and the junior choir white dresses.

Services in the Holy United church generally follow the pattern of the Methodist Prayerbook. There is less participation by ordinary members than in the churches previously described, with the minister playing the all-important role in preaching and leading prayers. As is usual in most churches in Soweto, men and women tend to sit on different sides of the room during services (which side varies from church to church). The ordinary Sunday service lasts from 11 a.m. to 2 p.m., and the important services are held at Christmas, New Year, Good Friday, Easter, Ascension Day and during the November Conference.

The Holy Communion service takes place quarterly, in the day-time, and only full members are allowed to take part. The service starts with the reading of the ten commandments, and then communicants make their confessions individually to the President or a senior minister. The rest of the service follows the normal Methodist pattern, with communicants being given bread and wine. Only the President is allowed to administer communion. After taking communion members are prayed for by the President, who lays hands on them. A foot-washing ceremony is held on Good Friday.

The Holy United church differs from independent churches of Zionist type in that it practises infant baptism by sprinkling, following the Methodist pattern. Children are confirmed as full members towards the end of their teens, and adults who join the church may become full members after a trial period which varies from three to six months. Members have to obey a set of church rules, including keeping the ten commandments, and prohibitions on smoking, drinking, dancing, attending parties or film-shows. The church insists on monogamy, and requires a civil wedding followed by a church service, as none of the ministers is a marriage officer.

The Holy United church differs markedly from most Zionist-type churches in a number of important ways, including dress, form of services, and rules of baptism and communion. It is therefore interesting to note that it does hold healing services, which are similar in certain respects to some of the healing services held by Zionists. In this church it is usually the women who do the healing through laying on of hands and prayer. During healing the congregation dances in a circle round the patient and healer, asking the Holy Spirit to work through the healer. However, the healers in the Holy United church are not prophets, they do not hold individual consultations, and use neither herbs nor other substances in healing.

The leader of this church believes that prophets 'have power from God — they can tell you why you are sick and then help you'. He said that he would like to have a prophet in his church, and was looking for one. This attitude was in response to a need felt by his congregation for the type of services provided by a prophet. At the same time, the church does not believe that spirit possession should be encouraged, and where there are signs during a service that a member is about to become possessed, a minister will immediately approach that member and stop the possession by laying on of hands and prayer. As the leader of the church said: 'The Spirit must work quietly.'

The official policy of this church, too, is that ancestors have no power to affect the church, either for good or ill. The leader of the church claims that he does not communicate with his shades: 'Why should I?' he said. 'They are dead and in the grave. They are waiting for the Second Coming.'

The specific case of the Holy United church would bear out the contention in chapter 2 that a division between Ethiopian- and Zionist-type churches is not clear cut. If we take the same factors shown in Tables 1 and 2 (pp 19, 20), we can see that the Holy United Church occupies a position roughly midway on the continuum, and that other Methodist offshoots would occupy positions on both sides.

TABLE 3 : INDEPENDENT METHODIST CHURCHES

	Prophets	*Drums*	*Night Communion*	*Dancing*	*River Baptism*	*Healing*
ABMC	No	No	No	No	No	Yes
IMC	No	No	No	No	No	Yes
Holy United	No	No	No	Yes	No	Yes
AMAC	Yes	No	Yes	Yes	Yes	Yes
BMAC	Yes	Yes	Yes	Yes	Yes	Yes

Key:
ABMC = African Bantu Methodist Church
IMC = Independent Methodist Church of South Africa
AMAC = African Methodist Apostolic Church of South Africa
BMAC = Bantu Methodist Apostolic Church of South Africa

Were the Holy United church to find a prophet, this might cause a change in other factors in the church, particularly in river baptism and spirit possession. Although prophets do not usually have formal positions in church hierarchies, they wield considerable authority through visions and predictions. Thus a prophet who stated that she had received a vision from God that the church should practise river baptism would probably find that river baptism would be introduced.

The Holy United church, being an Ethiopian-type church, does not have the same attractions as do the two churches discussed earlier. This became particularly clear in a survey of members of the church at the main branch, where in contrast to the two churches mentioned (in both of which more than 80 per cent mentioned healing as the reason for joining the church), no members stated that they had joined the church because they had been healed. Some members had followed the leader when he broke from his previous church; some had joined by marrying into the church, and some had followed relatives, but the majority — 75 per cent — had joined because they were particularly impressed with some aspect of the church or its leader. A few people were impressed by the personal qualities of the leader, and by the friendly atmosphere of the church, but the reason given most often was that as members of the church they had been helped, both financially and with advice. A number of members stated that they had received financial aid from the church to help with funerals, or in times of illness.

SOME COMPARISONS[7]

The selected churches described above were founded in 1932, 1938 and 1963, the youngest thus is 8 years old and the oldest is 39 years. It is sometimes suggested that the South African independent churches are shortlived because they are plagued by leadership disputes, but the evidence collected in this study does not bear this out. The average age of the 252 churches in surveys A and B was 22 years — that is establishment about 1949 — with a range from 1898 to 1971.

As will be discussed in the next chapter, an important crisis-point occurs in the life of every independent church with the death of the founder: at this point unless the church is well established it risks becoming defunct. Of the 58 churches in survey A, 25 (44 per cent) had survived at least one change in leadership, while the other 33 were still under the leadership of their original founders. Another interesting finding was that in only two cases had a founder been succeeded by a descendant. This will also be discussed more fully in the next chapter. In the three selected churches discussed, two had survived changes in leadership (in one case a change from founder to a relative) and the other was still under the leadership of its founder.

The leaders of the selected churches were aged between 49 and 51 and had a level of education ranging from standard two to standard six (between four and eight years' schooling). The average age of the leaders of the 252 churches in the combined surveys was 57 years, and only seven of those — less than 3 per cent — were under 40 years of age. The same leaders had a level of education of an average of approximately 5½ years' schooling — between standards three and four. All three selected church leaders had had some elementary theological education, and in comparison 90 per cent of the 58 church leaders of survey A had also had some theological education. While the three selected leaders were all in some form of employment, 63 per cent of the leaders in survey A were employed, while the remaining 37 per cent were full-time ministers, although some of these had various sorts of income which did not come from the church, for example wages from other members of the family, rents, and so on. The importance of married clergy has been stressed above, and the only one of the 252 leaders in the

7. The comparisons here are drawn from two major surveys, and one minor one. Survey A was a personally conducted analysis of aspects of 58 independent churches in various parts of the country. Survey B was a briefer survey of another 194 independent churches, not dealt with in survey A, carried out with the aid of a research assistant. Survey A 2 dealt in more detail with 13 selected churches from survey A. See Appendix 1 for details. In all references to the age of churches or individuals or groups, the present is taken as 1971.

combined surveys who was not married had recently been divorced.

The brief analysis of members and congregations in the three selected churches suggested that they cut across language and residence ties: all the churches had members who spoke a number of different languages, and all had congregations in at least two provinces of South Africa, if not farther afield. In survey A, church leaders were asked what languages were spoken in church services, and the answers involved combinations of the following languages: Zulu, Xhosa, Swazi, Ndebele, Tsonga, Venda, Southern Sotho and Tswana. The average number of languages spoken per church was three. Only 10 per cent claimed to have unilingual church services, and most of these were small churches in rural areas with predominantly one language spoken in the area. Only one urban church claimed to be unilingual.

A slightly different question was asked of the 194 churches in survey B: not what languages were spoken in church services, but what languages were spoken by church members. Again Zulu, Xhosa, Swazi, Ndebele, Tsonga, Venda, Southern Sotho, Pedi and Tswana were mentioned, and the average number of languages spoken by church members in each church was five. In this survey no churches claimed to have members who came from only one linguistic group.

Church leaders in both surveys were asked in what areas they had congregations of their churches. If the results of the two surveys are combined, of the 252 churches 95 per cent had congregations in the Transvaal, and 70 per cent were in Natal, 67 per cent in the Orange Free State, 48 per cent in the Transkei and Eastern Cape, 25 per cent in the rest of the Cape Province (mainly Northern Cape), 52 per cent in Lesotho, 57 per cent in Swaziland, 38 per cent in Botswana, and 21 per cent in other neighbouring territories. While these figures might initially appear rather large, it should be remembered that independent church leaders claim congregations even where there are only one or two members, or even a single family, who remain members of the church although they have left the headquarters area. The figures given above, then, are more an indication of the mobility of members of congregations than an indication of numerous established and flourishing congregations. The usual pattern is for a church to have one or two fairly large congregations — and these are often spread over different provinces — and then small pockets of followers in a number of other areas.

Independent churches vary in size of membership from fewer than ten members to more than two hundred thousand, although of course both extremes are rare. The largest independent church in South Africa, founded and led by members of the Lekganyane family, is believed to be the Zion Christian Church, which is con-

sidered to have 200 000 members or more. There are two main
problems in getting accurate estimates of independent church
membership: firstly, that accurate, up-to-date statistics are not
usually kept and, secondly, that some church leaders tend to
exaggerate their estimates to impress the inquirer.

In the surveys including all 252 churches, 6 per cent claimed a
church membership of 100 or less; 64 per cent claimed a membership between 100 and 500, 20 per cent claimed up to 1 000 members, and 10 per cent claimed more than 1 000 members.

The range of membership-size claimed was from 35 members to
18 000, but it will be seen that fully 90 per cent of the churches
surveyed had a membership of 1 000 or less, and that most of these
were in fact below 500. It has already been mentioned that during
the period of fieldwork, the average size of individual congregations
at Sunday services was observed to be between 20 and 30 people.
On important occasions such as major church festivals the number
of church members attending might rise to the region of 100 people.

It will therefore be seen from the data given on the number of
congregations and their spread around the country, that the average
independent church tends to have a number of small congregations
rather than a few large ones. There are two basic reasons for this,
the first being that accommodation is nearly always limited — in
survey A, 78 per cent of the churches had no buildings of their own
anywhere — and transport is often difficult and expensive; the second
reason will be argued more fully in later chapters, but is based upon
the hypothesis that small congregations are better able to meet certain
needs among members of their churches than are large congregations
— mainly in providing greater leadership opportunities and in ensuring
that relationships are not impersonal but face to face.

All three of the selected churches combined with other independent
churches of similar type for specific reasons: joint fund-raising, special
services, etc. In survey A, 88 per cent of the churches confirmed that
they combined with other independent churches for specific purposes.
The selected churches were also members of the African Independent
Churches' Association (AICA). As has been mentioned previously,
there are a number of associations of independent churches in South
Africa, and while in the combined surveys 48 per cent of the 252
churches did not belong to any association at all,[8], we may nevertheless expect a considerable degree of co-operation between independent
churches for certain specific purposes (see chapter 8).

8. Survey A, for reasons explained in chapter 1, was heavily weighted in
favour of churches which were members of AICA. Subsequent analysis showed
no basic differences between AICA churches, and those which belonged either
to another association, or to no association at all.

The incidence of healing practices, prophets, night communion, river baptism, drums and dancing has already been shown for the churches in survey B (Table 1, p. 19). A further survey was made of thirteen selected churches in survey A. Of these, four could be classified as Ethiopian-type and nine as Zionist-type. Of the nine Zionist-type churches, all had healing, spirit possession and prophets; eight had dancing, seven had river baptism and night communion, and five had drums and a belief in the power of the shades.[9] Of the four Ethiopian-type churches, all had some incidence of spirit possession, three had dancing and two had healing ceremonies. None of the other factors was present.

It is interesting to note from the above that healing was common to nearly all churches, and spirit possession occurred in all churches. The fact that spirit possession occurs, however, should not be taken to mean that the phenomenon is necessarily approved of by all church leaders. Generally, it is approved of in the Zionist-type churches, and played down as much as possible in those that are Ethiopian-type. In the latter, very often a minister will approach the person being possessed, and try to quieten the attack by prayer and laying on of hands.

It is also interesting to note that no leaders of Ethiopian-type churches said that the church believed in the power of the shades either to harm or help their church, and that only just over half of the leaders of Zionist-type churches said that their churches believed in the power of the shades. These official statements do not necessarily mean that the leaders interviewed do not personally believe in the power of their own shades. To take one example, the leader of one of the Ethiopian-type churches denied flatly that his church had anything at all to do with the shades. He initially denied that he himself had anything to do with his own shades. However, after some discussion, he suddenly said: 'I had better tell you the truth.' He proceeded to recount a recent occasion when he had dreamed of his father, and that in his dream his father was hungry and he gave him some money. The next morning he told his wife about his dream, and she said that they should make an offering to his father. A little while later the congregation of the church was summoned to a special service where a sheep was slaughtered, and were informed that it was a thanksgiving because the leader and his wife had recently safely returned from a long journey, and

9. Some explanation should be offered of the use of the terms 'ancestor' and 'shade'. 'Ancestor is used here to refer to a general category embracing all those who have died, whether or not they are believed to be able to affect the living. 'Shade' is used in a more precise context to refer to those specific ancestors who are believed to exert influence on the living.

because the church was still going well. No church members were
informed of the real nature of the feast, which was held after the
service (although it is possible that some suspected) and only close
members of the family were aware of the special significance of
the occasion.

While all four Ethiopian-type churches practised baptism of
infants by sprinkling, all the Zionist-type churches insisted on
baptism by immersion, although they differed in rules regarding
what age was required for baptism. Of the nine churches, two had
an age limit of 12 and above, two of 15 and above, three of 16 and
above, one of 18 and above and one of 19 and above. All these
churches insisted on baptism by immersion as the only valid form
of baptism. Baptism is regarded as vital to salvation, and must take
place as soon as possible — often it is a matter of urgency with
churches to have new members baptised. As one bishop said: 'What
would happen if they die tomorrow, and they are not baptised?'

As regards finance, none of the churches in either survey A or B
could be regarded as wealthy. In survey A, 63 per cent of the church
leaders were in full-time employment, and 78 per cent of the churches
had no property. In the same survey, church dues varied from R1,80
per member per year to a maximum of R4,40 per member per year.
The average for the 58 churches in this sample was approximately
R3,00. Of course this refers only to formal income. A general observation has been that most independent churches tend to collect
money for specific purposes only — for example for a special service,
to start a building fund, or to help a church member in need. For
these purposes money is raised by levy, and also by the combined
services already mentioned above. A few churches try to augment
their income by making door-to-door collections, mainly in white
suburbs in the main urban areas, but this was frowned upon by
most leaders who were questioned on this topic. Their attitude was
that door-to-door collecting tended to give their churches a bad
name, and that it was not permitted.[10]

The thirteen selected churches in survey A also showed a similarity
in church rules, and important services. All insisted upon monogamy,
and eleven forbade smoking or drinking. When asked for other specific
church rules, six leaders mentioned the ten commandments, six said
that their churches did not allow scandal-mongering or quarrelling,
three did not allow their members to attend dances, and two did not
allow cinema-going. Of the thirteen churches, the Ethiopian-type

10. Part of the reason for this attitude was that in certain cases, although by
no means all, door-to-door collectors have not been genuine members of independent churches. Door-to-door collections were felt by some leaders to 'put
a church on the same level' as the imposters.

churches tended to have fewer restrictive rules than those that were
Zionist-type.

CHAPTER **4 Bishops and Prophets**

In much of the literature dealing with African independent churches, the importance of leadership is stressed — the churches are seen as allowing outlets for expression of leadership qualities, and as a corollary are faced with a high incidence of leadership disputes, with resultant tensions and fission. In this chapter we shall look at church leadership in some detail, as one important aspect of the urban independent churches.

An early study of a particular independent church in South Africa (Mqotsi and Mkele 1946) continually stressed the importance of the leader of the church, although it did not attempt a sociological explanation, and two years later Sundkler wrote: 'The obsession for leadership in the Church is of course only a symptom of other underlying factors, one of the most important being that in the South Africa of racial discrimination and colour bar, it is the Church which has provided the only legitimate outlet for the African's strong urge for leadership.' (Sundkler [1948] 1961: 100.) He went on to compare independent church leadership in some ways with Zulu traditional leadership — thus he says (1961: 102), 'The kingship pattern of Zulu society is imprinted on the leadership of *all* the independent Churches. The leader whether "Bishop", "Overseer" or "President" is a king, *inkosi*, and the Church is his tribe.' Much later, Wishlade, also working in a rural area, drew attention to parallels between independent church leaders and village headmen (Wishlade 1965: 80).

It must however be questioned whether this type of analogy is valid when dealing with urban independent churches. There are no chiefs or traditional headmen in Soweto, and to compare a bishop in Soweto with a tribal chief in Zululand would, in Epstein's words, 'suggest a profound methodological error for (it implies) the assessment of urban conditions against a model of the traditional tribal system. . . .' (Epstein 1964: 99.) In addition, no single 'traditional tribal system' exists, for as has been mentioned before, the population of Soweto speaks various languages and comes originally from most parts of South Africa. For these reasons, independent church leadership in Soweto should be treated on its own merits.

A further problem suggested by an analysis of the literature is that attention has been largely centred on the leaders, and not much enquiry has been made about those who hold lesser positions in the hierarchy. With the elaborate hierarchies in the independent churches in Soweto, it seems important to distinguish between leaders at the top of their particular hierarchy, and those who hold other, lesser positions of leadership.

Sundkler also suggested (1961: 106) a distinction between a chief-type leader (typical of the Ethiopian-type church) and a prophet-type (typical of the Zionist-type) leader. This simple dichotomy does not apply in Soweto — although it is true that leaders of Ethiopian-type churches are never prophets. It is therefore necessary to examine more closely what sorts of leadership are in fact found in these independent churches.

If a dichotomous distinction is to be made, it may best be based on the distinction between those exercising charismatic authority, and those exercising legal authority:

> ... charismatic authority ... shall refer to rule over men, whether predominantly external or predominantly internal, to which the governed submit because of their belief in the extraordinary quality of the specific *person*. ... Legal authority is based on an *impersonal* bond to the generally defined and functional 'duty of office'. (Max Weber, trs. Gerth and Mills, 1946: 295, 299.)

This distinction is basically similar to that made by Firth (1969: 32) between a priest and a prophet, and to De Jouvenel's distinction between *dux*, the leader into action of a stream of wills, and *rex*, the man who regularises or rules (De Jouvenel 1957: 21). Although both types of leader are to be found in the independent churches in Soweto — ideally the *dux* in the Zionist-type church and the *rex* in the Ethiopian-type church — in fact a norm appears to be a combination of the two types: the embodiment of the *dux–rex* duality to which De Jouvenel refers.

The large number of small independent churches in Soweto allows potential members a wide degree of choice in deciding which church to join. As the broader advantages of the independent churches are common to all, the specific decision to join a particular church often rests either on the personality of the leader, or on the healing abilities of certain people in the church, or on a combination of these and other factors. The homogeneity of the churches, added to their acceptance of the movement of members from one church to another, makes it simple for individuals to change their affiliation, and consequently church leaders are not generally able to rely on purely legal authority, in the Weberian sense, in maintaining the allegiance of their congregations.

Thus it is seen that most church leaders exercise both legal and charismatic authority over their congregations. In the Zionist-type churches, however, the position is a little more complex. A large number of these churches in Soweto, according to the two surveys undertaken, have hierarchies in which the senior prophet, or prophets, stand outside the 'formal' hierarchy, and are therefore not leaders of churches. This was seen, for example, in the analysis of the BBCAC and Full Gospel churches in the preceding chapter, where both churches were led by bishops, but also had influential prophets.

The existence of a bishop and a prophet in the same church is of particular interest, and as it is a fairly common occurrence it should be discussed in some detail. Sundkler formulated the concept of the prophet-type leader of Zionist churches at an early stage in the history of the independent church movement; in the 1970s in Soweto it seemed that the Zionist-type churches were more firmly established than in the Zululand of the 1930s and required a more bureaucratic type of leader. But at the same time we have seen that the Zionist-type church requires a prophetic presence as well. These two types of authority are required if the move is to be made from an informal to a formal group, and involves very often the institutionalisation of the leadership. As Wilson has pointed out (1967: 138ff), this can give rise to severe role conflicts.

In some cases a prophet-type leader has had administrative talents. This is potentially a highly successful combination, as can be seen from two of the largest independent churches in South Africa, the Zion Christian Church of Lekganyane and the Nazareth Baptist Church of Shembe, which both had leaders of this type. But in most other cases the roles are separated, and this can lead to internal tensions (cf. Peel 1968: 278ff): for example, a prophet leader might resent the control of bureaucratic subordinates, and conversely subordinates who are prophets might resent the control of a bureaucratic leader without their charismatic gifts. This sort of situation can easily lead to fission, unless some way is found of accommodating both types of leadership. One apparently successful example is that of the Church of the Lord (Aladura), where the formal hierarchy has two streams, one stressing 'visions, revelations and prophecies' and leading to the position of Apostle, and the other stressing 'pastoral, preaching or administrative' gifts leading to the position of Bishop, with the overall leader being the Primate, who is expected to have both sorts of gifts (Turner 1967, vol. ii: 36–41).

However, in Soweto most prophets are women, and this provides a convenient solution to the problem. Women do not hold office in the formal hierarchy of the churches, and the presence of a woman prophet is usually no threat to the established male hierarchy. This seems to have facilitated the development of two streams of authority which are important in many Zionist-type churches. The relationship between the bishop and the prophet is also worthy of further discussion. As has been shown, and will be elaborated on later, healing is the most important factor in drawing new members into Zionist-type churches. Thus the prophet's role is vital in *attracting* members. Subsequently, other factors are also important in *retaining* members: for example leadership opportunities, emotional outlets, a supportive community of like-minded people, and so on. Many of these non-healing factors are provided by the institutional church, of which the bishop is the key figure. Thus the prophet attracts new members through healing and, while healing may still be very important to them, they are retained in the church to a large extent by the institutional framework provided by the bishop.

The bishop and prophet therefore co-operate, although in many cases the prophet may feel in a slightly stronger position. In fact, the relationship of a follower to the bishop and the prophet may be of different strengths at different times. Following healing, the one may be stronger than the other with a dependence on the prophet rather than the bishop, but if the follower is healed and remains well the relationship with the bishop may then be regarded as more important. By its nature, the relationship with the prophet is more susceptible to breakdown than that with the bishop, as it is a personal single-strand relationship depending on supernatural power. For the same reasons, of course, it can be a stronger relationship than that with the bishop. One solution to the problem of instability in the bishop–prophet co-operation was found in some churches where the prophet was the bishop's wife (e.g. in the BBCAC), although as mentioned the usual sexual differentiation of the offices also played its part.

So on the one hand there is what might be called a routinisation of charisma (Gerth and Mills 1946: 262) as Zionist-type churches move towards a more institutionalised form, and on the other hand two forms of authority develop parallel to facilitate the change. In this way these churches are able to incorporate and contain charisma within certain established forms (O'Dea 1966: 50).

The presence of women prophets raises the question of the power of women in the independent churches in Soweto. This subject will be returned to later, but it should be pointed out that while women are in the majority in the independent churches they are rarely in positions of direct authority except in their *manyano* groups. Their influence, however, is considerable. Women are not only numerically in the majority, but are also the major fund-raisers in their churches. The women maintain separate and independent organisations through their *manyano*, and are therefore in a strong position to influence church leaders, if necessary by threatening to stop raising funds for the church.

While *manyano* groups provide leadership opportunities for many women members, women have some opportunities to influence the churches more directly, particularly as prophets. In the Zionist-type church, the prophet is the interpreter of the will of God through the Holy Spirit, and is also able to predict. A message from the prophet, as it is believed to come from the Holy Spirit, would not be ignored by church leaders whatever their views on its content might be, and prophets are generally consulted on most important matters pertaining to the church. These may range from colours to be used in church uniforms, to suitable days for special services, or to assessments of candidates for leadership positions in the church. Thus the prophet, either as 'messenger' or 'oracle', will often wield more influence in church affairs than many men in the formal hierarchy.

There are a few cases, however, where women are part of the formal hierarchy of their churches. For example, only three of the 252 churches in the combined surveys were led permanently by women (two with the title 'Bishop Mrs' and one with 'Bishop Mrs Prophet'). These churches placed great emphasis on healing, and their leaders were all prophets. It is nevertheless usual for a male to be head of a church of this nature, although in some cases he may be a nominal leader.

The clearest example of this is the St John's Apostolic Faith Mission Church, whose founder was a prominent healer, Mrs C. Nku. While Mrs Nku was the effective leader of her church, it had an archbishop, who was constitutionally head of the church. The problems over leadership thus created are discussed later in this chapter. Two churches in survey A were good examples of a similar situation in which there were no leadership problems. In both cases a woman had felt the call to become a prophet while a member of a mission church, and had been forced to leave because of her healing activities. Both had left to form independent churches, with patients as the first members, and both had made their husbands become bishops. In both cases the husbands were not dynamic leaders, and were in a sense 'reluctant bishops', who left the running of their churches to their wives. This was particularly clear in services on important occasions, where the bishop might open the proceedings with a prayer, but would then hand over the rest of the service to his wife. Women thus can and do exercise considerable influence on their churches, although they rarely hold formal office, and even more rarely become leaders of their churches.

In analysis of church leadership I shall deal first with those at the top of their respective hierarchies. Titles are particularly important to independent church leaders, and by far the most popular is Archbishop or Bishop. Of the 252 church leaders in the surveys, no fewer than 80 per cent were titled Bishop or Archbishop, 15 per cent were Presidents, 3 per cent were Moderators, and 2 per cent had lesser titles.

Bishop was formerly the title most used by Zionist-type churches, and President by those that were Ethiopian-type, but in Soweto it appears that the title Bishop has gained considerable ground, and is now used by some leaders of Ethiopian-type churches.[1] At the same time, the title President is often incorporated into the Zionist-type hierarchies. Thus in 42 churches in survey A which were led by Archbishops or Bishops, 60 per cent had Presidents or Vice-Presidents lower in the hierarchy.

In the independent churches age is very important in conferring status, and so also is marriage. The ideal leader, in addition to being male, is at least middle-aged, and married. This was particularly clear in the 252 churches of the combined surveys, where very nearly 98 per cent of the church leaders were over 40 years of age (average 57 years), and all were married, although one had been recently divorced. The ideal leader should not be illiterate, but it was apparent that a high degree of education was not required. The leaders in the combined surveys had an average of 5½ years of schooling — most having reached standards three or four. Some form of theological education was considered desirable, and in survey A, 90 per cent of the leaders interviewed had had some elementary theological education.[2]

Church leaders are not of course confined to any particular language group, and in the combined surveys it was found that 48 per cent were Zulu-speaking, 16 per cent spoke Xhosa, 13 per cent Southern Sotho, 8 per cent Swazi, 6 per cent North Sotho or Tswana, 3 per cent Venda, 3 per cent Tsonga, 2 per cent Ndebele, and 1 per cent other African languages. The preponderance of Zulu-speaking leaders has been suggested to be general by some people acquainted

1. No adequate explanation has been offered for the popularity of the term. It is suggested that (a) the title confers prestige because of the prestige of bishops in the mission churches, and (b) it is used rarely enough in the mission churches to make it uncommon, thus allowing relatively exclusive use by independent churches — for example, the only bishops in Soweto are from the independent churches. The term is also convenient as it distinguishes church leaders specifically — the title 'President' may be held by a variety of secular office-bearers.

2. This result is most probably over-weighted, as a majority of leaders interviewed in this survey were members of AICA, which has a specific policy of providing theological education for its members, and provides them with more opportunities than most other leaders would get.

with the independent church movement, and while no definite conclusion can be drawn from the above evidence as it in no way consti-
tutes a random sample, the above figures do add some weight to
that hypothesis. It should also be noted that Natal (including Zululand) has been the most important growth-point, other than the
Reef area, for independent churches (see Van Zyl 1968: 4).

It is important to note also that church leaders tend to be multi-
lingual, at least in Soweto. Thus the church leaders in survey A
spoke an average of four languages, including their own. With the
exception of one man, all claimed to be able to communicate in
either English or Afrikaans or both: 31 per cent could speak English
only, 19 per cent Afrikaans only, and 48 per cent could speak both
languages. Only 10 per cent of the leaders interviewed claimed to
be able to speak only one African language. The ability to speak a
number of African languages, and at least an Nguni and a Sotho
language, is of great importance in Soweto given that members of
each independent church congregation nearly always have a variety
of home languages.

As will be discussed later, it is in the nature of the independent
church movement that members should join rather than be 'born
into' any particular church, and the same is true of the church
leaders. Of the leaders in survey A, only 3 per cent had been born
into the church they now led. Of the rest, 59 per cent had originally
belonged to a mission church as their first church, and 38 per cent
had belonged to some other independent church.

In the same survey, the majority of leaders were also the founders
of their churches: 56 per cent were founders, while another 4 per
cent were direct descendants of the original founder. The remaining
40 per cent had gained office by election, acclamation or appointment by the preceding leader. Of these leaders 37 per cent were
full-time ministers, 24 per cent were self-employed (as shopkeepers,
owners of small businesses, builders, tradesmen and so on), and the
other 39 per cent were in full-time employment, mostly of an unskilled nature. Thus 61 per cent of the leaders had some degree of
freedom to conduct church business during working hours.

From the above information it is seen that the average leader of
an independent church will be middle-aged, married, with five or six
years of education, and is likely to be in some form of employment
which does not pay particularly high wages. In fact, therefore, he is
likely to be very much like the ordinary member of his congregation.
This is an important aspect of church leadership, and one which
became increasingly apparent during fieldwork — that independent
church leaders are 'men of the people', facing the same problems of
lack of education, employment, etc., that are faced by members of

their congregations. This was often pointed out by independent church members as a positive factor compared with African ministers of mission churches, who often had a much higher level of education than members of their congregations, and who were usually supported financially by their churches.[3] It was suggested that these ministers were not as much in touch with the needs and problems of their people as were the independent church leaders.

At the same time it must of course be asked what makes independent church leaders into leaders if they have so much in common with the ordinary members of their congregations, and do not outshine them, for example, in terms of education or economic achievement. The answer clearly lies in their charisma and organisational ability. Dealing with religious leadership among the Shona, Murphree (1969: 97–8) distinguishes three criteria which combine in leaders — seniority, office, and reputation — and it is useful to apply this analysis to South African independent church leaders.

Taking seniority first, this is clearly of particular importance in the independent churches — it has already been shown that it is extremely unusual for a man under forty years of age to become leader of a church, and that the usual age is well over fifty. It is clear that the older a leader becomes, the more respect he is accorded. In African society generally, it is necessary to be married to achieve full adult status, irrespective of age, and all leaders interviewed were married men. It has already been mentioned that the independent churches are extremely strict about having married leaders, no matter where they fall in the church hierarchy.[4]

Office, of course, is also important. The church leader, particularly in the Zionist-type churches, has an impressive title and impressive robes, both of which are exclusively his by virtue of the office he holds. Zionist bishops wear elaborate robes of different colours, and usually stoles and mitres on special occasions. Most also have a staff of office. All leaders, even if they are founding a new church, have to be formally installed in office, usually with a great deal of ceremony, and in the presence of a number of people from different churches.

3. It should be stressed again, that in nearly all cases where independent church ministers claim to be full-time ministers, the church is unable to support them fully and they have to find other sources of income — for example, wages from relatives and children, renting rooms, etc. Thus one full-time minister of a large independent church said of his house — 'that house educated my children', as he had only been able to afford to pay for their education by renting out rooms.

4. See page 23n. Some independent church leaders pointed out that the unmarried status of Catholic priests as well as other celibates in some of the mission churches was a problem in view of this attitude on the importance of marriage.

Consecration services usually follow a basic pattern, and the more important points of one such service — conducted by the BBCAC leader — will now be given. The candidate for consecration as a new archbishop approached the BBCAC leader and asked him to conduct the service. He approached this particular leader partly because he had met him in a common association, and partly because he was known to be experienced in conducting consecrations. There followed a number of meetings and discussions between the two, as various details were settled, including questions of a new uniform and a certificate of consecration.

The main service started about 9 p.m. on a Saturday night, and was initially conducted by two ministers of the candidate's church. There were the usual opening hymns, prayer, Bible-readings and short addresses, until the candidate entered in procession with the BBCAC leader and the archbishop of another church. This was accompanied by joyful singing and some dancing, and then the BBCAC bishop started the consecration service itself. By this time, there were three archbishops (including the candidate) at the table in front of the congregation, thirteen ministers flanking them, and between 150 and 200 people. In all, five different churches were represented.

The service took place in a specially hired school classroom, which had all its windows papered over. The only light was from oil-lamps and candles. At the start the main table had seven candles and an oil lamp on it, but the oil lamp was removed after an objection by one of the archbishops, who maintained that the table should have only seven lights on it. The presiding bishop then made seven men from the candidate's congregation stand, and asked them publicly whether they were willing to accept the candidate as their archbishop. After they had agreed, the bishop asked for chairs to be brought forward, and the candidate and his wife were told to seat themselves in front of the main table.

Neither of the other archbishops had his wife with him on this occasion (one was ill and the other at a funeral wake) and eventually after discussion the elderly widow of a former minister in the BBCAC, as the most senior woman present, was asked to assist in the robing of the new Lady Archbishop. The new robes were produced, and after a short reading from the Bible (Exodus 29:5) — 'And you shall take the garments and put on Aaron the coat and the robe of the ephod, and the ephod and the breastpiece, and gird him with the skilfully woven band of the ephod' — the couple were formally robed. This was followed by a hymn. A new mitre was produced, and the next verse from the same passage read — 'And you shall set the turban on his head, and put the holy crown upon the turban'

(Exodus 29:6). The mitre was solemnly placed on the candidate's head, and another hymn was sung. A small bottle of oil was then prayed over, and the candidate was anointed after reading the next verse: 'And you shall take the anointing oil and pour it on his head and anoint him' (Exodus 29:7). Again, a hymn was sung.

Finally, with further readings from the Bible and hymns, the candidate had hands laid upon him by both the other bishops present. He was then congratulated, and exhorted by the two bishops on his episcopal duties. The congregation was then asked whether they had anything for their new archbishop, and a new stick of office and a Bible were brought forward and given to him. The new archbishop and his wife, who had also had hands laid upon her and been exhorted to assist her husband in his duties, were then presented to the congregation and there followed singing and dancing. After this the presiding bishop handed over to his colleague, who addressed the gathering. The essence of his address was that he disliked attending consecration services, because some bishops did not always fulfil their duties properly, or live up to their titles. He said he hoped this would not be the case in this instance, and advised the new archbishop to get a certificate of his new rank, so that the authorities would be able to see for themselves — 'they always want proof'. The service concluded with prayers and more singing in the early hours of the morning. Another service, along conventional lines, was held the following morning, and ended with a final feast.

An interesting part of the consecration was that the new vice-bishop, who should have been given new robes and consecrated at the same time, was not in fact consecrated because his wife was ill and could not attend. Great pains were taken at the service to inform all those present that the vice-bishop was in fact a married man, and that he would be consecrated as soon as his wife was well. This again shows the importance, already alluded to, of being married in the independent churches. Two Sundays later, the vice-bishop and his wife were consecrated by the BBCAC leader, given new uniforms and exhorted to fulfil all their duties properly. At the same service, the new archbishop was formally given his certificate of office. It carried the BBCAC name at the top, and announced that the new archbishop of the Ethiopian Salvation Light of Christ Church in South Africa had been properly ordained, and asked all in authority to assist him in his duties. Much of the wording of the certificate was illiterate, but it was accepted with great joy by the new archbishop, who showed it to the congregation and told them that everything was now all right, and that his work was now safe.

This service has been described in some detail because it points to some important aspects of leadership in the independent churches. Firstly, a leader must be properly consecrated, and this must be done in the presence of other church leaders — this is a general rule for independent churches in Soweto, where it is usual for at least three leaders to be present at another's consecration. The second interesting point concerns the asking of members of the congregation whether they are willing to accept the new bishop — showing clearly that he is dependent upon his followers for support in his new role. Thirdly, and this applies to Zionist-type churches mainly, spiritual authority is conveyed at consecration through laying on of hands and anointing with holy oil. Fourthly, the duties and obligations of the new leader are made public during an admonition/exhortation by the presiding bishop,[5] and in the case cited above, were reinforced by an address by one of the other leaders present. The final point that should be observed is the desire that exists for leadership to be officially sanctioned, and the great faith pinned on certificates in this regard. This will be discussed in more detail below.

While a consecration service is important in establishing a new leader in his office and proclaiming this to his congregation, there still remains the third of Murphree's aspects of leadership: that of reputation. This is of great importance in building up an independent church because, as has been mentioned before, the smaller independent churches in South Africa are very similar, within certain broad categories. Prospective members are faced with a number of possible choices, with their decision usually being based on the reputation of the church — which in most cases is closely bound up with the reputation of the church leader. It seems that a church leader may build up a reputation in either or both of two different ways. The first is to achieve a reputation as a strong leader and administrator, preferably someone who has some effect when dealing with those in authority (ideally, this would reflect an Ethiopian-type leader), and the second way is to achieve a reputation either as a strong prophet, or as a holy person (ideally, a Zionist-type leader). (Sundkler 1961: 106–9.)

5. The admonition of a bishop and his wife usually follows a set pattern, and is normally based on a biblical text, which is then elaborated upon by the speaker. The favourite appears to be 1 Timothy 3:1–7: 'The saying is sure. If any one aspires to the office of a bishop, he desires a noble work. Now a bishop must be above reproach, married only once, temperate, sensible, dignified, hospitable, an apt teacher, no drunkard, not violent but gentle, not quarrelsome, and no lover of money. He must manage his own household well, keeping his children submissive and respectful in every way; for if a man does not know how to manage his own household, how can he care for God's church? He must not be a recent convert, or he may be puffed up with conceit and fall into the condemnation of the devil; moreover he must be well thought of by outsiders, or he may fall into reproach and the snare of the devil.' See also Titus 1:7–9.

Some leaders build up their reputations through establishing bureaucracies within their churches — involving synods and con-ferences, councils and circuits, district meetings and local meetings. Each group thus created will have its own small hierarchy, owing allegiance to the church leader and thus strengthening his position. It is also possible to develop a reputation, which may or may not be deserved, for being good in dealing with those in authority. The prime example of this involves dealings with the Bantu Administra-tion Department in Pretoria. Sundkler describes the sort of leader who 'is supposed to be very learned, and very clever, and to be constantly interceding on the Church's behalf with the Government in Pretoria'. (Sundkler 1961: 150.)[6]

Other dealings with authority, which are more important, concern local officials who actually have authority to grant concessions and remove privileges. These are much more difficult for an 'unofficial' independent church leader to handle, and consequently there are very few who have a reputation in this regard.

A leader who happens to be a prophet may build a reputation through his healing ability, which will become known through successful treatment of patients, who will generally come from different residential areas and different churches. However, it has already been pointed out that many leaders of Zionist-type churches are not prophets in their own right, and the reputation of their churches in this respect usually comes from the efforts of their female prophets, who do not stand within the formal male hierarchy. Male leaders, however, may also achieve a reputation for being 'holy' — that is, leading blameless lives, and being blessed by the Spirit. Thus although the leader of the BBCAC, for example, was not a prophet, it was stated by some followers that they followed him because he was a 'good man'. It was also pointed out that he could heal in some cases because he was 'holy', even if he was not a prophet.

This is an important point about Zionist-type leaders: it is believed that the Spirit may work through them, even if they are not prophets in the sense that they cannot predict, divine and heal. The working of the Spirit is clearest perhaps in blessing — in many churches, ser-vices end with the bishop blessing individual members of the congre-

6. See page 24 and note. Many churches remain in communication with the Bantu Administration Department in Pretoria, sending copies of minutes, reports of baptisms and ordinations, etc.

Communications are generally acknowledged by the Department in non-committal terms, and the impression can be given by church leaders that useful discussions are taking place which are assisting the church. One leader of an association of independent churches in Johannesburg has gained support by acting as an intermediary between semi-literate church leaders and the authori-ties, particularly in the matter of registering churches, which no longer takes place.

gation. This is sometimes accompanied by spirit possession, and is taken to show the power of the bishop. Some leaders also build a reputation for being able to drive out evil spirits. An example of this occurred during an Ascension Day service held by the Full Gospel church.

The service in question was held, not at the headquarters as was customary, but at the inauguration of a branch in another part of Soweto. The bishop sent detailed instructions to the circuit convenor, as the branch leader was called (he held the rank of evangelist), and on the appointed day the bishop arrived. He was annoyed to find that nothing had been started: some members were still out of uniform, the candles had not been lit, there was no drum, and the service was not yet under way. This occasioned a fierce address in which the congregation, and especially the local leaders, were castigated for not carrying out their duties properly. The bishop swiftly put everything in its place, and this start set the tone for the service, as the bishop completely dominated everyone present and subdued them with his anger.

It was in this atmosphere that the circuit convenor, later in the service, read out the names of two members of the local circuit, a married couple. They were told to come forward and stand before the altar. The bishop had been informed in advance, but the couple were unsuspecting, and stood before him showing signs of considerable trepidation. The bishop announced to the congregation that he had been informed that there was bad feeling between the couple, and that this 'bad spirit' would have to be driven out. He then launched into an impassioned sermon against the evils of drinking and dagga-smoking (cannabis) and against the dangers of dissension within the congregation. He worked himself up to a high pitch while the couple stood trembling before him, and then while the congregation sang to the accompaniment of drums he stepped forward and laid hands on each in turn, touched them with his stick, and prayed in a very loud voice for the evil spirit to leave them, so that they could live in peace and leave behind all the evil things they had been doing. As he touched them, they both trembled quite violently with the Spirit.

It is difficult to describe the atmosphere of this incident, except to say it was extremely tense, and that the bishop was most impressive for his ability to dominate the proceedings utterly. It was also clear that the couple underwent a traumatic experience, and it was reported later that their quarrel had stopped, there was no more drinking in the house, that the man had got a steady job, and that they had settled down in the congregation. The incident must also have had a salutory effect on other members of the congregation, and probably heightened the esteem in which the bishop was held.

SUCCESSION

It has already been mentioned that 56 per cent of the churches in survey A were still being led by their founders, and that of the remaining churches no fewer than 40 per cent had a leader who was not a relative or direct descendant of the founder. It has often been pointed out that the first major crisis experienced by an independent church is likely to occur with the death of the founder, and the subsequent appointment of a successor. In this regard it is very interesting to note that as many as 44 per cent of the churches in survey A had apparently survived this crisis, and that in the majority of cases a new leader had been selected who was not a relative or a descendant of the original founder.

Succession to the leadership of an independent church can be resolved in a number of different ways. Firstly, the leader of a church can designate his successor during his life-time, as happened in the BBCAC, and this may be accepted by the church after his death. In a very few instances, for example that of the Full Gospel church, a leader may retire and personally supervise the selection of a successor. In either instance, the designated successor may or may not be a relative, although in certain churches it is 'traditional' where possible for father to be succeeded by son. The most prominent examples of this are two of the largest independent churches in South Africa: the Nazareth Baptist Church founded by Isaiah Shembe in Natal is now led by his son (Sundkler 1961: 111 and 119), and the Zion Christian Church of the Transvaal founded by E. Lekganyane, was later led by his son, and then by his grandson, the son of the second leader. However, most of the churches interviewed in Soweto which had survived the death of their founder were not in fact being led by a relative.

Sundkler (1961: 117–21) mentions the importance of inherited leadership in the independent churches in Natal but also points to some of the difficulties experienced by successors who did not have the full approval of all members of the congregation. One way of resolving this sort of problem is to combine principles of inheritance and election in one system: for example, by allowing the election by a church council of one of a number of possible heirs.[7] In the independent churches, however, this is an unusual system to be *prescribed*

7. Regarding succession to chieftainship, of course, this sort of system is not unknown among some African peoples of South Africa. The clearest example is that of the Swazi (see Kuper 1947: 88ff.) but even more rigid systems where succession was rigorously prescribed could sometimes be 'bent' to allow succession by another person of the same house, who was deemed to be more suitable (for the Sotho, for example, see Goody 1966: 61).

— what is more likely to happen is for a church council to decide to elect a new leader who is a relative of the former leader. Difficulties may arise here when a relative is elected above another candidate whom some of the congregation might deem to have superior qualities. In these cases splits in the church are likely to occur.

In churches where the principle of inheritance is not important, there are a number of other ways of resolving succession. The simplest is where, particularly in small churches, there is only one possible successor, who is usually the second-in-command anyway, and who takes charge of the church without the need for elections. This we term succession by acclamation, in that it involves general approval by church members. In these cases a formal consecration follows to set the seal on the church's decision.

The system of election by a church council, or some like body, is also relatively simple, provided they elect someone who has the general approval of the majority of church members. Difficulties occur when an election takes place in which the wishes of the majority are not followed. In only one case during the fieldwork was a leader elected by universal suffrage; in most cases the leader was selected by a small group of leaders in the church. These men might select somebody other than the candidate with the best claims in the view of the ordinary members, through personal jealousies, or through a wish to appoint a relative of the late leader.

Further complications arise when there are a number of candidates who claim special qualifications for the position of leader of the church. Typically the man who is second-in-command of the church expects to succeed on the death of the founder. However, it appears to be a principle in the independent churches in Soweto that a leader will not appoint a second-in-command who is likely to outshine him: such a deputy would be likely to split off and form his own church. The result seems to be that those who remain as deputies are generally not of the same calibre as their leaders. Within the hierarchy, in Soweto at least, the position most likely to be awarded on merit and ability is that of general secretary, which is often held by a minister. The general secretary is appointed for his education and ability to keep minute books, write letters, etc. On the death of a leader the general secretary, as the man with the most education, and the man who often has possession of some church documents and correspondence, may regard himself as the ideal successor and oppose the claims of the generally older and less-educated second-in-command. One or two cases occurred during fieldwork when this happened, and in one of them the inevitable split did not occur because the church concerned owned property which both sides wanted.

This particular church, which we shall call the African Church, is an offshoot of the Methodist Church of South Africa, and was founded in 1926. Details of the dispute will be given here as an example of the sort of complexities that occur. The President of the church retired in 1967 and a dispute over his successor soon followed. The Revd T., who said that he had been 'born into' the church, claimed that he had been elected President in 1968 after having been acting leader in 1964 and 1967. He was a young man, and fairly well educated in independent church terms. His opponent, the Revd R., joined the church in 1964 (perhaps significantly during the period T. claimed to have been acting leader). R. was an elderly man, not a dynamic leader, and of little education. Observers in other independent churches who followed the dispute with interest stated that T., in view of his education, had been acting as church secretary whilst R. was second-in-command to the former leader. Both possessed some of the church correspondence, although some had been lost. Each accused the other of having destroyed the lost correspondence.

A staff member of the Christian Institute of Southern Africa, who visited the former leader in his retirement shortly after the elections, said that he was satisfied that the Revd R. had been properly elected with his former leader's support. The latter had changed his stance after the Revd T. had 'worked on him', and was no longer prepared to state categorically who was leader. An executive member of the African Independent Churches' Association, of which the African Church was a member, also said that from their records it appeared as though R. had been properly elected President.

Both leaders had their own group of supporters, largely concentrated in the area in which they each lived — R. lived a few kilometres from Johannesburg, and T. lived in Soweto. Under normal circumstances it is most likely that the two groups would have split to form separate churches, as there was certainly no sense in their forming a corporate body (Wilson 1964: 8). However the church owned fixed property in the form of a church building in Soweto which was in the last stages of completion, and both sides laid claim to it. While the dispute had simmered for nearly three years, it came to the boil over the question of dedicating the new church. Both leaders claimed the right to do this, and the dispute later narrowed down, after an agreement that both would be present, to who should turn the key to open the new building. It was eventually decided that the President of AICA should open the building, and turn the key in the presence of both leaders.

On the day of the dedication, both leaders appeared with their followers. The Revd R. came with about thirty of his supporters, although they were all from several kilometres away, but the Revd T. could muster less than half a dozen. R., possibly profiting from the weak support of his rival, took the opportunity of presiding at the service which followed, although most of it was conducted by the AICA President. T. sat near the main table with a number of ministers from other churches who were also present. The AICA President in his sermon exhorted both sides to pray and make up their differences, but no other reference was made to the dispute. The service itself was dull and without any spark to it, and the singing was lacklustre. A couple of visitors afterwards commented on the dullness of the proceedings, and attributed this to the dispute.

AICA leaders made an effort to resolve the dispute by suggesting that a church conference be held at which all members could vote for a new President. This was agreed to by both parties, who went away and separately organised conferences at which their supporters unanimously elected them President. Meanwhile, the dispute still centred round the church building in Soweto. The Minister in charge of the building was the Revd S., who supported T. In view of this, R. and his conference pronounced that S. had been handling his parish incompetently for the last seven years, and transferred him to another area. They appointed another minister, the Revd M., in his place. However, S. refused to be transferred, and as he acknowledged T. as his leader he refused to discuss the matter with R.

After the church dedication, S. somehow obtained the key to the building, and refused to allow M. entry. At this stage the dispute became even more bitter, and the police were called in. There was reported to be some security police interest also. However, the dispute was too complicated for the authorities to sort out, and by the end of the fieldwork period it still did not appear that there would be any easy solution.

When no obvious leader with general support emerges, there is another way of resolving the sort of dispute that has been described above – and that is to appoint a 'caretaker' leader, who is not one of the candidates for the office but who has sufficient status to be able to hold the position. Perhaps the most usual instance of this, although it does not happen frequently, is for the mother or wife of the late leader to become temporary leader of the church. This has two advantages, firstly that a woman cannot usually be the permanent leader of the church (although she may preside temporarily, nobody would regard this as a threat to the male candidates), and secondly that women – particularly elderly wives or kin of leaders – may reach positions of great authority within independent churches, even if they do not hold formal titles.[8]

8. A parallel may be drawn here with some traditional African political

One of the largest and most prominent independent churches in the Transvaal, the St John's Apostolic Faith Mission Church, gives a good indication of the problems that can arise when a woman founds and leads an independent church. This church was founded by a prominent prophet and healer, Mrs C. Nku, who holds the title 'Founder and Life General President' of the church, which is known all over the Reef area and beyond as 'Ma Nku's Church'. The church has a number of bishops, and significantly has an Archbishop, which is the senior male position in the church. Elections for this office were due to have been held in January 1970, but 'because of certain misunderstandings within the church's branches',[9] they were postponed until August 1970.

There were two candidates for office, Bishop P. J. Masango, and Bishop J. Nku, the son of the founder and Archbishop before the elections. The church was prominent enough to have news of the election in the African newspaper *World*, and on the day following the election the results were announced with a banner headline '9 000 elect Masango as new St John's Archbishop'. The report stated that after a secret ballot lasting from 11 a.m. to 4 p.m. Bishop Masango beat Bishop Nku by 4 618 votes to 3 935. The report continued, 'The results . . . have shocked thousands of churchgoers who favoured Archbishop Nku. Tongues are wagging that some church members voted twice.' According to the paper Mrs Nku 'dropped a bombshell . . . when she announced that Bishop Masango's term of office would only last four months in terms of the new constitution. She said that according to the new constitution she, as head of the church, was required to appoint bishops, ministers and church elders. Mrs Nku also announced that Bishop Masango would occupy the archbishop's seat temporarily until early next year when she would appoint another archbishop.'

A few days later, under another banner headline 'Big Split Threatens Nku's Church', a further report was carried including rumours of a split and an interview with the secretary-general of the church, who claimed that 'there were a lot of irregularities during last week's

systems. For example a woman of royal blood has acted as Regent in Lesotho (Goody 1966: 72). See also the role of the Queen Mother among the Swazi (Kuper 1947).

9. All quotations from the *World*, published daily in Johannesburg. The elections were dealt with in issues of 23.8.70 and 24.8.70. Rumours of a split and a denial appeared on 3.9.70 and 4.9.70. Further statements followed on 25.9.70, 10.9.70, with the resignation of Bishop Nku on 27.9.70 and 8.10.70. The expulsion and rejection of this by Bishop Masango followed on 14 and 15.10.70. The subsequent court case was dealt with on 1.11.70, 8.11.70 and 30.1.71 and 3.2.71. Masango's warning to church members was on 28.4.71. *World* also ran several letters to the editor on the subject in the latter part of 1970, and has covered developments in the dispute extensively since then.

elections, despite the presence of the two advocates and members of
the South African police.' More significantly, the secretary-general
also stated: 'Another bone of contention is that the founder of the
church has been reduced to nothing except a figure-head who is like
a constitutional monarch. Unless this is put right, especially the
clash of personalities which has crept in, I have fear that the church
is tottering towards an inglorious end.' The following day Bishop
Masango stressed that he had been properly elected, and that there
was no split looming.

A week later Mrs Nku made an important statement on the dispute,
in which she said that 'the Revd Johannes Nku and the Revd Petros
Masango have no authority in this church in my lifetime. . . . I am
not going to take orders from the Revd Johannes Nku nor the Revd
Petros Masango. . . . I am not at all prepared to turn this church into
a non-spiritual structure or into a political body. . . . If (they) refuse
my spiritual orders they can leave the St John's Apostolic Faith
Church and start their own churches. . . . I am not interested in being
misdirected by man.' She concluded by saying that she alone had the
right to appoint church officials, and that no new constitution could
be accepted without her 'written approval'.

Some weeks later, the *World* announced that Bishop Masango
would be holding the traditional November feast in his own area,[10]
and not as usual at Evaton, Mrs Nku's centre. He said this was
because his area was now the headquarters of the church. Some
days later Bishop Nku announced that he was resigning from the
church and going into business, and was sharply attacked by his
mother. A week later Mrs Nku announced that she was expelling
Bishop Masango from her church as he had questioned her leadership. She stated, 'I have saved his life, ordained and anointed him,
and made him what he is today directed by the Holy Spirit. . . .
For him to tell me to take orders from him . . . I consider as a direct
insult.' Bishop Masango replied immediately that he refused to quit
the church as the expulsion was unconstitutional, and that he still
regarded Mrs Nku as head of the church.

Some weeks later the Supreme Court in Pretoria issued a temporary interdict, ordering that Bishop Masango be given full access to
all church documents, until the action was decided. The case was
postponed several times, and finally settled in March 1971 when it
was ruled that Bishop Masango was the legitimately elected Archbishop of the church. Subsequently the *World* carried a warning
from the Archbishop that all church members should recognise his

10. As Bishop Masango has spent considerable time in Swaziland, this feast
may have links with the Swazi *Incwala* rituals (Kuper 1947: 35, 197ff) which
take place at the same time.

authority — if they failed to do this, he might be forced to demolish the church buildings of dissenters. He also stated that he hoped to work in harmony with Mrs Nku, and that their church was more important than any of them.

A number of interesting points come out of the dispute. Firstly, a clear conflict developed after the founder's choice for the position of Archbishop (her son) had been rejected in favour of another candidate, who drew wide support among ordinary church members from different areas.[11] When this happened, the founder unilaterally announced that the new Archbishop would only serve for a token period, and this was contested. At the same time members of the church contested the elections themselves, and the whole matter was taken to court.[12] In the dispute that followed it was quite clear that there was disagreement between Mrs Nku and Bishop Masango over the degree of authority each should wield, and that Bishop Masango wanted more say in church affairs than did Bishop Nku.

As Life General President, with authority claimed from the Holy Spirit, Mrs Nku also clearly felt that she could control the affairs of her church as she wished, but she was hampered by her church constitution and the fact that Bishop Masango was prepared to go to court over its interpretation. This is yet another case where it can be fairly safely assumed that the church would have split into two groups, had it not been for the church property involved (cf. Wilson 1964: 8). The St John's Apostolic Faith Mission has the largest independent church building on the Reef at Evaton, Mrs Nku's home, and has other buildings elsewhere. Neither side was prepared to lose these symbols of the church's status and security, and it is significant that Bishop Masango, in a clear reference to the Evaton church, threatened to demolish the church buildings of those who would not recognise his authority.

The church's problem, stated simply, was that although it had a leader she was female, and it was felt necessary to have a senior male leader as well. Instead of allowing the leader to appoint a man to this position, a constitution was adopted which allowed elections. The person elected in this case was not prepared to play second fiddle, whereas the leader's nominee would have. This position can be contrasted with that of the Bethsaid Healing Faith Mission, an

11. Bishop Masango was well known in the church for his travelling to visit the various congregations of the church. For example, Sundkler mentions his efforts in Swaziland (Sundkler 1961: 318, 320).

12. It seems to be more and more popular among some independent churches to threaten legal action over disputes, particularly where questions of elections or interpretation of constitutions are concerned. Another prominent independent church to be involved in litigation over leadership during the fieldwork period was the Presbyterian Church of Africa. This also received press coverage.

independent church in Soweto which was founded by a woman who was unable to use her healing powers to the full in her old church. She therefore founded a church stressing healing, and became the driving force in it. At the same time she felt that the church should have a male bishop as its titular head, and her husband was elected to this position, one he accepted rather reluctantly, as he had been only a layman in their previous church. The latter situation is much more common, and a number of independent churches in survey A were in a similar position. However, this was only the case with Zionist-type churches, where women prophets had felt it necessary to found churches in which they could exercise their healing gifts.

Having discussed succession to the highest office in the independent churches, we shall now turn to those who hold lesser office in the churches, but who are nevertheless numerically more important.

SOME HIERARCHIES

As has been mentioned, 80 per cent of the leaders of the churches in the combined surveys were titled Bishop or Archbishop, while 15 per cent were titled President and a smaller number either Moderator or were some variation of Minister. In discussing other titles in independent church hierarchies, it is useful to distinguish between those who hold titles higher than Minister (*Umfundisi*), and those who are of the rank of Minister or below. While the second category shows a great deal of uniformity throughout the churches surveyed, there is considerable variation in the first, which can lead to confusion as the same titles can refer to different positions in a given hierarchy. The hierarchies discussed here are taken from 57 churches in survey A.

Nearly all independent churches have a second-in-command who is usually designated by a title higher than that of Minister — only 9 of the 57 churches under discussion had a second-in-command with the rank of minister. The titles used were: President (15), Vice-President (13), Vice-Bishop (12), Minister (9), Bishop (2), Moderator (2), Vice-Moderator (1), Presiding Elder (1), Archdeacon (1), and Superintendent (1).

Whatever the formal title, most deputy-leaders are known simply as *i-Vice* or sometimes as *Mongamedi* (in Zulu), or *Mookamedi* (in Sotho). This is often rather loosely translated to be either Vice-President *or* Vice-Bishop, and these two titles should more accurately be taken together, which would make them clearly the most popular for a second-in-command. The other titles give some indication of the variety and confusion that may arise. For example, four out of the ten titles cited may also designate the leader of a church in another hierarchy — Bishop, President, Moderator, and Minister. A further complication is that four of the terms used here for deputy-leader — President, Vice-President, Moderator and Archdeacon — are used also to denote people who are third or lower in the hierarchies of other churches in the same survey. In certain cases hierarchies are further complicated by the fact that more than one person will have the same title: thus two churches in the survey had three Vice-Bishops each, and one had three Presidents. Other titles above the rank of minister which occurred were General Secretary (5), Dean (1), and Senior Minister (1).

Much more uniformity was shown in titles from Minister down. All 57 churches had Ministers, while 32 had Deacons, 50 had Evangelists and 54 had Preachers, in that order of precedence. The only variations were that three churches had Elders instead of Deacons, one had Stewards instead of Deacons, and one had Prophets instead of Evangelists. Only two churches had ranks below that of Preacher — one had Deacons and Sub-Deacons, and the other Circuit Stewards followed by Leaders.

Some of the variety in leadership hierarchies may be seen in the selected hierarchies presented in order of precedence in Table 4, on page 70.

A number of writers have commented on the elaborate hierarchies that are so often found in the independent churches. Wishlade (1965: 91) refers to the high proportion of officials to members, while Sundkler (1961: 127) suggests that one of the main weaknesses of the independent churches is that they are overstaffed to an extent 'which could often be described as absurd'. While this may be the judgement of outsiders, it is quite clear that the elaborate hierarchies mentioned are extremely important in providing opportunities for exercising leadership, and this has been pointed out by Sundkler and others (Sundkler 1961: 100; Pauw 1960: 77; Wishlade 1965: 76).

It is important to realise that while independent churches may be regarded as 'overstaffed' by some, members within their respective hierarchies have clearly defined rights and duties. The lowest rung of the ladder is the office of *umgosa* or Steward (sometimes referred to in English as 'Doorman' or 'Porter') which is not usually listed in the ecclesiastical hierarchy. The steward's function is to care for the church building (be it church, garage or classroom), to usher members to their seats, and to supervise the opening and closing of the door during services.

The lowest rung of the ecclesiastical ladder is held by the Preacher. A Preacher's specific role will vary depending on whether or not he is in charge of a congregation. Usually he is not, and has more senior officials over him, and his role will be confined to preaching, praying and reading passages from the Bible during services. In Zionist-type

TABLE 4 : SOME SELECTED HIERARCHIES

1	2	3	4
President	Moderator	Bishop	Archbishop
Vice-President	Vice-President	President	Vice-Bishop
General Secretary	Ministers	Vice-President	President
Ministers	Deacons	Ministers	Ministers
Evangelists	Evangelists	Deacons	Deacons
Preachers	Preachers	Evangelists	Evangelists
		Preachers	Preachers

5	6	7	8
Bishop	Bishop	Bishop	Bishop
Vice-Bishops	Bishop	Superintendent	Bishop
Senior Minister	Archdeacon	Ministers	Moderator
Ministers	Dean	Elders	Ministers
Deacons	Ministers	Evangelists	Preachers
Evangelists	Deacons	Preachers	
Preachers	Evangelists		
	Preachers		

9	10	11	12
Bishop	Archbishop	Bishop	Bishop
Vice-President	President	Archdeacon	Moderator
Ministers	Vice-President	Ministers	President
Deacons	Ministers	Deacons	General Secretary
Evangelists	Deacons	Evangelists	Ministers
Preachers	Evangelists	Preachers	Evangelists
	Preachers		Preachers

churches he is often not distinguished from ordinary full members in uniform. The Evangelist is the next step up, and most Preachers can expect to be made Evangelists after a period of time. Evangelists also preach, pray and read the Bible at services, and in many churches an extra duty is to baptise new members.[13] In most churches a man will not be made a Deacon unless the intention is for him to be made a full Minister after a probationary period, usually one year. Deacons are therefore probationary ministers (often distinguished by wearing reversed clerical collars) who fulfil much the same functions as Evangelists.

The step from Deacon to Minister is particularly important, as far as both status and duties are concerned. A Minister, *umfundisi* (Zulu)

13. In a number of baptism services attended, the Bishop would conduct the service from the bank, and an Evangelist or Minister would enter the water — in only one case during two years was a Bishop observed personally baptising in the water.

or *moruti* (Sotho), is treated with respect, and has the right to wear
a stock and clerical collar, as well as to put 'Reverend' before his
name. The importance of the Minister is also indicated by the fact
that his ordination is more elaborate than that of Deacons, Evangelists or Preachers. The Minister is more often in charge of a specific
congregation, and will have the right to baptise, admit new members,
ordain lesser officials in the church, and administer Holy Communion,
at the discretion of the Bishop.

Preachers, Evangelists, Deacons and Ministers can either be elected
by church conference or appointed directly by a Bishop, and this
varies greatly from church to church — but in most cases it would
appear that the Bishop's wishes are respected, whether or not appointment is by election. In many cases promotion occurs annually
up to the rank of Minister (with the rider that no one will be appointed Deacon who is not going to be promoted to Minister within a short
period of time). With the increasing emphasis on the need for theological education it is possible that it is becoming more difficult to
be ordained a Minister, as certain educational standards are now
required, but this does not as yet appear to have affected the numbers
of ordinations, as educational standards are still extremely low
(Sundkler 1961: 125; see also pages 30 and 53).

With regular promotions from Preacher through the hierarchy up
to the rank of Minister, certain problems of rank within the hierarchy can arise in the larger churches where there are numerous ministers. To some extent ambitions can be fulfilled by assigning control
of separate congregations to different leaders, but this does not solve
hierarchical problems of precedence. Many churches have thus created
positions below that of leader, but above the rank of Minister. Of the
57 churches in survey A there were only 9 that did not have one of
these 'intermediate positions', and the remaining 48 churches had
77 such positions.

In a few cases these 'intermediate positions' are easily instituted
by virtue of the tradition from which the independent church comes.
Thus the African Free New Church follows Anglican tradition,
because its leader broke from the Anglican church, and therefore
has more than one Bishop, as well as an Archdeacon and a Dean.
The Presbyterian Church of Africa, on the other hand, follows its
parent church, the Church of Scotland, in having a Moderator with
several Provincial Moderators under him. In this case, as in some
others, holders of these positions are given authority over certain
geographical areas — thus, to give another example from a Zionist-
type church, the First Catholic Apostolic Jerusalem Church in Zion
of South Africa has a Bishop and under him three Presidents who
are responsible for different areas of the country.

But in many other cases titles in this range do not confer any real extra power above that wielded by a full Minister, and the purpose is largely to clarify the order of precedence within the hierarchy. To take one example, the Bantu Bethlehem Christian Apostolic Church of South Africa, at the time of fieldwork, had an Archbishop, a Vice-Bishop and a President holding the top three positions in the hierarchy. In this case, the Vice-Bishop was the deputy-leader, and the President was rather vague about his duties, which he described as 'I look after the whole church'. In fact the President had less power in the church than the General Secretary, who held the rank of Minister, and his rank was given to him on account of his age — 77 years — and his seniority within the church: he had joined the church at its foundation and had risen to the rank of Minister in 1957. He was promoted to the rank of President when the present leader vacated that office to become Archbishop (see page 23ff).

The fact that more independent church leaders — including some in the Ethiopian-type churches — are using the title Bishop makes it easier to give prestigious titles to those of lesser rank: in addition to Vice-Bishop, the titles President, Vice-President, Moderator, etc. may be used. It is also not uncommon for the church leader himself to be promoted; this not only allows promotions lower in the hierarchy, but also indicates some sort of objective judgement regarding leadership titles.

Attention was drawn to this early in the fieldwork by a report in the *World* under the heading 'Founder of Church is made Archbishop',[14] which referred also to the fact that the leader of the church had recently been promoted. In survey B, church leaders who were founders of their churches were asked for the date the church had been founded, and also for the year in which they had been consecrated. Of the total of 194 churches in this survey, 151 churches filled the requirements, and it was found that 32 per cent of their leaders had been consecrated in the same year that the church was founded while no fewer than 68 per cent had been consecrated a year or more after their founding of the church. The average delay was four years. This figure is possibly a bit exaggerated, as it is possible that some leaders claimed to be the founder of their church, when in fact this was not so. But even accepting this, it is clear that there is some degree of self-judgement involved.

14. *World*, 3.11.69. The report read: 'Rev Clemence Boy Mopu, 49, founder of the Apostolic Church–Jerusalem Association, has been promoted to Archbishop. Rev Mopu. who founded the church in 1946 while working in Durban, becomes the second-in-command to the president of the church, Revd Z. Z. Tabane of Krugersdorp. Revd Tabane has also been recently promoted by a church conference. The two men will be confirmed in April during a nine-day church conference in Krugersdorp.'

One example of this is the leader of the Holy United Methodist Church, who at the time of the research held the title President. He explained that he would eventually be consecrated as Bishop, but only when his church had been going successfully for a number of years, and when the congregation had grown to a more suitable size. To give another example, the leader of the First Apostolic Church of Christ in Zion of South Africa, a Bishop, said that he would become an Archbishop after he had been in office as a Bishop for ten years — he felt that at that stage he would have had sufficient experience to become an Archbishop.

While people holding 'intermediate positions' may take precedence in rank over those below them, they do not always hold commensurate power in the church. I have mentioned above the case of a church President who holds less authority than does the church General Secretary, and this is not uncommon. The tendency for deputy-leaders to be people who do not outshine their leaders has also been mentioned, and the same is true in some measure for those holding lesser positions. The importance of the General Secretary, as an educated official having responsibility for church correspondence, etc., was also indicated. The General Secretary is often a figure of more importance than his rank in the order of precedence might suggest. Of some importance, too, is the position of Treasurer, in those churches where it exists.[15]

Leadership in the independent churches is thus vested in clearly defined hierarchies, with individual members having defined duties and powers. In most independent churches some authority is vested in certain groups of leaders. The most common is the church Conference where all in positions of leadership come together once a year to decide various matters, notably promotions. In some of the smaller churches, particularly Zionist-type, a church Conference can act merely as a rubber-stamp for the Bishop, while in other churches, particularly Ethiopian-type with their slightly more egalitarian leadership, Conferences may hold some significant power, including in some cases the right to elect the church leader at regular intervals. In Zionist-type churches, leaders tend to be elected for life; in those that are Ethiopian-type, particularly the larger ones, leaders are elected for a specific period, usually of the order of five years.

While most churches have at least a church Conference, a number

15. Many leadership disputes in the independent churches centre around financial matters, and many church leaders prefer to keep direct control of their church finances. Treasurers are therefore less important than Secretaries, and in some churches there are no Treasurers at all, duties being shared by the leader and his Secretary.

have other bodies also, with different powers and duties, although the constitution and powers of these bodies vary considerably from church to church. The larger Ethiopian-type churches tend to have more such bodies than other independent churches. Thus, for example, the three small churches discussed in chapter 3 had very few combined leadership groups, what they had being church Conferences and in one case a church Council which dealt mainly with matters of church discipline. In contrast, the 6 000-strong United National Church of South Africa has a Conference, two Provincial Synods, and numerous District Conferences and smaller Circuits. The 37 000-strong Presbyterian Church of Africa has a more elaborate system consisting of a National Assembly, with various committees attached to it, six Provincial Presbyteries, with numerous sessional committees, and a large number of Circuits with authority over individual Stations.

DISPUTES

The role and extent of disputes within the African independent churches has often been exaggerated to the extent that someone unfamiliar with the movement might suppose that disputes were their most important characteristic. While disputes undoubtedly occur frequently they are by no means always followed by enmity and bitterness. Perhaps because secessions are so common, a pattern seems to have been worked out which allows them to take place with a minimum of disruption.

Disputes usually result in a split in the church, and usually centre round problems of leadership. They occur in different ways for different reasons. Firstly, there can be disputes within specific hierarchies. Some may be based on 'genuine' grievances — for example the leader embezzling funds, or an official usurping the rightful role of another, or a contravention by a leader of the church constitution. Other disputes may be contrived. This often happens when a subordinate feels that he should be the leader of the church (either through self-estimation, or through pressure from supporters) and then seeks some excuse for a confrontation with the church leader. It is in these cases that it is particularly difficult for the fieldworker to ascertain the 'real' reason for a particular dispute. Unless there is the complication of ownership of property, disputing groups are able to drift apart — for example they may just stop attending services and start off on their own. In some cases the reason for the split may never be made entirely clear, and a leader may simply find that he has lost a congregation. This type of secession is particularly easy, given the highly decentralised organisation of most independent churches and the difficulties of communication caused by both distance and lack of education.

Where specific reasons are given for leadership disputes, it appears that the most common arise from disputes about money. Few independent churches keep, or through lack of training are able to keep, adequate financial records (West and Van Zyl 1970), and it is a relatively simple matter for disputes to arise over income and expenditure. One example was given in chapter 3, where the leader of the Holy United Methodist Church broke with his former leader because the latter could not account adequately for money that had been collected to buy church badges. Other disputes arise through contraventions of the church constitution (as was alleged in the dispute in the St John's Apostolic Faith Mission) and through ignoring or usurping rightful duties (one leader in survey A broke with his bishop because the latter had ordained a minister in his area without prior consultation or approval of the congregation in the area).

It should be made clear, however, that where disputes occur they are internal in most cases — as in the examples cited. Friction tends to occur *within* hierarchies, and not *between* churches. And hierarchies are in a sense self-stabilising — in most cases disputes are resolved through one party's splitting off to join another church or found a new one, and both parties return to an equilibrium position. While it is necessary, as will be shown later, to co-operate with leaders of other churches, there are sufficient independent churches in Soweto for it to be unnecessary for either party to come into contact with the other, and so what hostility might have existed tends to wane or disappear. Moreover, it seems to be realised by many leaders that secession is, so to speak, a professional hazard (most leaders having seceded themselves) and cases are often treated rather fatalistically. As one leader said, in order to have peace in the church it is better that those who are dissatisfied leave and go elsewhere.

It can be seen that the African independent churches provide scope for leadership which includes numerous and varied positions with different responsibilities and degrees of authority. There is wide scope for promotion within individual hierarchies and, with certain provisos about those holding what we have called intermediate positions within these hierarchies, there are usually specific rights and duties associated with specific offices. The average church leader is relatively poor and relatively ill-educated — and it is important to note that opportunities for exercising leadership are available for these people in the independent churches to a degree that is not paralleled in other fields of activity.

CHAPTER **5 Church Followers**

A lack in many studies of African independent churches has been in
the attention paid to ordinary members, the rank and file, who do not
generally hold high office, but who comprise the majority of all
church members. Some studies have brief evaluations of general
membership (e.g. Peel 1968: 191–217; Turner 1967, vol. ii: 10–19),
others refer to church members in relation to their leaders (e.g.
Sundkler 1961: 100–79) and some do not have specific sections on
followers at all. In this chapter we shall examine church followers
in some detail, drawing information from a survey of followers in
the main congregations of the three churches described at the beginning of chapter 3 (this survey of followers was called survey C, see
Appendix 1).

In the survey mentioned above, only 34 per cent of the followers
of the three churches who were interviewed were male, so membership was almost two-thirds female. This is roughly the proportion of
men to women in the independent churches which was observed
during fieldwork. The preponderance of females in churches has been
noted many times, and Bryan Wilson (1961: 298) goes so far as to
generalise that 'almost all religious denominations attract a larger
proportion of women than men'. Noting that in a survey of inhabitants of a Rhodesian township over 50 per cent of the women
belonged to church groups compared with 16 per cent of the men,
Thomas (1970: 283–4) suggests that churches fulfil certain specific
needs for women in an urban environment. Lehmann, dealing with
independent churches specifically, suggests something similar: that
'the churches replace the functions of customary institutions which
have been weakened by culture change'. (Hayward 1963: 66.) This
aspect of the churches will be discussed in the final chapter.

The average age of all the members interviewed in survey C was
46 years. The average age of members of the BBCAC was 47 years,
of the Full Gospel 48 years, and of the Holy United church 42
years. These figures should be compared with the average age for
church leaders, which was found in the combined surveys A and B

to be 57 years. Survey C dealt only with full members of the congregations, and therefore does not take into account churchgoers in
their early teens and below. From observation during fieldwork over
nearly two years, it appears that most independent church congregations consist of young children and people of middle age and older
— there appears to be a fairly uniform dearth of members in their
twenties and early thirties.

While church leaders were found to have had an average education
of between standard three and four (about 5,5 years of schooling)
the average of members of the three selected churches was slightly
less: between standards two and three (4,7 years). There was some
variation in the three selected churches, with the BBCAC having the
highest average length of schooling (5,6 years), the Full Gospel members having 4,7 years and the Holy United members the lowest
average of 3,6 years.

One reason for the slightly lower score of Holy United members
is that many of them were brought up in rural areas in the Northern
Transvaal, where access to schooling was limited. It is also important
to note that 44 per cent of their members claimed to have had no
schooling at all, compared with 22 per cent of the BBCAC and 17
per cent of the Full Gospel church — giving an average for the three
churches combined of 26 per cent without any education at all.

Of the members interviewed in survey C, nearly all were either
employed full-time or else were housewives (most of the latter doing
part-time domestic service). Of these members, 67 per cent were in
full-time employment, 27 per cent were housewives and 6 per cent
were retired or unemployed. In comparing the occupations of leaders
and followers, leaders were more skilled (71 per cent as against 25
per cent of followers) and many more were self-employed (24 per
cent as against 7 per cent). Most followers, then, were in unskilled
employment, but the differences in employment and in income and
education are not as wide as those between leaders and followers in
many of the mission churches.

It is perhaps significant that only 19 per cent of the members
interviewed in survey C were born either in Johannesburg, or in one
of the surrounding urban areas. The remaining 81 per cent were
born elsewhere, the large majority in rural areas. Also important
was the length of time spent in Johannesburg by those who were
not born there. Of those born outside Johannesburg, 76 per cent
were able to recall the year they had come to the city. Taking 1971
as the base year, these members had been in Johannesburg for an
average of 24 years. Comparing this figure with the average age for
the same members it is clear that the members interviewed had spent
on average approximately half their lives out of the city, having

arrived as young adults. With one exception, all had joined their present church in Johannesburg.

The fact that church members came initially from different areas in the country meant that they also came from a number of different tribal groups. This can be seen in the three selected churches discussed in chapter 3. Thus members of the BBCAC had five different languages as their home language, and all spoke more than one other African language. BBCAC members spoke the following home languages: Zulu (44 per cent), Xhosa (26 per cent), Southern Sotho (22 per cent), Swazi and Tswana (4 per cent each). Full Gospel members interviewed had a narrower spread: Southern Sotho (44 per cent), Tswana (30 per cent) and Zulu (26 per cent). The Holy United church had the widest range of home languages, however: Tsonga (44 per cent), Southern Sotho (25 per cent), Zulu (13 per cent), and Venda, Xhosa, and Swazi (6 per cent each).

It can therefore be seen that members of the three selected churches who were interviewed were on average middle-aged (though younger than their leaders) and of little education, with a significant number having had no formal education at all. Those who were employed were largely unskilled, and therefore poor. Very few had in fact been born in the city, and most had come to Johannesburg from various rural areas as young adults seeking work. The church they joined in Johannesburg thus cut across ties of language and residence, but brought together people of similar age, education, and level of employment.

Although fission of churches is an important aspect of the spread of the independent church movement, movement of ordinary members between churches is also important, although sometimes disregarded. It is interesting to note firstly that the average length of stay in their present church of the members interviewed was 6,2 years (base year 1971). Table 5 below gives the average length of stay for members of each church, as well as the proportion of members interviewed who had been in the church five years or less — this last figure is to indicate where the average length of stay might be somewhat inflated by one or two members having been in the church for very long periods.

TABLE 5 : LENGTH OF MEMBERSHIP OF FOLLOWERS

Church	Average length in years	% 5 years or less
BBCAC	4,7	70
Full Gospel	7,8	56
Holy United	6,1	19

Table 5 shows certain differences that can in part be explained fairly simply. The Full Gospel, being the oldest of the three churches, has some members who have been in the church for a long time (up to 35 years), which has tended to inflate their average. More interesting, perhaps, are the differences in the column showing the percentage of the congregation who have been in the church five years or less: here the Holy United Church, while being by far the youngest of the three, appears to have a more stable congregation. The most likely explanation for this centres on the type of church: the BBCAC and Full Gospel churches are Zionist-type churches where the emphasis on faith-healing and the control of the Holy Spirit is particularly strong. In contrast, the Holy United church is Ethiopian-type. As will be shown below, a high proportion of members of the first two churches have joined through healing, under the direction of the Spirit, while this is not a factor with the Holy United church. While Zionist-type members may wander from church to church under the guidance of the Spirit, or in search of a better healer, this does not apply to Ethiopian-type churches unless their members specifically wish to change *type* of church. Thus where membership is determined largely by successful faith-healing, and direction by the Spirit, congregations are likely to be somewhat less stable than others where these factors do not apply.

When dealing with movement of members of independent churches, it is also necessary to trace their church histories to see what churches they originally came from, and how many different churches they have been members of. The independent church movement, at least in South Africa, is essentially a movement which is *joined* by specific decision, and not a single member interviewed in survey C was actually 'born into' his present church, or had joined that church as his first church: all those members who were interviewed had previously had some ties with at least one other church. At the same time it is interesting to note that no fewer than 73 per cent of those interviewed (ranging from 79 per cent for the BBCAC to 70 per cent for the Full Gospel and 69 per cent for the Holy United) had first belonged to a mission church. (The churches cited included Methodist, Anglican, Roman Catholic, Dutch Reformed, Lutheran, Presbyterian and Apostolic Faith.) The 27 per cent without mission church contacts had first belonged to independent churches, and these included both Zionist- and Ethiopian-type churches. As a further indication of movement between churches, it is interesting to note that 43 per cent of the members interviewed had joined more than one church before their present one — in other words, they had been affiliated to three or more churches.

This leads inevitably to the question why individual members in fact joined their present church. Here again there is a clear difference between the BBCAC and Full Gospel churches on the one hand, and the Holy United church on the other. Table 6 sets out the different reasons given for joining, and the percentage of members of each church who cited them.

TABLE 6 : FOLLOWERS' REASONS FOR JOINING

Reason	BBCAC	*Full Gospel*	*Holy United*
Healing	83%	83%	– %
Attracted by Spirit	13	–	–
Followed a Minister	4	–	12,5
Impressed generally with church	–	9	75
To escape fighting in former church	–	4	–
Marriage	–	4	12,5
	100%	100%	100,0%

Taking the BBCAC and Full Gospel churches first, the tremendous importance of faith-healing is at once seen, with no fewer than 83 per cent of members interviewed in both churches stating that they had joined their church because they had been healed in it. In the BBCAC a further 13 per cent cited the attraction of the Holy Spirit in the church — giving that church a total of 96 per cent who were attracted by specifically Zionist-type attributes. As these factors are clearly so important a few cases will be described.

Mr J. M. of the Full Gospel: 'I was a strong Roman Catholic — I didn't think there was any church better than the Catholic Church. I was an organist. Whenever I played I cried and I didn't know why. One day I was troubled by my stomach — I had a pain. I went to the Apostolic people that pray, and they gave me blessed water to drink. Whenever I drank from that water my stomach became better. From then onwards I always blew wind and screamed — I became hysterical and jumped under the Holy Spirit. I didn't know the Bible, but I was taught by the Holy Spirit how to explain it to the people. From then on there was no look-ing back for me: I went with the Apostolic people, but not forgetting my church. I used to go to my church in the early morning and then to the Apostolics.[1] They helped me a lot. After that I became a Zionist, from there I didn't look back until today. I left the Zionist church

1. This is but one indication of what Barrett (1968: 6) has referred to as the 'ice-berg analogy', where supporters, or potential supporters, of indepen-dent churches remain within the mission churches.

because there was a difference, because I liked the teaching of the Bible and they spent more time propheting. We that have a bit of education like to learn more about the Bible. If it weren't for the sickness of my wife I wouldn't have found the Full Gospel church.' (Mrs J. M. had been ill and had been brought by a relative to a Full Gospel prophet who had healed her. Mr J. M. subsequently had a dream that he should join the church, 'because they were looking for me'.)

Mrs E. S. of the BBCAC: 'I was very sick, and a friend said I must visit Mrs. R.; and she helped me with holy water. I was very happy and I found a place to stay.'

Mrs C. R. of the BBCAC: 'I was sick. They gave me holy water, and I got well again.'

Mrs L. N. of the BBCAC: 'I was always sick, then this church helped me a lot.'

Miss E. M. of the BBCAC: She had had 'mental illness' for some time, and had been having visions since the age of 10 (she was 34 years old). After trying two churches without success, she went to stay with a 'strong sangoma' (diviner) in Swaziland. She stayed for two years, but was not helped, even though she paid the diviner, and worked for her. She then returned to Johannesburg, and was told about the BBCAC prophet. She consulted her, and subsequently joined the church — since then she has been helped considerably.

Mrs E. M. of the Full Gospel: She was born of Zionist parents, and later joined the African Methodist Episcopal Church (Ethiopian-type) when she married. She stayed in this church a number of years, 'but I always liked the Apostolics'. She became sick, and was healed by a Zionist prophet. After this she decided to join a Zionist-type church, and was urged to join the Full Gospel by her brother, who was a member. 'He said to me, "Sister, you must come where I am, this church is very hot".' She attended services and then joined the church, as she was very impressed with its leader: 'He is a powerful preacher, he makes you feel that you have got something, he is a hot preacher.' She had her husband's permission to join the church, and to take her children with her, while he retained his AME membership — 'He likes his AME, but he doesn't go often,' she said, 'but I like my church — when I am in church I like to feel I am in church.' She was accepted at once as a full member, without having to serve a probationary period — 'they knew me'.

The individuals cited above either joined their respective churches specifically because they had been healed, or because they were impressed with it after having come into the Zionist-type movement through healing. In the Full Gospel church, 9 per cent of the members interviewed joined the church because they were impressed with it — usually with the leader's personality and abilities — and

4 per cent joined to escape from disputes in another Zionist-type church. It is interesting to note that nobody in the BBCAC who was interviewed, and only 4 per cent of those in the Full Gospel, had joined through marriage, that is joined the husband's church on marriage.

The importance of healing and prophets has already been stressed. I believe that the figures given for the BBCAC and Full Gospel churches of members who joined through healing are representative of most healing churches. To take just one example of another church, nearly all members of a small congregation at a service of the First Catholic Apostolic Jerusalem Church in Zion of South Africa testified that they had joined their church because they had been healed. Two testimonies were as follows:

Mrs M.: 'Peace be with you. I would like to say how I became Apostolic or Zionist.[2] I was from Wesleyan (Methodist Church); I was married there. Through sickness I came to the Zionists. I used to pray, it didn't help. I went to doctors, it didn't help. Since I came here I was healed. I couldn't walk, I couldn't sleep. When I had medicine it didn't help. Only through water and prayer did it help. I was in Baragwanath (Hospital) for four months, but it didn't help. I could not drink their medicines. But when I came to the Apostolics I took a stick for the first time, and now I can walk. That is why we are here, that is why we follow the Apostolics.'

Mrs A.: 'I didn't come an easy way. I came from the Bantu Baptist Church. There I got sick, and there was no doctor who could help me. I went to Heidelberg and Pretoria, I tried African and European doctors. When I came to the Apostolic Church I rested for three months. I went to Bishop M.'s place, where I was healed. I was healed through water, not by drinking medicine. Even through love of God. Even today I am well. Since I started with the Apostolics I have never had trouble. For 19 years I have been all right. So I will have to stay here, in this Apostolic church where I am. This Apostolic church pulled me from difficulties, otherwise I do not think I would be living at this time. Even my children are here, and I wish they will stay here.'

In contrast to members of the first two churches, to whom healing and the attraction of the Spirit were so important, most members (75 per cent) of the Holy United church who were interviewed said that they had joined because they were impressed generally with the church or attracted by specific attributes, while 12,5 per cent had

2. The two testimonies given here are by members of a self-styled Zionist church, and one which has the word 'Zion' in its title. It is interesting to note that the first testimony equates Zionist and Apostolic, while the second refers only to Apostolics. For a discussion of differences between the two terms, see page 18 above.

followed the church leader when he formed his new church and
another 12,5 per cent had come into the church by marrying one
of its members.

One of the senior ministers of the Holy United church suggested
in an interview that people joined their church because the members
helped each other as a community, and because they were impressed
with the church leader. He said that the leader never turned away
requests for assistance, particularly from poor people who came to
him. (It should be pointed out here that the Holy United minister
was rather better-off than most independent church leaders as he
held a skilled and responsible job.) This contention was to a considerable extent borne out by the individual members who were
interviewed. Of those who were listed in Table 6 above as being
generally impressed with the church, 40 per cent mentioned no
specific attributes which impressed them, but no fewer than 33 per
cent said that they had been attracted to the church because of the
help they had received from it. Financial aid during periods of sickness, and also help with funeral expenses were mentioned. Of the
remainder, 13 per cent said that the church made them feel happy
or contented, 7 per cent said that they were impressed by the leadership qualities of the leader, and 7 per cent said that the church increased their learning and understanding. But specific reasons
advanced by members are not the only important factors leading
people to join the independent churches, and I shall now turn to
some of the other, underlying aspects of the churches, which contribute in great measure to the success that they enjoy.

An important aspect of the independent churches is the small
size of their normal congregations. The average number of members
of most of the independent churches surveyed was between 100 and
500, with these numbers usually being divided into a number of
small congregations in various parts of the country and, as we have
seen, the average size of an ordinary Sunday congregation was
approximately 20 people. Most of the independent churches dealt
with here were therefore divided into a number of very small groups
for most of their activities. This is one of their attractions. That this
is so both in rural and urban areas is suggested by Pauw's observation
of rural churches in Taung, which can be applied equally to churches
in Soweto: 'The small size of the local church groups makes for intimate in-group relations. The intimacy of the relations is often increased by the fact that the church services are held at the home-
stead of a church leader, or one of the other members. Moreover,
some of the most important opportunities for joint activities and
social contacts are provided by the church.' (Pauw 1960: 66.)

Writing about the functions of churches in a Rhodesian urban area, Thomas suggests (1970: 284) that they fulfil certain social needs for 'sociability, status, security and approval', and these are clearly also attributes of the independent churches in Soweto. The small congregations of these churches consist in the main of close-knit groups of people who are bound together by common circumstances as well as common membership of the same church.

Independent church members are bound together by common experience of adversity. They share also a background of a rural birthplace and a move to the city as young adults. This shared background and experience would seem to be sufficient to counteract any language or ethnic barriers that might have existed — the 'inter-tribal' nature and composition of the independent churches in Soweto has already been stressed[3] — and makes assimilation of new members relatively easy irrespective of ethnic affiliation.[4] Wishlade suggests (1965: 105) that in independent churches in Malawi, 'congregations are groups into which strangers ideally are accepted, and within which they can make friends', and the same applies to churches in Soweto.

With this as a background we can look at some of the more specific attractions of the independent churches, most of which stem from the fact that operationally they form small groups. It is convenient to start with Thomas's (1970) four factors of sociability, status, security and approval, and then to extend them somewhat. As far as sociability is concerned, we have already seen that new members are accepted into a close-knit group, and may make friends there. The members of the three selected churches who were interviewed in survey C were asked (see Appendix 3) whether they had friends or relatives in their own church, in other independent churches, and in mission churches. Some of the results are given in Table 7.

It is perhaps not surprising that 100 per cent of those interviewed said that they had made friends within their own congregation: this does little more than confirm suggestions made by other authors. In view of the mobility of church members between different churches, and the homogeneity of the different types of independent church, it is not surprising either that 66 per cent of those interviewed also had friends in independent churches other than their own. More interesting is the fact that no fewer than 42 per cent

3. Cf. Pauw in a rural area: 'It seems probable that in some cases the element of ethnic origin also plays a role in deciding which church a person joins. A Nguni would rather join a church with a strong Nguni element among its members, I should think, than an exclusively Tswana church, while a Tswana would not be so easily attracted to a church which is very predominantly Nguni.' (Pauw 1960: 66–7).

4. During fieldwork, the only evidence of division on ethnic grounds appeared in one or two situations of leadership disputes, where it was stated by the loser that his ethnic group had counted against him.

TABLE 7 : CHURCH AFFILIATION OF FRIENDS AND RELATIVES

	Same church as follower	Other Independent Churches	Mission Churches
Friends	100%	66%	42%
Relatives	76%	53%	56%

stated that they had retained friendships with people who were in mission churches. Differences in religious affiliation, even when they are wide, are thus not necessarily sufficient to affect friendships. It might have been expected that members of the Holy United church, with its Methodist origins, might have had more friendships with people of mission churches than members of the two Zionist-type churches, but in fact while 31 per cent of Holy United church members had mission church friends, the figures for the BBCAC and Full Gospel churches were 43 per cent and 48 per cent respectively. While the majority of those interviewed (58 per cent) had no friends in the mission churches, a significant number did.

Table 7 shows also that members of the selected churches tended to have relatives distributed fairly widely in all three categories, with an expected weighting towards their own church. The high number of relatives in the mission churches may be explained by the fact that nearly three-quarters of those interviewed in survey C had started off in a mission church, usually in a rural area, and would often still have relatives, especially of their parents' generation, in those churches.

While the majority of those interviewed had links with members of other churches both independent and mission, a large minority were more exclusive, with links restricted to independent churches, and in some cases to their own independent church only. While this points to certain links between members of churches, it is not an analysis of social networks of individual members, and data are not presented, for example, on content, density or frequency in members' networks (Mitchell 1969: 17–29). It is therefore not possible to say which links are more important, or more frequent, than others. Superficially, it would appear that links between members of the same church, whether friends or kin, are both regular and important for various reasons. The significant factors are friendship, co-operation and mutual aid, and these can be seen in Thomas's factors of sociability, security and approval. Members of the same independent church may make friends on one level, but on another they are all kin — as evidenced by use of the terms 'brother' and 'sister' for fellow church members. As friends or quasi-kin, members will visit other members who are ill or in need, for example, and attend each other's rituals.

This last factor is particularly important. During fieldwork it was repeatedly noticed that church members would attend funerals, weddings, and thanksgivings, as well as other occasions, of individual members. In many of these instances there appeared to be more church members than kin and other friends present, and on more than one occasion a 'family affair' was taken over by the church. To take an example from the Full Gospel church, one of its members held what he called a 'family thanksgiving', which was suspected to be for his shades, although he would not confirm this. The main activity, after the slaughtering of an animal, was a lively church service held in a tent behind the man's house, which was completely controlled by the bishop. Approximately forty church members were present. While the church service was proceeding, four male relatives of the holder of the celebration were seen sitting in front of the house drinking beer.

A further example from the First Apostolic Church of Christ in Zion of South Africa indicates the importance of church members in family affairs. On this occasion a senior member of the church was 'raising a tombstone' with his elder brothers for his father, who had died and been buried in Soweto some years previously. The elder brothers were living in the country, and it was the brother in Soweto who organised the fund-raising in the family to buy a suitable tombstone. On the appointed day the elder brothers and other members of the church of the younger brother were invited to swell the ranks. An offering was followed by a night vigil and church service, before the actual laying of the tombstone on the following day. While one should beware of interpreting urban phenomena in terms of traditional practices, it is interesting to note the parallel between the modern raising of a tombstone, which often occurs some time after the death of an individual and the traditional 'bringing home of the spirit', which is well-known for example among the Zulu (*ukubuyisa idlozi*, Krige 1936: 169–70) as the ritual which incorporates a dead spirit among the ancestors, and which also takes place some time after death. In that ritual, senior kinsmen, family and villagers would attend, with the senior surviving son officiating: in the urban ritual described here senior kinsmen, family and church members were present. In this, and other cases, particularly weddings and funerals, where family and villagers in rural areas might attend, it is seen that independent church congregations, perhaps because they are relatively close-knit groups, play a role similar to that of villagers in another situation.

Security and approval are present in the independent churches through common membership, as is a certain status or standing in each other's eyes. Bryan Wilson's analysis (1961: 354) of some of the functions of what he calls 'sects' is relevant here:

> A sect serves as a small and 'deviant' reference group in which the individual may seek status and prestige in terms of whose standards he may measure his own talents and accomplishments in more favourable terms than are generally available in the wider society. . . . Its ideological orientation and its group cohesion provide a context of emotional security. . . .

It will be contended in a later chapter that the independent churches are particularly important as reference groups in an urban situation like that of Soweto, as a means of adjusting to an urban environment, and it is in this context that Wilson's analysis should be seen.

With the difficulties and frustrations of urban life in Soweto, the importance of the small independent church congregations as supportive, reference groups should not be underestimated. As Monica Wilson (1961: 66) has pointed out, 'The basic insecurity of men comes, not from poverty, but from the feeling that no one cares about them', and this is certainly a feeling that is absent in these congregations. They are caring communities, where concern is shown for all, but particularly for the sick, the aged, and those in adversity. An observer is struck by the mutual co-operation and aid that exists, and thus we see an emphasis on the duty to visit among the congregation in the Full Gospel church, faith-healing and collecting of clothes for the elderly in the BBCAC, and financial assistance of members in need in the Holy United church, to mention just a few examples. Aid and co-operation are both moral and material — ranging from spiritual reinforcement in services where members take part in giving testimonies, to women's groups finding employment for their fellow-members.

In addition to this, the independent churches provide specific opportunities of various kinds for their members — and here it is necessary to distinguish between male and female members. The major practical opportunities for men have been discussed in the preceding chapter, and centre on the provision of numerous outlets for the exercise of leadership abilities. In very few cases, however, does a position of leadership include any great financial advantage, or any employment opportunities.[5] In addition, men in Soweto

5. In only one case was it suggested that a certain large employer of African labour preferred to hire members of a particular church because they were believed to be hard workers who were generally abstemious. This, however, was unconfirmed. In fact it might be argued that a leadership position in an independent church hinders job satisfaction, in view of the conflict which must exist in an individual who is a respected bishop, for example, in one situation, and a menial servant in another.

have certain other outlets in other voluntary associations — for example sports clubs. It is contended that the opportunities for women in the independent churches are far more important to them, which is one reason why women are in the majority there.

A woman who joins an independent church will, either immediately or after a probationary period, depending on circumstances, become a full member of the church. In most of the small churches studied, full membership (which in itself means that a person is in good standing in the church) brings with it the right to attend the church *manyano*, or women's organisation.[6] In most of the churches studied, the *manyano*, with its regular Thursday afternoon meetings and other activities, was the only important group other than the congregation itself.

As Mrs Brandel-Syrier (1962) points out, life in the townships is particularly hard for women. While most men are able to 'escape' to some extent through being employed outside, it is the women who are largely saddled with problems that are a direct result of their environment: for example they have to try to make ends meet on an inadequate budget, and to handle delinquency problems caused by insufficient schools. While many women will have some employment, usually in domestic service, they are much more tied to the problems of the townships than are the men, and have fewer outlets; this is why church *manyano* are so important.

Brandel-Syrier's work refers largely to either mission church or Ethiopian-type church *manyano*, and stresses the emotionalism (in confessions, testimonies, services, etc.) as well as the 'legalistic' aspects ('giving the law', judicial roles, etc.). In the type of church to which she mainly refers, emotionalism is not as important as it is in independent Zionist-type churches, and it is possible that emotionalism is not quite as important in Zionist-type *manyano* groups — it has already been shown that emotional outlets in singing, dancing and spirit possession exist in ordinary Zionist-type services.

At the same time, independent church *manyano* groups fulfil many of the other functions cited by Brandel-Syrier. They tend to be smaller groups even than the church congregations — ten to fifteen people — and more close-knit. Early in her book Brandel-Syrier (1962: 28) quotes a *manyano* woman as saying: 'Where do you think

6. Brandel-Syrier (1962: 47–8) refers to 'very strict' rules regarding membership of *manyano*. Her book is important as the only work dealing in detail with this phenomenon, but it should be borne in mind that it deals with an extremely limited range of churches (Brandel-Syrier 1962: 233–6). A study of *manyano* groups was beyond the compass of this particular project, but an investigation of the influence of women and their *manyano* on independent churches would certainly be worthwhile.

we get the strength to persevere? It is in our *manyanos*.' Members
are bound through common ties of membership and friendship,
through common experience (in which personal confessions and
testimonies play an important part in drawing people together), and
through co-operative action – whether in visiting the sick or raising
funds for the church. As has been suggested for all independent
church members, the need for security is strong – 'This need to
belong, inherent in all human beings, but particularly strongly felt
by African women in their urban situation and in the absence of
their kith and kin, finds its most satisfactory fulfilment in the *Manyanos.*' (Brandel-Syrier 1962: 137.)

Manyano groups, being essentially separate from the church congregation, also provide leadership opportunities for their members.
To a large extent hierarchies are determined by virtue of the status
of the husband in the church: thus the leader will be the Lady Bishop, with under her the wife of the church second-in-command,
followed by wives of ministers, deacons, evangelists and preachers.
This is one reason why a man is usually ordained with his wife, and
after ordination both are formally led to their places in the congregation: the man, for example, among the ministers, and the woman
among the lady ministers.

While this hierarchy is to some extent fixed, in that a woman will
have a certain status by virtue of her husband's status, irrespective
of her own qualities of leadership, hierarchies do make provision for
the incorporation of people with particular qualities. For example,
the BBCAC (see page 24) had two influential *manyano* positions
held by elected people who did not hold any position through
ascribed status. As Brandel-Syrier points out (1962: 65), *manyano*
are ideally led by wives of church leaders, but if they are not of
'strong personality' leadership may be exercised by elected leaders:
this may be direct, or more often the church leader's wife is the
titular leader, while others lower in the hierarchy exercise 'the
power behind the throne'.

Manyano also have certain more practical functions, which have
already been hinted at. Many women members of the independent
churches are either full- or part-time domestic servants in the suburbs
of Johannesburg, and it is not uncommon for *manyano* to meet there
for convenience – in a back-room, servant's quarters, garage, or even
outdoors. These meetings provide useful intelligence about employment opportunities and conditions in the particular area, and often
an attempt is made to get a fellow church member employment in
the same area. Lines of communication operate between Soweto and
the suburbs, with information being exchanged about available jobs
and members seeking employment.

The practical importance of fund-raising should also be stressed (Brandel-Syrier 1962: 70ff) as a vital function of many *manyano*: they may in fact be instrumental in finding money to subsidise ministerial salaries, assist the aged or those in need, augment church building-funds, and for various other purposes. Since women are the backbone of the independent churches, and the *manyano* are their driving force, a church is very often only as strong as its *manyano*.

CHAPTER 6 Healing

Healing has always played a part in Christianity, but its emphasis has varied considerably in time and place. Christian missionaries, particularly, have often been associated with healing, and mission hospitals have been prominent centres of conversion in many rural areas (see, for example, Vandervort 1968). It would seem that the bearers of a new religion, at least in Africa, have been expected by converts to show the same interest in health that was the concern of their traditional religions. This relationship and its outcome has been put succinctly by Monica Wilson (1971: 114):

> It will be recalled that the rituals of traditional religions which we examined were primarily concerned with health and fertility, and the service constantly sought from missionaries in Africa has been aid for the sick. All the early missionaries provided some sort of medical aid, whether they were medically qualified or not, but very soon the Churches were hastening to provide hospitals, and medical training for nurses, and later for doctors. This has been one of their major contributions. But medical work became so special-ised that the ordinary priest or minister ceased to take much share in service for the sick, and in most mission congregations healing and worship became quite separate.

This last point is highly significant, for the separation has been reversed in the independent churches.[1]

The importance of the re-integration of worship and healing will be dealt with below, but first the importance and nature of healing in the independent churches must be analysed. In preceding chapters I have tried to show how important faith-healing is in independent churches: thus 100 per cent of the 194 churches in survey B held special healing services and 88 per cent had prophet-healers, while over 80 per cent of the congregations of two selected churches stated

---

1. In this respect the independent churches discussed here are already put-ting into practice Professor Wilson's suggestion: '. . . I ask myself whether a closer link between healing and worship should not be sought by Christians. If indeed the incidence and course of disease is profoundly modified by mental attitudes, must we not rethink the relationship?' (M. Wilson 1971: 114-5.)

that they had joined their church because they had been healed in it. While the importance is uniform, methods of healing vary from church to church although they share certain overall features.

For the purposes of analysis, faith-healing in the independent churches can be divided into three categories: healing during church services, healing by immersion, and healing through consultation with a prophet. Generally, in Ethiopian-type churches healing is restricted to church services where the sick are prayed for and have hands laid on them. Some of these churches may have healing in a river, and some may have prophets, but this is not common. In the Zionist-type churches, where healing is of such importance, it takes place in all three ways. It is also useful to distinguish between what we shall call 'direct' and 'indirect' healing. In indirect healing it is not necessary for the healer or healers to be aware of the specific complaints of individual patients — they are healed through the power of the Holy Spirit, *uMoya*, acting through the agency of the healers, and often of the church congregation as a whole. Direct healing takes place where the healer is specifically aware of the patient's complaints, and prescribes specific cures for them.

Healing in church services can be both direct or indirect, the latter being more common. Perhaps the most common form of healing is through prayer and laying on of hands, and this usually takes place in one of two ways: either the patients are called up in front of the congregation, kneel and are prayed for, or else they are placed in the centre of a circle and prayed for while members of the congregation dance round the perimeter. A typical example of this is the BBCAC, where at the end of each Sunday service a skin is removed from the floor to reveal a Holy Place, and the seats are moved to the side of the room. On one occasion John 10:1–5 was read and two people were called forward to stand in the centre of the Holy Place. All those participating removed their shoes, and a hymn started. While singing and drumming continued, ordinary members of the congregation followed the lead of the Senior Prophet in dancing round the Holy Place. After a while the prophet entered the circle and started to pray for the sick people in the centre — this she did by praying while holding her hands in blessing above each patient's head, and by holding a prophet's stick above the head and then passing it over the body.

After a while other lesser healers entered the circle and also prayed for patients after they had been treated by the Senior Prophet. When the first two had been prayed for they left the centre and joined in the dancing; others then took their place until all who wished had been prayed for. After the healing had been going for a short while, the atmosphere in the room became tense and exciting: the room was full of people singing and dancing rapidly round the perimeter of the Holy Place, first in one direction and then the other, the drumming was loud and rhythmic and every now and then the prophet's entreaties could be heard above the din. The general movement and noise heightened the atmosphere as the healing continued, and there were several cases of spirit possession. When all ordinary members who so desired had been prayed for, the lesser prophets stood before the Senior Prophet in turn, and were also prayed for.

While this account is typical of ordinary church healing services where patients are prayed for, it was interesting to note that two of the patients were probably treated 'directly', in that it was known that they were ill before the session started, and their names were specifically called out because they had been to the prophet beforehand; the rest were treated 'indirectly', because the healers generally would not know what specific complaints individuals had, nor was there time for questioning during the service.

In the service described, as in others of its type, the Holy Spirit is believed to heal through the agency of the healers and also through the efforts of the congregation: the dancing in a circle round the Holy Place is believed to ensure the presence of the Holy Spirit, which comes down on patients, healers and congregation alike. As has been described above for the Full Gospel church, dancing often takes place even when there is nobody needing to be healed — in these cases its purpose is to call down the Holy Spirit on the congregation. (In fact when he is possessed, to give an example, the leader of the Full Gospel church can be seen to raise his hand to 'catch' the Holy Spirit while dancing, and re-direct it towards the congregation.)

Holy Places or healing circles are common to many of the Zionist-type churches. The Holy Places of the BBCAC and Full Gospel churches have already been described, and their symbols (stars, crosses, moons, suns for the BBCAC; tent, cross and stones for the Full Gospel) are also regarded as very important in ensuring the efficacy of the healing which takes place about them. In general these Holy Places are fixed on particular sites, but one instance was encountered of a 'mobile' Holy Place, used by a prophet who spent considerable time travelling from place to place. This particular Holy Place consisted of four pieces of linoleum cut in the shapes of a cross (Christianity), a heart (people/patients), a moon (heaven) and a star (the prophet's personal sign). The prophet said that the advantage of this particular Holy Place (which had been revealed to her in a dream) was that it could be folded and stored away when not in use, so that it would not be defiled by people walking over it, and that it could be easily transported. It was treated with the same veneration that 'fixed' Holy Places were, and when in use people were required to remove their shoes before approaching it. On the other hand healing circles are not treated with the same veneration when not in use — examples of these which can be seen in many suburban parts of Johannesburg are small rings made in the grass on open places, which have been worn away by repeated use. These are not protected in any way when not in use, but are regarded as holy during services, when they may be augmented with candles and sticks. In the suburbs these places are used mainly by domestic servants during free time on week-ends.

The other very important way of healing during church services is by giving holy water to the congregation to drink. Here a distinction can usefully be made between healing and purification — a distinction which is also particularly relevant to healing by immersion. Holy water may be given to members of a congregation to heal them of something specific, or else it may be drunk to purify and protect against illness and misfortune. Obviously the dividing line between healing and purification is not sharp, and in this case both would usually fall into the category of indirect treatment.

The administering of holy water appears to be fairly uniform. Sufficient water (either from a tap or a spring) is put in a large container and then prayed for by a prophet, or by all the prophets and other senior officials of the church. In some cases the blessing of the water may include stirring it with a holy stick. The water is then given to congregation members to drink, usually in small glasses, at a particular time in the service. In the Full Gospel church, for example, drinking of holy water often takes place at the same time as members are treated at the Holy Place. During the dancing they may come to the table which has the holy water on it, be given a glass to drink and then receive a blessing and laying on of hands by a prophet. This is a rather informal approach, but in other churches the drinking of holy water may be much more formal. We shall take as an example of this the service of the Bethsaid Healing Faith Mission.

In this case drinking of holy water is a regular part of the ordinary Sunday service, which is held in a rented classroom in Soweto. Water is placed in a large container and blessed by the senior prophet. While the congregation sings (usually a short phrase repeated over and over — a favourite is 'We are walking in the Light', *Re tsamayang Leseding*), water is poured into a number of small glasses. As the singing continues ten or twelve members of the congregation come up to the front and kneel (this is done in order of importance — first the important men, then the important women, followed by male and then female full members, followed by other adults, followed by

children). The Senior Prophet assisted by lesser prophets takes the
glasses to the kneeling members, and each drinks. After each group
has drunk, the prophets present bless them collectively, collect the
glasses and refill them while the next group comes to the front. This
continues until all have taken the holy water. Finally the lesser
prophets drink, and then the whole congregation is blessed by the
Senior Prophet.

Another important but less frequent method of healing is by
immersion in a river or stream, or even on occasion in a public
swimming-bath. The form is essentially similar to that for baptism
— members of the congregation go down to the river (usually in the
early morning) and, after prayers and sometimes dancing, one or
two senior men will enter the river and will immerse patients in
turn. When the patients emerge from the river they will be blessed,
usually by the bishop or senior official present. Very often both
baptism and purification rites take place at the same time, and this
may account for some confusion where observers have suggested
that Zionist-type churches often have repeated baptisms.[2]

Purification rites in the river may either be directed at healing a
specific complaint, or else they may be protective. From limited
observation it has seemed that people are immersed most often in
cases where they are deemed to be possessed of an evil spirit —
although of course immersion is used for a variety of complaints.
This type of healing usually is prescribed by a prophet, and will
thus be discussed below. Protective immersion is more general in
Zionist-type churches, and may occur for a number of different
reasons. A prophet may, for example, direct a congregation to go
to the river to be purified after a death in the church, or after illness,
or to avert some possible misfortune which the prophet may see
threatening the church. It is also very common in many of these
churches for the whole congregation to go to the river to be purified
at the beginning of a new year. It has been mentioned that many
churches hold big services at New Year rather than at Christmas, and
purification at the river is often an important part of such services.
Similarly general purification may take place on other important
occasions — for example at Easter, or at the time of the church
conference.

It should be clear from the discussion of healing practices thus
far that prophets are of some importance. Before coming to the

2. In general the rule of the Zionist-type churches in Soweto was found to
be that baptism by immersion was essential — any form of baptism by immersion was recognised as valid, while baptism by 'sprinkling' was not. Confusion
may have been caused through new members often being taken for *purification*
on joining a new church — but this is not the same as *baptism*.

third type of healing — by personal consultation with a prophet — we should examine briefly the types of healer present in Soweto, and very generally what they do. For the purposes of analysis we shall distinguish three basic types of healer, but it should be remembered that these categories are not entirely discrete. They are: the faith-healer, the prophet, and the *isangoma* or diviner.[3] All three have it in common that they heal largely by supernatural means, and as we are concentrating on this aspect of healing we do not include herbalists, western medical doctors or pharmacists.

The faith-healer (probably the smallest group, although no figures are available) is a Christian who may belong either to a mission or an independent church. The power to heal is believed to come from God (although in some cases it may be thought to come from God indirectly through the shades), and a period of training as a healer may or may not have been necessary. As will be seen from the description of a prophet below, a faith-healer may be close to a prophet (if the ancestors are involved and the healer has had training, for example), or he may not. Two examples are given, one from an independent church, and one of a healer who does not belong to a formal denomination, but who regards himself as a Christian.

The Revd M. M. was already adult, and a prominent lay member of a mission church, before he realised that he had healing gifts. He had no history of illness, but had a vision while asleep in which his shades called him to be a healer, and said that they would help. M. ignored this as he did not believe that he could be a healer, and continued to think nothing of his vision for about a year. He then started having visions of a similar sort again, and felt increasing pressure on him. Finally he had a vision that the next day a girl would come to his house with stomach-ache, and that he should recite the Lord's Prayer over her. He said that he forgot about this until on the following day a young girl did come to the house en route to a doctor as she was suffering from a stomach-ache. M. said that he then greatly surprised members of his family by praying for the girl. She returned the following day to say that he had cured her, and from then on M. started to heal, using the ancestors to help him. He uses prayer, laying on of hands and holy water in his healing, but does not wear elaborate robes. To be more free to do his healing he left his mission church and subsequently founded his own, independent church. His powers developed as he continued, and he needed no training.

Mr S. M. had been having dreams and visions since the age of 12. As an adult he had a vision that he should go to a certain Anglican priest

3. Strictly speaking, *isangoma* refers to a Zulu diviner, but the word is used generally in Soweto (usually 'sangoma' with the prefix dropped) by people of various languages to denote a 'tribal' diviner.

(although he was not Anglican himself) and be prayed for and blessed — in his dream the priest had to wear a white cassock while doing this. Mr S. M. went to the priest, who refused to do what was requested, and said that in any case he was in a hurry as he had to keep an appointment outside Johannesburg. He then left in his car, and Mr S. M. waited at the church. Eventually the priest returned, saying that he had felt sick on the road and had decided to return. Mr S. M. regarded this as significant, and said, too, that he thought that the priest, an African, was worried about being bewitched as he had noticed protective medicines around the church building. He confronted the priest with this, and the priest was embarrassed, and agreed to don a white cassock and pray for him in the manner directed. After this Mr S. M. was able to predict, divine, and heal. He required no further training, and is helped by the shade of his maternal grandmother, who was a herbalist and was fond of him while she was alive. He uses prayer, water, ash and steam in his treatments of patients, and also immerses them in a pool on the outskirts of Soweto (which he has specially modified by deepening, building a bank of concrete, and planting grass about it). While he regards himself as a Christian, Mr S. M. does not belong to any formal church as he says that if he did the consequent rivalries between members and also churches would hamper his work. Unlike the Revd M. M., he makes offerings to his shades, and trains patients he finds to have gifts of healing. He is adamant that he is in no way an *isangoma.*

The Soweto sangoma, who is usually a woman, is regarded as a 'traditional' diviner, even though her techniques may be different from a rural tribal diviner. A sangoma may be a Christian, although usually she is not, but her healing power is specifically not Christian, and comes directly from guiding shades.[4] Healing techniques vary — although most sangomas use herbs — and so do methods of divination. Some will throw bones to divine, and others will rely on dreams or other communication with their guiding ancestors. One example of a Soweto sangoma is given below.

Mrs B. M. had been ill and had been having dreams from an early age. No western treatment had helped her, and finally she was helped by a sangoma, who informed her that her ancestors were calling her to become a sangoma. Before starting her training she returned home and offered a goat to the shades to inform them of her intention. She then started a

4. Of interest in this regard is a statement by a sangoma living in the Transvaal who herself is a highly qualified nurse with a postgraduate university education. In a personal communication she wrote regarding the sangoma's power: 'This power is in actual fact innate, in which case it could be regarded as a gift from God. . . . The work of a sangoma when undistorted is very Christianised — there is nothing a sangoma, under the direction of a guidance, can do that would defeat the ends of Christianity.'

period as a novice with an established sangoma. This involved offerings, use of emetics, analysis of dreams, etc., until her guiding shades started to communicate, and she found herself able to prophesy. After her training she returned home, where an ox was offered, and a final feast was held. Later she was directed to go to a river and purify herself by immersing herself and also using an emetic — after this she was able to see under water, and to work with water. This she was able to do because she had a water snake as a clan animal. In her healing she uses water, sea water, salt, vinegar, ash, certain roots and also various coloured beads. Unlike many sangomas she does not use drums.

The prophet is a healer who is found mainly in the Zionist and Apostolic churches, who has the ability to predict, heal, and divine, and who draws power to do this from God, although in many cases this power may come from God through the more direct agency of certain guiding shades. The importance of prophets in many independent churches has already been stressed, and it has also been suggested in passing that prophets have varying powers. The strongest prophets are those who heal through private consultations, and who take the lead in healing-services, while weaker prophets tend to act as assistants and limit their activities.

Most prophets have a history of illness which has been cured by another prophet. Any patient who has been through the healing rites is in some respects a candidate to become a healer; the position is much the same as Turner reports for the Ndembu: '. . . the patient in any given cult ritual is a candidate for entry into the cult and, by passing through its rites, becomes a cult adept.' (In Kiev 1964: 232.) While all patients may be candidates, not all are deemed to have powers to become prophets. It seems, however, that there is a strong desire on the part of many female patients to become prophets or, failing that, the next best thing, which is a prayer-woman. Prayer-women are in some ways what one informant called 'half-prophets': they are given holy sticks with which to pray for the sick, and are given authority by the church to visit the sick and pray for them.

Prayer-women are usually given office in a special ceremony. To take one example, the Full Gospel church has a number of prayer-women who rank below their prophets. The bishop explained that often a woman would come and say that she had had a dream that she should pray for the sick. This would be taken as an indication of the wishes of the Holy Spirit, and arrangements would be made to give the blessing of the church for this work on a suitable occasion. One such occasion attended was an Ascension Day service held at one of the local congregation centres. When the service was well advanced a candle was brought forward for the bishop to bless and light. The

Zionist healing service on the outskirts of Johannesburg

A small Zionist congregation of domestic servants meeting in a Johannesburg suburb

Zionist wedding in Soweto

Interdenominational communion service

Bible-reading in two languages at a midnight consecration service

A powerful preacher — the
Bishop of the Full Gospel
Church

The Bishop of the BBCAC
blessing new members

Two ordained ministers of
a Zionist church (women
rarely become ministers in
their own right)

Counting the Sunday collection in the Holy United Methodist Church (Ethiopian-type)

Procession of a *manyano* of the Gardner Mvuyana African Congregational Church (to keep faith needs the strength and tenacity of the leopard, hence the hats)

The leader of the African Free
New Church, a breakaway from
the Anglican Church

A former President of AICA
addressing a conference in Cape
Town

AN ORDINATION

(1) The ordinand and his wife kneel before the bishop

(2) After the ordinand receives his clerical collar, the bishop sprinkles him with holy oil and lays his hands upon him

(3) The bishop lays his hands also upon the ordinand's wife (who is required to be present at the ordination)

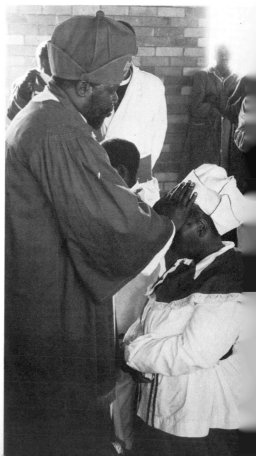

(4) All the ministers present (including a visitor from another church, in a dark robe) lay hands on the ordinand in the final act of ordination

Ordaining an evangelist and his wife in the Holy Free Corner Stone Church in Zion

Prayer at a Zionist midnight service

A young member of the
Full Gospel Church being
held by her mother while
in a state of possession

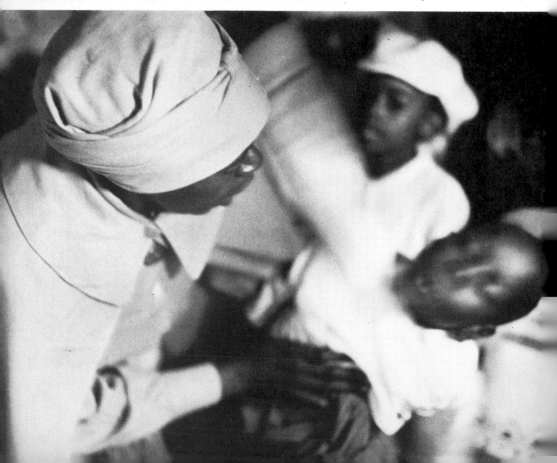

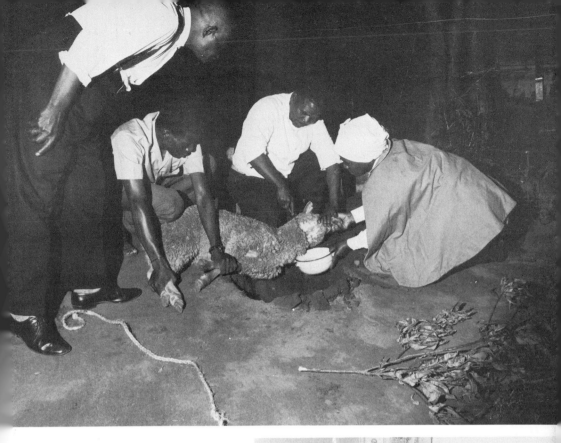

(1) A midnight sacrifice of a sheep in St Francis Church. The occasion was a thanksgiving for a successful healing

(2) The prophet, Mrs A.N., prays over the blood of the sheep in front of the congregation

A young Zionist watches a healing rite in a river near Soweto, and a young Zionist girl waits for baptism

Baptisms and healing at dawn. A number of churches are represented

An unusual meeting — a prophet (Mrs A. N.) and a sangoma (diviner)

The Bishop of the First Catholic Apostolic Jerusalem Church in Zion at a healing service in a hired classroom

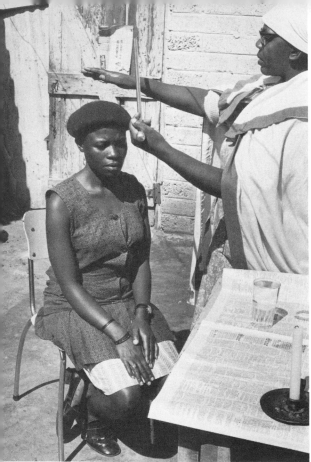

Mrs L.R. of the BBCAC, praying for a patient, and in consultation with her

Healing rites in a river near Soweto

Zionist bishop and prophet

lighted candle was given to the lady bishop to hold behind the new prayer-woman, who had been summoned to stand in front of the bishop and congregation. A minister read a short passage from the Bible — Esther 5:1–3 — and the short silver healing-stick was unwrapped. The woman, rather confused, tried to take the stick, but was prevented as it had not been paid for. She produced R1, but the officials said that the stick had cost R2. She did not have the extra sum, but embarrassment was avoided by one of the evangelists, who lent her the extra money. The bishop took the stick and blessed it and handed it to the woman. He blessed her, laying hands on her and exhorting her to use her stick wisely and properly. While the congregation sang a hymn the other ministers and officials present came up in turn to pray for the woman. After each had prayed, they all shook hands with her, and the ceremony closed with the senior women dancing up to congratulate their sister, who was then led back to her place in the congregation. In this case the prayer-woman was not given a certificate, but in many churches a special certificate is given to show that the bearer has authority from the church to do certain things.

While prayer-women have authority to pray for the sick, they differ from prophets in that they have no specific training, other than in some cases assisting a prophet during consultations. Prophets, on the other hand, have training and specific initiation. The life history of a typical prophet (see chapter 9) is in many respects parallel to that of a traditional diviner, and includes a call, a period of illness which could be successfully treated only by another prophet, training, purification, and initiation as a prophet. Very often, too, a prophet will have had one or more prophets or diviners in the family. Before discussing prophets in more detail, I shall give one or two case histories.

Mrs M. R. is a successful prophet in Soweto with a wide clientele, coming from many different churches, who consult her. She is the wife of the leader of the BBCAC, and thus holds the title of Lady Bishop as well as being a prophet in her own right.

Mrs M. R. had a history of visions and fainting spells going back to childhood. They were sufficient to interfere with her schooling, and were not curable by western medicine. For a long time she consulted various prophets, who were able to help her to some degree. She found that from the age of 12 she was able to heal people, to divine causes of illness, and also to predict. She began working on a small scale until she visited a 'strong prophet' who lived in Springs, near Johannesburg. This prophet assisted greatly in her training, and brought her to her present position.

In common with other prophets, Mrs M. R. has had relatives who were themselves healers, on both paternal and maternal sides. Her paternal

great-grandfather was an *isangoma* and his sister was a 'fortune-teller'.
On her mother's side, her grandfather was also an *isangoma*, while one
of her maternal uncles was a prophet. But, unlike some other prophets,
Mrs M. R. does not believe that any of her shades assist her in her work.
The spirits of the ancestors, *omoya wamadlozi*, exist, but they are sleep-
ing and waiting. Her visions have been specifically Christian — on occasion, for example, she has felt herself approached personally by Jesus
Christ, which has frightened her and made her run — and her power to
heal, predict and divine comes directly from the Holy Spirit.[5] Her cosmology includes God, Jesus Christ, the Holy Spirit and the good powers
of heaven symbolised by the stars, the moon and the sun. The powers of
evil are represented by the Devil, who is the father of *amademone*, the
lesser evil spirits.

According to Mrs M. R. sickness comes as a result of man's fall as recounted in the story of Adam and Eve. People become sick because they
have sinned, but also through the action of the Devil and *amademone*.
Illness and misfortune are caused supernaturally and also through the
human agency of individuals, who may be witches or sorcerers. Witches
may cause harm either wittingly or unwittingly, whilst sorcerers, *abatha-
gathi*, specifically use the power of the Devil, *umoya kaSathane*, to do
harm. The prophet has the power through the Holy Spirit to see what is
happening, why it is happening, and what remedies should be employed.

Of her consultations with patients, Mrs M. R. says of her work:
'uMoya leads me to do it — sometimes I am led by dreams, but specially
it is the Holy Spirit.' Thus the Spirit prescribes what the prophet shall
wear during healing, and what remedies she shall use. Mrs M. R. wears a
cape, usually blue or yellow, but also occasionally green, red, or white.
She says that the Spirit guides her which one to wear, although she admits
that she wears yellow — symbolic of the Holy Spirit — when she has a
'big work' to do. She usually also wears protective cords of coloured
wool, and at her desk she has a candle and a Bible. She has two healing-
sticks — similar to those used by prayer-women — one small one about
15 cm long, which she can carry about with her unobtrusively, and a
larger one of about 45 cm which she uses in healing. Her authority for
using a stick is taken from Exodus 7:9. In treating patients she prays for
them, administers holy water, prescribes protective cords of colours to
be tied round different parts of the body, and uses a variety of other

5. This view is contested by some — for example a sangoma referred to Mrs
M. R.'s powers as being 'quite good powers, really', but said that she used the
power of her shades — 'that is what her *umoya* is'. Whether or not this is the
case in this specific context, some prophets are reluctant to admit the continuing belief in the shades for fear of being regarded as 'primitive', 'backward' or
'pagan'. On more than one occasion an independent church minister was prepared to admit the influence of his shades only after he felt assured of a sympathetic hearing.

substances which will be described later in this chapter. Her authority
for healing is taken from I Corinthians 12:1–6, where it is said various
people will be given various spiritual gifts, including 'gifts of healing by
the one Spirit . . .', prophecy, . . . and 'the ability to distinguish between
spirits'. Her title of prophet, as in most independent churches interviewed,
is taken from Ephesians 4:11: 'And his gifts were that some should be
apostles, some prophets, some evangelists, some pastors and teachers. . . .'

Mrs A. N. was born in a rural part of the Orange Free State. She
started having dreams in about 1938, when she was 19 years old, but
said that she could not see things clearly because 'the way wasn't right'.
This was the beginning of seven years of illness with symptoms of insomnia, lack of appetite, and fainting spells. She was not helped by western
medicine, and eventually she was taken to a diviner, who helped her and
said that she was being called by her shades to become a diviner. While
believing in the powers of her shades, Mrs A. N. was also a member of
the Anglican church, and she prayed to her shades to allow her to become
a Christian prophet rather than a sangoma. This was allowed, and it was
as a prophet that she came to Johannesburg in 1942. Because she became
ill if she did not carry on with her healing work, she continued to do so,
and remained in the Anglican church as her activities had the blessing of
her local parish priest. When he left to go to another congregation, however, his successor disapproved of Mrs A. N.'s work, and she left the
church. She went to a Zionist church and then joined the Methodist
church when she married. Finally she and her husband founded their
own church, where she takes a very active part in directing its affairs.

Before reaching her present position as an influential prophet, Mrs
A. N. had to undergo a long and expensive period of training with
another prophet. This involved offerings of animals at various intervals,
purification by immersion in a river and through use of emetics, as well
as observation of her trainer at work with patients and sessions of dream
analysis. When her training was completed, a final offering was made.
Mrs A. N. believes that her power to predict, divine and heal comes from
God through certain guiding shades — particularly her paternal great-
great-grandmother, who was a diviner and after whom Mrs A. N. was
named. Others of her shades who were healers also assist her in her work.

An indication of the power of Mrs A. N.'s shades was given by her
when she said that she had become very ill when moving to Soweto and
had found that in addition to being ill she could not use her healing
powers. She consulted another healer who informed her that her shades
were annoyed that they had not been formally informed of her movements — she was advised to return to her birthplace and to offer a cow,
inform her shades of her movements, and ask them to accompany her.
This she did, her illness disappeared and her healing powers returned.

In early discussions Mrs A. N. stated that she would have nothing to

do with sangomas, or with the medicines they use. Subsequently it
turned out that she did in fact work with one sangoma with whom she
was on very friendly terms. This sangoma, Mrs M., was a Roman Catholic
who had become ill in middle age. When doctors couldn't cure her she
knew that she was being summoned by her shades. They sent her to train
for short periods with two different diviners, and she became a fully-
fledged diviner after a final offering of a cow. Unlike Mrs A. N.'s case,
Mrs M.'s shades informed her that they did not want her to go to church,
and she then left the Roman Catholic Church. Mrs A. N. regards the
differences between them as being firstly that Mrs M.'s powers are from
the shades only, whereas hers come from God *through* the shades, and
secondly that their healing techniques differ: Mrs M. uses herbs and other
medicines whilst she uses mainly prayer and holy water. The cases they
treat, however, are substantially the same, and they exchange supernatural messages from time to time.

Much of Mrs A. N.'s work is aided by dreams and visions. In one
vision God spoke to her and promised that while certain objects were in
the house of a patient, no death would occur, but that if death was
coming she would be informed. These objects were also revealed in
dreams, and while not all are used directly in healing, they are all protective. They are three 'flags' which are pieces of oilcloth with certain
scenes painted on them, and a seven-candle candalabra. The flags are
used for different purposes, and are based on various biblical passages.
One comes from 1 Samuel 7:12 — 'Hitherto the Lord has helped us' —
and is used specifically during Mrs A. N.'s annual December thanksgiving
for being able to exercise her powers. Another is based on Genesis
16:7-16, which recounts a story that parallels a period of Mrs A.N.'s
own life — how she conceived a child at a very advanced age after having
been barren. The final flag is based on Genesis 32:25-32 which recounts
Jacob's struggle 'with God and with men' and how he prevailed. This
flag was made by Mrs A. N. to prevent her from being endorsed out of
a particular area by the authorities, and was successful. Thus the three
flags symbolise the support Mrs A. N. receives in her work, and the
favours shown to her which are evidence of her special calling.

In her healing consultations Mrs A. N. is very similar to Mrs M. R. —
she wears a cape and healing cords, and uses a prophet's stick, candles
and a Bible. In addition she has a portable Holy Place, as described
earlier. When healing she relies mainly on prayer and holy water,
although she uses one or two herbs and a number of other substances.
Mrs A. N. is a little unusual in that she has a more than usually sophisticated system of giving holy water. The water itself is divided into a
number of types: sea water, fresh water from a tap, fresh water from a
spring and rain water. In her house she keeps a cupboard full of bottles
of water — each bottle has been prayed for specifically to cure a parti-

cular illness, and is labelled. When Mrs A. N. is away from home her
daughter is able to dispense holy water according to a patient's complaint.
A fuller account of Mrs A. N.'s consultations will be given in a special
section below.

Mrs A. N.'s cosmology includes God, Jesus Christ, the Holy Spirit,
the Devil and the shades. There are also evil spirits which can be used by
men to harm others — this is one reason people may become ill, but
other reasons are linked to the fall of man. God may send illness as a
punishment and as a reminder — 'We must get sick — if we can't get
sick we will forget God.' Mrs A. N. can tell with her powers in what way
illness has been caused, although she is reluctant (like many other prophets) to point directly to witchcraft. As a prophet with powers coming
from God she is stronger than those who exercise evil powers, and thus
she is able to heal.

Mrs S. M. also started having dreams from an early age — about 20. She
was ill for a very long time with symptoms including a distended stomach,
general pains over her body and bad headaches. Western doctors were
unable to help her, and she eventually went to a prophet in Soweto, who
was able to give her some relief. At that time she was a member of the
Presbyterian Church of Africa, an Ethiopian-type church, and shortly
afterwards she married and joined the Methodist church of her husband.
Later they both left the Methodist church and joined the Presbyterian
Church of Africa. Mrs S. M. found that her condition deteriorated after
marriage. Again western doctors were unable to help, and she was 'sick
but walking' for some time. She had operations and numerous injections
without success, and then in 1960 she finally consulted another prophet,
who healed her and told her that she would not recover permanently
until she herself became a prophet. This she agreed to do, and she went
through a series of rituals including purification by immersion in a river
and through use of emetics, offerings to the shades and to God, and of
course the usual observation of the healer at work and sessions of interpretation of dreams. Thus Mrs S. M. became a prophet, and began seeing
things in church 'like a bioscope'. This was unacceptable to the Presbyterian Church of Africa, and she was asked to leave. She and her husband,
who was an elder in the church, then formed their own healing church
with their first congregation members being patients who had been
healed by Mrs S. M. A prominent feature of this church is healing through
giving holy water.

Like the other prophets described above, Mrs S. M. feels that illness
can be sent by God as punishment for sin as well as being caused by the
Devil or by evil spirits. When she heals she wears a cape and also uses a
healing-stick, prayer, holy water and various other substances. She is
assisted in her work by her shades, who intercede on her behalf with

God. As her powers come from God through the shades, they are superior to those of evil spirits which do not come from God. Unlike sangomas, she can only heal through the power of God — 'I trust God. *Madlozi* (the shades) can't be strong with God, God is strong with *madlozi*. I can only help when I trust in God.'

The three cases cited above are in most respects typical. The pattern that emerged from those prophets interviewed was as follows. Most prophets appear to be females, who have had a long and early history of illness which usually has rather vague symptoms such as fainting, loss of appetite, headaches and the like. This illness has not been cured by western medicine, and the sufferers have consulted either diviners or prophets, who have helped them. Part of the diagnosis has been that the patients are being called by the shades to be healers, and that they should accept the call if they wish to be completely well. The call is then accepted and the patients become initiates who go through a series of rituals including purification and offerings to the shades, as well as to God.

After the final rituals a prophet is able to heal independently, but this will depend on the strength of her powers. Weaker prophets will do their work mostly in church services, whilst the stronger ones are likely to attract a clientele which extends beyond church membership, and therefore to start healing by private consultation. In private consultations prophets will heal with the guidance of the Holy Spirit, either direct or more commonly through certain shades. Methods of healing vary in detail, but show considerable uniformity.

CONSULTATIONS

I shall now deal in some detail with patients seen over a five-month period by Mrs M. R., the senior prophet of the BBCAC. The information that follows is drawn from a diary, kept at my request between January and May 1971, of the names of patients, their complaints, and how they were cured.

During the five-month period, Mrs M. R. had 361 consultations with patients, which means a daily average of 2,4 and a monthly average of 72. The 361 consultations were attended by 162 different patients. Just under two-thirds (62 per cent) of the patients were women, and a minority of 42 per cent were members of the BBCAC — the other patients came from a variety of churches, both mission and independent, while some had no formal affiliation with any church. It can be reasonably assumed that the more successful a prophet becomes the more patients will be attracted from outside her own congregation, and the fact that Mrs M. R. has more patients who are not members of her church is an indication of her standing.

Since there were more consultations than individual patients, many must have returned for more than one session with the prophet. In fact, 60 per cent of Mrs M. R.'s patients came only once in the five-month period, and 32 per cent came between two and five times; to put it another way, 92 per cent of the patients came five times or fewer. Only 8 per cent came more often, the range being between six and twenty-two visits.

The patients attracted to a prophet from outside the church are drawn by word of mouth, as there is no advertising. Mrs M. R.'s 162 patients came from Soweto and environs, other Johannesburg suburbs (largely domestic servants living with their employers), other African townships within approximately an 80-kilometre radius, and in two cases from other provinces.

According to the diary, 94 per cent of the patients came from the Johannesburg district, of which most came from Soweto itself. Further analysis of the homes of patients in Soweto showed a concentration nearest the township in which Mrs M. R. held consultations. While only 10 per cent of patients came from her own township, 59 per cent of all her patients came either from her township or from one immediately adjacent, and 70 per cent came from no farther than two townships away.

Mrs M. R.'s patients revealed a wide variety of complaints over the five-month period under review. As patients were not interviewed personally, either by myself or a doctor or psychiatrist, it is not possible to analyse complaints in detail. Any given complaint must therefore be taken largely at face value — for example a person may say he is complaining about stomach-ache whereas his real trouble may be non-physical such as depression or some personal problem. To try to bring some order, however loose, to the large variety of complaints they are presented below in two categories: *category A* deals with complaints that were presented in physical terms — for example, sore feet — and *category B* deals with complaints of a less physical nature — such as bad luck or trouble at home. The list of complaints is given in Table 8 together with the number of times each complaint was mentioned.

In Table 8 there are 74 separate complaints listed a total of 684 times — which means that many people mentioned more than one symptom (average 1,89). Of the 684 complaints 70 per cent were in category A and 30 per cent in category B, but a more accurate reflection of the proportion between these two categories may be seen by examining each consultation and separating those that mention *only* physical complaints from those in which non-physical also occur. In this distinction 'sore feet and pimples' would fall in category A, whilst 'sore feet, pimples and trouble with my husband' would then fall into category B. With this analysis of the 361 con-

TABLE 8 : COMPLAINTS TO MRS M.R. IN 361 CONSULTATIONS

Category A				Category B	
Stomach-ache	79	Mouth sores	3	Troubles with spouse	33
Body pain	60	Pregnancy pain	3	Bad luck	22
Headache	59	Insomnia	3	Work troubles	21
Sore feet	47	Flatulence	2	Trouble with children	17
Back pains	33	Loss of hair	2	Holy Spirit troubles	17
Fainting	22	Bleeding	2	Trouble at home	12
Heartache/Failure	22	Coughing	1	Run away from home	10
Sore ears	17	Body sores	1	Nightmares, visions	9
Dizziness	12	Weakness	1	Trouble with kin	8
Menstrual problems	12	Worms	1	Haunted	8
Pimples	12	Loss of voice	1	Housing problems	7
Sore eyes	10	Suffocation	1	Love problems	5
Neck pains	9	Loss of weight	1	Crying	5
Skin complaints	8	Constipation	1	Poverty	4
Sore legs	7	Hiccups	1	Barrenness	4
Kidney troubles	6	Boils	2	Drinking	4
Cramps	4	Bad blood	1	Money problems	3
Loss of appetite	4	Food poisoning	1	Madness	3
Wounds unhealed	4	Blindness	1	Nerves	2
Blood pressure	4	Stiffness	1	Troubles over pass	2
Chest complaints	3			Loss of memory	1
Tiredness	3			Unnatural pregnancy	2
Diarrhoea	3			Loss of temper	1
Can't feel pain	1			Poisoning, evil agent	1
Vomiting	3			Lack of education	1
Sore teeth	3			Talking in sleep	1
Sore knees	3			Fainting before driving	1

sultations, 60 per cent fell into category A and 40 per cent in category B.

In both cases given above, the apparent emphasis is on category A complaints.[6] People citing category A complaints may have a physical problem, but in many cases they may have other problems which are expressed in physical terms — for example acute depression may be expressed as 'pain all over the body'. A third possibility is that a non-physical problem may result in a physical complaint —

6. I am indebted to Professor L. S. Gillis, Head of the Department of Psychiatry in the University of Cape Town, for advice on this point. It was his opinion that many, perhaps most, category A symptoms had category B causes, which would be in line with findings of psychiatrists dealing with the same sort of people. Mr Gerald L. Stone, clinical psychologist, examined the records of the 361 cases in detail, and suggested that a minimum of 47 per cent fell into category B. (See also Field 1960, and Daneel 1970: 30f.)

worries over children, for example, may result in 'severe headache'. In other cases patients with a personal problem may first sound out a prophet with a minor complaint before coming out with what is really bothering them.[7] Some indication of this can be taken from the record of the patients themselves rather than the individual consultations: 49 per cent cited only category A complaints (no matter how many consultations they had); 25 per cent cited both categories (either in the same interview or at different times) and 26 per cent cited only category B complaints.

From this we can see that 51 per cent of all Mrs M. R.'s patients at some stage mentioned a category B complaint, and from all available evidence it seems as though most patients will consult Mrs M. R. because they have category-B-type complaints, even if they are not always articulated as such. Prophets are often aware of this: Mrs M. R., for example, discussed one of her regular patients and said that he had started off with a complaint about sore feet, but once he had got to know her the 'real trouble' turned out to be a marital one.

We now turn to the actual healing part of the consultations. Mrs M. R. interviews her patients at a small table on which is placed her healing-stick, a Bible, a candle and a glass of water (the latter is not always present). She herself will be wearing a cape, the colour of which is normally determined by what she sees to be the guidance of the Holy Spirit, although on occasion she will select a colour she herself deems to be appropriate. After interviewing a patient she is guided by the Spirit as to which of her remedies she should use in that particular case. Table 9 gives the different remedies and the number of times they were each used in the consultations.

Some explanation of these remedies is required. It should be noted that in all consultations the patient was prayed for, and this includes laying on of hands and blessing with a healing-stick. Water is important in a number of the remedies, but most important as holy water; holy water is prayed for by the prophet and then given to the patient to drink in a glass. Sea water is also administered in this way, and is believed to be a particularly potent remedy. The importance of holy water in healing can be seen by the fact that it was given to patients in 79 per cent of consultations.

Baths were given in 52 per cent of the consultations. Variations are as usual determined by the guidance of the Spirit, and include the use of hot or cold water, and the placing of candles around the bath. In her diary Mrs M. R. specified the number of candles in over

7. It is interesting to note that in fact just over 12 per cent of Mrs M. R.'s patients mentioned a category B complaint on a second or subsequent visit, having first given category A complaints.

TABLE 9 : REMEDIES GIVEN BY MRS M. R. IN 361 CONSULTATIONS

Prayer	361	Milk	14
Holy water	285	Bicarbonate of soda	9
Baths	189	Oil	9
Enemas	161	Methylated spirits	6
Steaming	153	Vaseline and sulphur	4
Emetics	78	Epsom salts	3
Candles	89	Vinegar and sugar	3
Ash	59	Sugar	2
Sea water	25	Sulphur	2
Vaseline	24	Food	2
Vinegar	19	Advice	2
Rosewater	17	Petroleum jelly	1
Vaseline and methylated spirits	14	River immersion	1

three-quarters of the cases where they were used. The numbers were 2, 3, 4, 6, 7, 12 and 14, the most popular being 7 (used in 51 per cent of the specified cases) and 12 (in 25 per cent of cases).

In many cases baths were given in conjunction with steaming — the steam being made either by boiling water or by pouring hot water on to heated stones. Patients were given steam treatment in 42 per cent of consultations. Usually the whole body was subjected to steaming, although in some cases it was only a part of the body — perhaps the head, or the feet.

Enemas and emetics were frequently used to purify the body: enemas were given in 45 per cent of consultations, and emetics were used in 22 per cent. Either an emetic or an enema was administered in 53 per cent of consultations, with 30 per cent of these having both. Enemas were most usually administered with water, although milk was used in a few cases. A greater variety of substances was used in the emetics, the most popular appearing to be water mixed with vinegar and sugar, although plain vinegar and occasionally vinegar mixed with ash were also used.

Ash was also used fairly frequently (in 16 per cent of consultations), as a rubbing agent and also to protect a house — by sprinkling the ash outside. Most of the other substances mentioned in Table 9 — including vinegar, vaseline and methylated spirits mixture, vaseline and sulphur, vaseline, methylated spirits, sulphur and petroleum jelly — were mainly used to rub on afflicted parts of the body. Oil was used only for sore ears, rosewater was sometimes used in baths, and bicarbonate of soda and epsom salts were generally given to drink. On two occasions Mrs M. R. rendered very practical assistance by giving food to patients who complained of poverty.

Mrs M. R. did not record all remedies in her diary, the most significant omission being the use of 'holy wool' — wool of different colours tied round afflicted parts of the body for protective purposes: this was not recorded because the wool was regarded as protective rather than curative. In only two cases was 'advice' given, without any other remedies. Advice to patients is clearly part of a prophet's work and probably one of the most important parts, whether or not the prophet is aware of it. In this regard one prophet said, 'It is not only my holy water which helps — sometimes they just want to talk about their troubles and get advice.' It should be noted that in many cases Mrs M. R.'s advice included the suggestion that a patient visit a doctor or a hospital. This was not always recorded in the diary, but even so patients were advised to seek the help of western medicine in 12 per cent of consultations where it was recorded, and the true total is likely to be much higher. Mrs M. R. visits a doctor herself, and is in no way opposed to western medicine. However she does suggest that patients who have medicine prescribed for them should bring it to her to be prayed for.[8] Most of the prophets interviewed in Soweto were not opposed to the use of western medicine, although there were one or two who regarded it as unnecessary because their type of healing was superior.

To amplify this section on consultations, we shall now look at one or two specific patients, their complaints and how they were treated. The examples will be taken from more regular patients, so that the differences in complaints are seen, as well as the similarity in treatment.

Mr A. M., the most regular patient, was an elderly man who had been a cook but had been out of work for some time because of trouble with his feet. In all he visited Mrs M. R. twenty-two times in the five-month period. Below are the complaints he cited (quoted from Mrs M. R.'s diary), together with the treatment in each case:

Visit 1: 'He used to have swollen feet, couldn't go to work nor could he walk.'
Treatment: Prayer, steam, bath, emetic with vinegar and sugar.

Visit 2: 'The troubles he had, the thing that is worrying him now is the Holy Spirit.'
Treatment: Prayer, holy water, steam, bath with 7 candles.

Visit 3: 'Swollen feet a bit better but not quite.'
Treatment: Prayer, holy water, steam for feet, vaseline to rub feet.

Visit 4: 'Still doing treatment and the feet are improving, only a little bit swollen.'

8. Mrs M. R.'s treatment sometimes shows the influence of western medicine: for example, when she prescribed a bottle of holy water to be taken 'two spoons every four hours'.

Treatment: Prayer, holy water.

Visit 5: 'He says at night he sees some things and sometimes he dreams of being out in a lonely spot praying hard.'

Treatment: Prayer, holy water, steam.

Visit 6: 'He had swollen ankles and itching feet underneath and tired legs.'

Treatment: Prayer, holy water, vaseline for feet.

Visit 7: 'He had bad luck at marriage and at home, and sickness, sore stomach, pains and Holy Spirit.'

Treatment: Prayer.

Visit 8: 'He is being attended for treatment.'

Treatment: Prayer, holy water, enema.

Visit 9: 'He used to have a lot of trouble about swollen feet and sore headache.'

Treatment: Prayer, holy water, steam, bath with two candles, vinegar for feet, advised to go to a doctor.

Visit 10: 'He had swollen feet and swollen stomach, now what worries him is the Holy Spirit.'

Treatment: Prayer, holy water, sea water, steam, bath.

Visit 11: 'He is still going for treatment, now he is much better.'

Treatment: Prayer, holy water.

Visit 12: 'He used to have lots of trouble for sickness and Holy Spirit.'

Treatment: Prayer, holy water, steam, bath with candles, enema.

Visit 13: 'He used to have stiff legs and other troubles with sickness and the Holy Spirit.'

Treatment: Prayer, holy water, sea water, steam, bath with 14 candles, emetic with vinegar and milk, enema.

Visit 14: 'He used to have sore stomach-ache and pains in his back and Holy Spirit.'

Treatment: Prayer, holy water, bath with 12 candles, told to go to a doctor.

Visit 15: 'He used to have Holy Spirit, and sore feet and headache and stomach-ache and sore back.'

Treatment: Prayer, holy water, steam, bath with 7 candles, enema.

Visit 16: 'He used to have troubles with the Holy Spirit and stiff legs and cramp the whole body.'

Treatment: Prayer, holy water, steam, bath with 12 candles, enema.

Visit 17: 'He used to have a lot of troubles with sickness.'

Treatment: Prayer, holy water, bath, enema, emetic.

Visit 18: 'He says that at night he sees some things and sometimes he dreams of being out in a lonely spot praying hard.'

Treatment: Prayer, holy water, advised to go to a doctor.

Visit 19: 'He used to have pains, he still talks in his sleep.'

Treatment: Prayer, holy water, bath, emetic.

Visit 20: 'He used to have troubles about sickness.'
Treatment: Prayer, holy water, bath, enema.

Visit 21: 'He used to have a lot of troubles about sickness.'
Treatment: Prayer, bath, enema.

Visit 22: 'He was very sick, now he is much better, the only trouble now is the Holy Spirit.'
Treatment: Prayer, holy water, bath, emetic.

There are a number of interesting things about this case. It should be noted that a category A complaint was mentioned first (swollen feet) and complaints of similar type continued (itching feet, stiff legs, stomach-ache, headache, back pains and cramps). After an initial interview category B complaints came to the fore – including being troubled by the Holy Spirit, bad luck in marriage, talking in his sleep and visions at night. It is interesting that Mrs M. R. regarded his major problem as an unhappy marriage, although this was only once given as a specific complaint. It appeared as if Mr A. M. thoroughly enjoyed his regular visits to the prophet, which took up much of his time whereas before he had little to do: he subsequently became a member of the church, and at the end of the fieldwork period was made a preacher. It was learned late in 1972 that Mr A. M. had been found to have exceptional powers, and that he was expected to become a fully fledged prophet himself by the end of the year.

Another interesting aspect of the case is the type of treatment given in relation to the specific complaint. It will be noted that different treatment is given for the same complaint at different times (e.g. visits 5 and 18) and that a new complaint does not necessarily mean a new remedy (e.g. visit 7). This point will be taken up again below.

Here, for comparative purposes, are two other cases, without individual analysis:

Mrs M. C.

Visit 1: 'She had period pains, pains in the back and sore feet.'
Treatment: Prayer, holy water, steam and vaseline for feet.

Visit 2: 'She did not have children who lived, and the doctor said that it was something wrong with her womb.'
Treatment: Prayer, holy water, ash, enema.

Visit 3: 'She used to faint when she went to work and sore stomach-ache.'
Treatment: Prayer, steam, bath, emetic.

Visit 4: 'She used to have pains when she was going to get a baby, she used to have sore stomach-ache.'
Treatment: Prayer, holy water.

Visit 5: 'She used to have bad luck in marriage and at work.'
Treatment: Prayer, holy water, bath with 2 candles.

Visit 6: 'She used to have pains and sore stomach, now she is better.'
Treatment: Prayer, holy water, enema, vaseline and methylated spirits
to rub.

Visit 7: 'She used to have sore neck and headache and stomach-ache
and pains all over her body.'
Treatment: Prayer, steam, bath with 7 candles, emetic, enema.

Visit 8: 'She used to have sore stomach, and sore headache and pain-
ful feet.'
Treatment: Prayer, holy water, bath.

Visit 9: 'She used to have pain and sore headache and sore feet.'
Treatment: Prayer, holy water, steam, enema, advised to consult a
doctor.

Visit 10: 'She used to have troubles with her husband and she was
sick.'
Treatment: Prayer, holy water, bath with rosewater.

Visit 11: 'She used to have a lot of pain in her back and sore stomach.'
Treatment: Prayer, holy water, bath with 7 candles, enema.

Miss D. G.

Visit 1: 'She had pimples over the whole body and sores round the
mouth.'
Treatment: Prayer, holy water, bath, steam, ash and vaseline for pimples.

Visit 2: 'She had lots of trouble with her mother and bad luck with
everyone.'
Treatment: Prayer, holy water, ash.

Visit 3: 'She used to faint and have headaches, she used to have
womb troubles.'
Treatment: Prayer, holy water, bath with 4 candles.

Visit 4: 'She had a bad wound in her leg which would not heal for
some years through bad blood.'
Treatment: Prayer, holy water, ash.

Visit 5: 'She used to have sore ears and sore heart and pains all over
the body.'
Treatment: Prayer, holy water, bath, oil for ears.

Visit 6: 'She used to have heart troubles and stomach-ache and
dizziness and couldn't see properly.'
Treatment: Prayer, holy water, bath, enema.

Visit 7: 'She used to have troubles because she couldn't have a baby;
she tried all over but she couldn't have a child.'
Treatment: Prayer, holy water, emetic, enema.

Visit 8: 'She used to have troubles about sickness.'
Treatment: Prayer, holy water, bath, emetic, enema.

Visit 9: 'She used to have sore pains in her back every month.'
Treatment: Prayer, holy water, bath, enema.

Visit 10: 'She used to have pains every month in her back.'
Treatment: Prayer, holy water, bath, enema, vaseline.

From the above cases we can see something of the variety of
complaints that one patient may bring forward during consultations.
It also shows that the same treatment may be given for different
complaints in some cases, whilst in others the same complaint may
be treated in different ways at different times. This would be con-
sistent with Mrs M. R.'s claim that she is merely being guided by
the Holy Spirit, but there are certain remedies which appear to be
used systematically — for example, oil was always given for sore
ears, sore feet were either steamed or one of a limited number of
mixtures was prescribed for rubbing them.

THREE PROPHETS — SOME COMPARISONS

The three prophets described earlier — Mrs M. R., Mrs A. N. and
Mrs S. M. — all kept diaries of their consultations, but for various
reasons Mrs A. N. and Mrs S. M. kept their diaries for a shorter period
than did Mrs M. R. In addition, they had fewer patients, partly because they were both employed and had limited time for consultations. Mrs A. N. worked part-time as a domestic servant, and Mrs
S. M. sold fruit and vegetables. They also differed from Mrs M. R.
in that a large proportion of their patients were treated during church
services, and were therefore not recorded in their diaries. Table 10
gives a comparison of the consultations of the three healers for the
period January to February, 1971:

TABLE 10 : THREE PROPHETS: CONSULTATIONS JAN. – FEB. 1971

	MRS S. M.	*MRS A. N.*	*MRS M. R.*	*TOTAL*
Consultations	19	56	172	247
Males	26%	25%	38%	34%
Females	74%	75%	62%	66%
Patient's church affiliation				
Prophet's church	–	9%	45%	33%
Other or none	100%	91%	55%	67%
Complaints				
Category A	37%	48%	60%	56%
Category B	63%	52%	40%	44%

From Table 10 we can see that although Mrs M. R. had more than
twice the number of consultations of the other two put together, the
ratio of male to female remained substantially the same. The fact

that Mrs A. N. and Mrs S. M. did much of their healing in church
accounts in part for the fact that a very much smaller proportion of
their consultations was with members of their own church, as it
would be more likely for church members to be healed during services
than in private consultations.

Table 10 shows also that both Mrs A. N. and Mrs S. M. had a higher
percentage of category B complaints than Mrs M. R. – it has already
been suggested, however, that many, if not most, of Mrs M. R.'s
patients were hiding category-B-type symptoms behind category A
complaints. It will be seen from what follows that Mrs M. R. had a
wider range of physical remedies than the other two prophets, and
it is possible that by reputation she attracted more patients with
that type of complaint. We shall now look very briefly at the consultations of the other two prophets.

From Table 10 it can be seen that Mrs A. N. saw 56 patients in
the two-month period. A very important difference between her
patients and those of Mrs M. R. was that they came from a much
wider area of South Africa. While Mrs M. R. did nearly all of her
healing at home, Mrs A. N. was prepared to travel to her patients,
and in the period covered in the table she travelled to a congregation
of the church in Pretoria and also to Ficksburg, her birthplace, in
the Orange Free State. Of Mrs A. N.'s 56 patients, 66 per cent came
from Soweto or Johannesburg suburbs, 14 per cent from Pretoria,
14 per cent from the Orange Free State/Lesotho area and 5 per cent
from Port Elizabeth. Mrs A. N., then, had a reputation which extended beyond the borders of Soweto, but the amount of time she
spent travelling, and the fact that she had a part-time domestic-
service job, reduced the number of patients she was able to see.
This is one reason why Mrs A. N. keeps a stock of bottles of holy
water at her home, so that they may be administered to a patient
needing urgent treatment during one of her absences. Her travelling
also necessitated the use of the portable Holy Place, already described.

Mrs A. N. of her own accord kept details of the church affiliation
of her patients. Only 5 of her 56 patients were in fact members of
her own church. It is interesting to note further that 61 per cent of
her patients came from independent churches, and of these she distinguished 23 per cent as being 'Zionists' and 27 per cent as being
'Apostolics'; the remainder were not classified. The rest of her
patients (39 per cent) came from four mission churches: the Anglican Church (20 per cent of the total number of patients), the Methodist Church (7 per cent), the Dutch Reformed Church (7 per cent),
and the Roman Catholic Church (5 per cent). The preponderance
of Anglicans may in part be explained by the fact that Mrs A. N.

had been an Anglican, and practised as a healer in that church, before she was forced to leave because of her healing activities. She has retained many of her patients in the Anglican Church, some of whom followed her when she formed her own church and some of whom continued to consult her while remaining within the mission church.

Regarding the complaints of her patients, Mrs A. N.'s diary is essentially similar to that of Mrs M. R., although there is a greater proportion of category B complaints. Her patients gave the same sort of complaints under category A: sore stomach and sore feet again were important, followed by menstrual problems, sore back, sore head, general pain and loss of appetite. Category B complaints again were very similar to those of Mrs M. R., although proportions differed. Trouble with children was most often mentioned, followed by bad luck, trouble at home ('no peace in the house'), love problems, troubles with husbands, haunting, madness, and barrenness. In one case a minister consulted her because his congregation were not coming to church.

This list of complaints is clearly not indicative of the total range of complaints that Mrs A. N. may handle, as the period under review was so short. It is therefore useful to list those complaints that Mrs A. N. said that she was able to deal with, as this should in fact be much the same as a list of complaints she would treat most often. In the order in which she gave them, Mrs A. N. said she could treat headaches, circulation problems, extremes of temperature, sore bones, colds, diarrhoea, insomnia, internal pains, loss of appetite, womb and gynaecological problems, problems with unborn children, loss of children or inability to conceive; she also prayed for people living in poverty, for spendthrifts and for those out of work; and she could predict things including difficulties over childbirth and the nature of infant illnesses.

Mrs A. N.'s treatment of patients showed broad similarities with Mrs M. R.'s, although it was not as elaborate. She, too, prayed for all her patients, and gave holy water to most of them (84 per cent). However, other remedies were used fairly sparingly — hot baths with steaming were given to 18 per cent of her patients (in nearly all cases with accompanying candles), and in only one case was an emetic given. Although she does use them on occasion, no enemas were given to any patients in this group. Unlike Mrs M. R., Mrs A. N. reported use of holy wool, and wool of various colours was given to 25 per cent of her patients.

It has been mentioned before that colours have significance in the independent churches, and that there is considerable accord about interpretation. Most prophets appear to have their 'own' colour, usually revealed to them in a dream. Mrs M. R.'s special colour was yellow, and Mrs A. N.'s was blue, which she regarded also as the colour of Mary, mother of Jesus. Yellow for her symbolised the Holy Spirit, red symbolised blood, green was for fertility and strength, and white was symbolic of purity. Different combinations are given to patients depending on the guidance of the Spirit and on the type of complaint. To take one example, Mrs A. N. usually uses a combination of green, red, and white wool plaited together as a protective cord for those who are seeking employment. Cords may be used for this sort of purpose, as well as an aid to healing — when for example they may be tied round a sore foot or arm.

Although Mrs A. N. says she disapproves of the use of herbs and other medicines as used by diviners, she admitted that she uses two herbs herself — one a root which is crushed, burned to ash, and administered to women with menstrual problems, and the other a red flower which is crushed and used for people who have problems with their shades. The importance of advice of a general nature has already been mentioned and, while all prophets give advice, Mrs A. N. stressed its importance particularly, and in 21 per cent of her interviews she recorded advice given as being an important part of the treatment.

Table 10 shows that Mrs S. M. saw fewer patients — only 19 — than the other two prophets, and that none of her patients belonged to her church. Although she saw too few patients for this to be of any great significance, it should be noted that her church concentrated more on healing during services than the churches of the other two did, and consequently fewer of her members would consult her in private.

Mrs S. M. kept a less complete diary than the others, but what she recorded accords well with their information. The proportion of male to female was much the same, and the church affiliation of patients was equally broad. No affiliation was recorded for 5 of the 19 patients, whilst of the remainder 7 were from independent churches, 3 were Roman Catholics, 2 were from the Dutch Reformed Church and 2 were members of the Lutheran Church. While Mrs S. M. recorded more category B complaints than the others did, the complaints recorded were much the same. Patients complained of bad luck most of all (7 times), followed by being troubled by the Spirit of God, general body pain, cramp, barrenness, madness, sore stomach and tiredness.

No record was kept of the remedies administered to these patients, and Mrs S. M. merely said that she prayed for them, gave them holy water, and in some cases gave them holy wool. She, too, used ash and vinegar in her treatment, and had given advice when this was what was needed. In interviews, Mrs S. M. said that she healed patients by prayer, laying on of hands, holy water, steam, salt, ash, vinegar and holy wool. As with the other prophets, the holy wool used was of various colours, each with a special significance: white for purity, red for blood, green for the Spirit and the sky (symbolising the power of heaven), and blue also for the Spirit and the sky, whilst yellow was for God. Different combinations would be used for different purposes: for example, red and green wool might be used to tie round a sore leg: red for the blood which had to be improved in order to heal, and green for fertility and power from heaven. Mrs S. M. also said that she used enemas and candles when healing; three candles symbolising the Trinity were often put round a patient. Like the other prophets, Mrs S. M. makes use of western medicine. As she said: 'If I see people are too sick, I send them to the doctor, to get medicine. Then I pray for it. Even I myself go to a doctor, because doctors help — like me.'

Unlike the other two prophets, Mrs S. M. does not have a Bible with her when she heals, but in common with them she wears a cape and protective cords, and uses a healing-stick. Usually when patients come to see her they put a small amount of money in a saucer of ash, which is placed on a table between the prophet and the patient. She looks at the saucer and, through her shades who act as intermediaries with God, she finds out the nature of the patient's problem and what she should do about it. Although she is in the hands of the shades who guide her, and of God, she does have specific healing routines for special complaints. If she senses that a person is being punished by God, she uses prayer, and gives the patient advice on how to mend his ways. A patient troubled by evil spirits or the Devil will be prayed for, while those with marital disputes will receive holy water. People seeking work are generally made to wash and are given holy water to drink. They are then given wool of blue, green and red, wound into a cord which they are told to wear. People with bad luck are given cords of red and green, while 'urgent troubles' are treated with a cord of five colours (blue, red, green, white and yellow). If a house has been bewitched, water and ash and salt are usually sprinkled about it. In common with the other two prophets, Mrs S. M. reports that many of her patients come to her not only to be healed, but also to find out why they are suffering. Often they suspect witchcraft, and wish to know who is bewitching them. Mrs S. M. is also unwilling to fan witchcraft accusations and plays down this aspect in her consultations.

From the above we can see certain differences in the prophets we have described, but more importantly we can also see certain parallels: in training, in types of patients, and in remedies used. With some idea of the specifics of healing, we now turn to a more general view of healing in the independent churches, and the role it plays.

THE ROLE OF HEALING

Soweto has a large general hospital near by. It has seven general medical clinics operating within the complex, as well as tuberculosis, dental, and child-care clinics. There are also a number of medical practitioners with consulting rooms in various parts of the area. Western medical services are not regarded as adequate (although over one million cases are seen annually by the clinics, and half-a-million immunisations are administered annually) and extensions are planned, but it should be noted that the existing facilities are spread throughout the townships, and it is possible for the ordinary citizen to make use of them relatively easily. At the same time, Soweto has faith-healers, prophets, diviners and herbalists who enjoy considerable patronage. Thus despite the provision of western medical services people still turn to the non-western healing techniques of the independent churches. In the next pages I shall try to explain why this is so.

Firstly, we should look at the types of complaint that patients bring to the independent church prophets. In our analysis of consultations we distinguished between category A complaints (where 'physical' symptoms were mentioned) and category B complaints (where 'non-physical' symptoms were mentioned). However, it was suggested that many of the category A complaints had underlying symptoms that would have been more accurately placed in category B. Margaret Field (1960: 113) noted the same phenomenon among visitors to the shrines in Ghana: 'The majority of those who come to the shrines complaining of sickness do not appear to have anything organically wrong, but they are in anxiety. They complain of palpitations, pains all over, headache, trembling, giddiness and darkness in front of the eyes.'

One should then ask whether western medicine is able to cure complaints of this nature. For example, could western medicine handle a complaint of being bewitched, or of inability to find a house, or of general bad luck? As Whisson points out (1964: 304), 'A most important factor in the healing process is that the treatment is given in clearly explicable terms. . . . The psychiatrist working within a frame of reference that excludes spirits would have great difficulty in curing any patient who believed himself attacked.' The frame of reference is clearly important, and it is the prophet not the western medical practitioner who works within the same frame of reference as the patient.

This raises the important question of 'African' versus 'European' categories of illness, a distinction made by many writers. Read, for example, quotes 'two medical workers of wide experience' as distinguishing in African systems between trivial complaints treated by home remedies, 'European diseases' which respond to western scientific therapy, and 'African diseases' which are not likely to be understood or treated by western medicine (Read 1966: 24). As Longmore points out, 'There are many psychological conditions caused by superstition, anxiety and fear among Africans which are not understood by European doctors, and which African doctors can and do cure. . . .' (Longmore 1959: 231.) This in turn tends to reinforce the idea of a difference between 'African' and 'European' diseases.

In many cases, too, it is the prophet who is more flexible. Many prophets use western medicine as well as their own techniques of healing. Field (1960: 117) mentions this to be the case in Ghana, where shrine therapists will tell patients with certain ailments to go to a hospital, and Murphree (1969: 144) refers to the use of western medicine by Vapostori members. On the other hand, western medical practitioners rarely make use of prophets to assist in handling what their patients might regard as 'African' complaints.[9] In this regard, of course, prophets claim to be able to cure a far wider range of complaints than do western practitioners: a glance at Table 8 and the list of complaints brought to one prophet is sufficient indication of the variety of complaints that patients feel a prophet is able to deal with, as well as evidence that the prophet shares their view.

Hellmann reports (1971: 10) that in Soweto 'there is the conflict between Christianity and resort to magical practices – a conflict which led interviewers in the Soweto survey to report that informants considered it "non-U" to admit to observing magical practices, although more than half, the majority professing to belong to a Christian church, stated that they did go to witchdoctors.' Given that mission churches as well as some independent churches forbid their members to consult diviners, it is interesting to note that many, at least in the survey mentioned, defied the instructions of their churches. It may reasonably be assumed that people were prepared to do this because diviners were able to satisfy needs that could not be satisfied elsewhere.

9. There are one or two exceptions to this. For example, Mrs M. R. has on a very few occasions been summoned by doctors at Baragwanath Hospital near Soweto to minister to a patient of theirs who demanded holy water, or prayer. There is no evidence, however, to show that patients are ever *referred* to prophets for private consultation.

It is important to note that in Zionist-type independent churches no such conflict exists because of the presence of prophets. It has already been suggested that prophets and diviners deal with much the same sort of complaint, albeit by slightly different means, and it will be contended later that one of the important reasons that people leave the mission churches and join independent churches is that they are able to satisfy certain needs that cannot be met in most mission churches. And healing, particularly of 'African' complaints, is an important factor.

In dealing with psychosomatic cases prophets are clearly successful, as the testimony of patients indicates, but they may also be effective in dealing with cases that, seen objectively, cannot be 'cured'. One prophet herself provided part of the reason for this when she said that it was often not her holy water that helped people, but her advice. Prophets, in fact, often provide 'tea and sympathy' for those patients who go to them to tell their troubles. Although their problems may not have been solved, patients feel better for having discussed them, and are given hope that they might be solved.

The variety of problems dealt with is also important. To take one example, a man might have the following complaints: stomach-ache, inability to get a house to live in in Soweto, and trouble with his children, who do not want to go to school. Making use of western institutions, he might then visit the clinic to have his stomach-ache treated, he might visit the housing official of his township to try to get a house, and he might consult a social worker or a parish priest about his troubles with his children. Will this be effective? If his stomach-ache is merely symptomatic of his wider problems, the clinic will be unlikely to assist. If he is not eligible for a house, or is on a long waiting-list, the housing official — even if sympathetic — will not be in a position to help. Even if he decided to consult a parish priest, or could find a social worker, they would probably not be able to help significantly in the face of a double-shift schooling system, very high pupil–teacher ratios, and all the other problems of African education (see Horrell 1964; Spro-Cas 1971).

In this sort of situation, and faced with likely frustration, many people turn elsewhere for assistance, and in many cases they turn to the prophets of the independent churches. That this is so is understood and to some extent condoned even by those who do not believe in the ability and powers of these prophets. For example, the leader of an Ethiopian-type church in Soweto said that he did not believe in the healing powers of Zionist-type prophets, but that he understood why people would consult them. He put it in these terms: 'My people do these things because they are suffering — if a man is suffering he will try anything to get better.' Some evidence for this can be seen in the fact that many people who are not members of the independent churches nevertheless consult prophets, and that it is common for these people to state in case histories that they had tried for relief through other channels before approaching a prophet.

We must then ask why prophets are successful in attracting patients, and whether they have specific attributes that assist them in this. Firstly it should be noted that prophets claim supernatural sanction for their activities. The prophet alone claims to work with the power of God — the strongest of supernatural sanctions. Against this, of course, the doctor or social worker has nothing comparable to offer. Even the diviner, who also claims supernatural power, cannot match the ultimate power claimed by the prophet. Faced with frustration or the inability of other people to assist, people are attracted — even if as a last resort — by the claims of the prophets regarding their source of power.

It is, of course, not only the power claimed by the prophet that is important in attracting patients. Equally important is the fact that the prophet is believed to understand the nature of complaints. As has already been pointed out, a distinction is often made between 'African' and 'European' diseases, and the prophet, while claiming to be able to heal both types, is certainly regarded as being better able to deal with the former category. The prophet has another advantage. Western medicine can usually only explain *how* a particular complaint was contracted, and even this may not be satisfactory for a person with little or no physiological knowledge. But even if the 'how' explanation is accepted, it does not often explain 'why' — why for example that particular patient and not somebody else should have contracted a particular complaint at a particular time. This the prophet claims to be able to do by means of divination.

Understanding why something has happened is extremely important, even if the prophet does not reveal to the patient exactly what has caused his illness. It has already been mentioned that many of the prophets interviewed were reluctant to tell their patients if they thought a particular person was causing them harm, for fear of spreading ill-feeling. A further factor is the Witchcraft Suppression Act of 1957, of which some prophets are aware, which would make explanations of this sort an offence (cf. Hammond-Tooke 1970: 27). It is important that the prophet should understand why the illness has occurred, because this aspect cannot be separated from the cure: to cure one must understand what has happened, and to understand what has happened one must know the why and the how. That the prophet fulfils these requirements is another strong recommendation.

The prophet is attractive, then, not only for the power which she calls upon to assist her, but also for the fact that she is able to understand not just the complaint itself, but why it happened — in short, she is concerned both with the complaint and if necessary its whole social context. From this the prophet is often able to provide a more convincing diagnosis (from the patient's point of view) than a western doctor. Diagnosis may be effective through simplicity — for example 'bad blood' and 'heart failure' cover a multitude of evils in simple terms — but more often what is important is the ability to explain misfortune in meaningful terms.

An analysis by Lévi-Strauss of the case of a woman who was being cured by a South American shaman is relevant to our discussion:

> The cure would consist, therefore, in making explicit a situation originally existing on the emotional level, and rendering acceptable to the mind pains which the body refuses to tolerate. That the mythology of the shaman does not correspond to objective reality does not matter. The sick woman believes the myth and belongs to a society which believes in it. The tutelary spirits and malevolent spirits, the supernatural monsters and magical animals are all part of a coherent system on which the native conception of the universe is founded. The sick woman accepts those mythical beings, or, more accurately, she has never questioned their existence. What she does not accept are the incoherent and arbitrary pains which are an alien element in her system, which the shaman, calling upon myth, will re-integrate within a whole where everything is meaningful. Once the sick woman understands, however, she does more than resign herself, she gets well. . . .' (Lévi-Strauss 1968: 197.)

This reintegrative function of the healer, whether shaman or prophet, is of great importance. Through the diagnosis the unknown becomes known, and fear is often replaced by understanding. Thus satisfaction may be given even if a complete cure is not achieved, and this satisfaction can come about only if the diagnosis is meaningful to the patient — that is, if the world-views of healer and patient in some measure coincide.

Finally, a satisfactory diagnosis and explanation by the prophet is followed by satisfactory treatment. As has been described above, the healing repertoire of a prophet can be spectacular with its ritual and variety of techniques. In the case of Mrs M. R., for example, her patients were given an average of nearly four different remedies each per consultation, and these were administered by a person in prophet's robes, claiming to represent the supreme power, with ritual involving prayer, blessing, candles, etc. This type of consultation may be much more impressive than a visit to a western doctor, for reasons such as those that were outlined to Jarrett-Kerr by an African medical attendant:

When a patient goes to an African doctor, the doctor doesn't ask him a lot of funny questions . . . the doctor should know all about that. He can smell the sickness at once. What does take a long time is not the questions at the beginning but the treatment at the end. . . . But when a patient comes to a White doctor, the doctor asks him many, many questions about what he should know already. Then when he comes to a prescription the doctor only writes something you can't read even if you understand English. The patient is not impressed with such things.' (Jarrett-Kerr 1960: 36.)

There is also an important difference between treatment by a prophet in familiar surroundings (for example, the same sort of room that you have in your home), and that given through hospitalisation. As Read points out (1966: 41), '. . . hospitalisation represents a traumatic break from intimate personal support in familiar surroundings to impersonal attention from professionals in a strange and forbidding environment'. Again the prophet has the advantage of treating in familiar, explicable terms: the emphasis is not on separation of the patient, but rather on reintegration. This concern is shown with specific reference to hospitals by the efforts of independent church leaders to get permits to visit members of their congregations in the local hospitals at all times, as well as the efforts of ordinary congregation members to visit fellow-members in hospital as often as possible, to be with them and to pray for them.

Thus far the specific attractions of the prophet have differed from those of a diviner only in that the prophet lays claim to a superior supporting power. This is not his only advantage; another which has wide implications is that the prophet is linked to a church, and thus — because it is an independent church — to a fairly close-knit community. For some patients, as we have seen, this is not important, and they visit the prophet in isolation from the church, but for many others the community to which the prophet is attached is most important.

Here we may return briefly to the point made at the beginning of this chapter: that the independent churches integrate healing with worship whereas this link has largely been broken in the mission churches. In healing, the congregation of the independent Zionist-type church plays a supportive role. Edgerton (1971: 269) has suggested that some important factors in 'primitive medicine' are the roles of suggestion, faith, confession, catharsis, and group support. Much of this is reinforced by the congregation: the common belief strongly suggests the efficacy of faith-healing, and members are encouraged to have faith. At the same time, many of the churches have a cathartic function for people by encouraging confession, dancing and spirit possession.

It has been suggested that many of the patients who are treated

in the independent churches have social problems which are often
manifested in states of anxiety. Whether or not this is perceived by
the healers or other members of the congregation,[10] the support of
the congregation for these people is clearly very important. In church
healing, or at the river, the participation of the group is essential, and
in many ways it is a shared experience. In the frequent visiting, both
at home and in hospital, the patient is assured of the support of the
group.

It will be contended in a later chapter that the independent churches are particularly well-equipped to deal with many of the problems
that arise specifically out of an urban environment, but we see here
that they play a special role in dealing with illness, and with other
problems which those who suffer them explain in terms of illness.
In many cases people come to the independent churches with problems which are associated with some crisis in life, a situation that,
as Park has suggested, often requires divination (Park 1963: 195ff.).
This the prophet is able to provide but the western doctor is not.
Further, the prophet is able to explain to the patient in meaningful
terms what has happened; he then proceeds to administer remedies
which are usually both simple and spectacular. Added to this, the
prophet's church provides a ready-made caring community, bolster-
ing the faith of the patient and providing support which stretches
beyond the specific complaint to its social context and to the whole
life of the individual concerned.

In times of crisis many people turn to religion, and it is the integration of religion with healing in the independent churches which
makes them attractive and meaningful to many people in Soweto
who have difficulty in either solving or coming to terms with various
forms of misfortune.

10. As has been mentioned, some prophets are aware of this, and others
not. Edgerton (1971: 263) mentions that a diviner he studied recognised
stomach-ache and headache (both very common complaints among the independent church patients) as being two symptoms highly indicative of excessive worry.

CHAPTER 7 The Wider Network

The independent church movement in South Africa is often seen
as consisting of numerous tiny churches, formed by continuing
secession, with little or no co-operation between them. Co-operation
between independent churches is not a subject normally dealt with;
the usual emphasis is on the divisive factors within the movement,
which lead to the proliferation of churches. For example, Sundkler
(1961) pays very little attention to this aspect of the churches — and
in fact it is possible that at the time of his study co-operation was
not particularly important. However, any study of the independent
churches in Soweto now must include an analysis of interaction
within the movement, as this is an important factor for groups and
individuals alike.

Most independent churches no matter how small are divided into
a number of congregations, which often meet independently. For
this reason interaction must be approached from an inter-congrega-
tion level as well as an inter-church level. I shall therefore distinguish
firstly between *intra-church* interaction and *inter-church* interaction,
on either a personal or a group level.

INTRA-CHURCH INTERACTION

The analysis of church followers in chapter 5 has shown that
urban congregations of the independent churches cut across ties of
kinship, language and residence. It has also been suggested that
congregations are small close-knit groups which satisfy many of
the needs of their members. It may be assumed that members may
interact more with fellow-members than with non-members: as
Sundkler suggests (1961: 86), '. . . the Bantu independent church
in the city is also the centre for a wider social life.' In the survey of
ordinary church members of a number of independent churches in
Soweto, 75 per cent said that they had relatives in the same church
and 97 per cent said that they had made friends within the church
they had joined: that is people they regarded as friends outside the
church situation. This result would tend to confirm the hypothesis

that independent churches fill a wider role in the lives of their members than the purely religious.

Friendly relationships among congregation members are often stressed in the independent churches, and visiting is encouraged. Individuals may also have contacts with congregations other than their own by attending services with a friend or relative, attending funerals, and sometimes by visiting a prophet in another congregation for private consultations. The quest for healing is an important factor in contacts between congregations and between churches.

There are also of course contacts between congregations of the same church, as groups. A limiting factor in this regard is distance, and consequently the closest contacts are those between congregations within Soweto. These congregations will usually meet together for important services: for example New Year, Good Friday and Easter, and the day of the church conference. There may also be less formal occasions linking congregations, and invitations may be extended by one congregation to others to attend services to welcome new members, or to give thanks for a particular event, or to witness the ordaining of prayer-women.

There are other occasions which formerly might have been attended by kith and kin only, but are now the preserve of the church, and these include weddings, funerals, thanksgivings, rituals to raise tombstones for relatives, and the like. Often fellow-members feel an obligation to attend these rituals, whether or not they are personally friendly with the protagonists, and it is not unusual for the church leader to take a leading part in the ceremonies. For example, I have already mentioned a thanksgiving held by a member of the Full Gospel Church which was entirely arranged by the bishop. At this gathering some male relatives of the person who was holding the thanksgiving took no part in the service and sat drinking beer in front of the house. I was present at a number of weddings and funerals which were attended by church members in full uniform. I was also present at the preliminary rites at the raising of a tombstone, for which the elder sons of the dead man had collected money. One of the younger sons was a prominent member of a Zionist church and he had arranged for church members to attend the night vigil, and for the bishop to take a leading part, despite the presence of the senior brothers.

The farther congregations are apart the less likely they are to have this sort of contact. The expense of travelling and the difficulty of getting time off from work severely limit contact between congregations that are far apart. Usually some considerable effort is made for all congregations to be represented on the most important days in the church's calendar, and particularly at the church conference.

But very often representation is restricted to a few officials, and ordinary members of farflung congregations may never have the opportunity to meet with other congregations. This is one reason why some church leaders alternate the venues of their important services so as to allow all church members to participate on important occasions on a reasonably regular basis. The Full Gospel church, to take one example, does not alternate venues for the church conference, and one conference during the period of fieldwork was attended by the nearest congregations only — those in Soweto and from Thokoza, a township a few miles away. Only one or two members came from congregations farther afield.

When this happens, some congregations of the church may continue for some time without any direct contact with the church headquarters: some in fact may be *de facto* independent, and it would be an interesting investigation — which was beyond the compass of this study — to see whether any important differences exist between the headquarters of churches and their semi-independent congregations. Some of the more independent congregations have in fact attached themselves to a Soweto church and have not been an offshoot of the central body. The contact between congregation and headquarters in this case is often restricted to a patron–client relationship between the bishop and the leader of the local congregation, and in many cases it seemed as though the bishop or one of his senior deputies was the only formal link with the more distant congregations, the link being preserved through visits. Most of the church leaders interviewed in Soweto who had farflung congregations tried to visit them all every one or two years on a general tour. These tours would be important occasions for the church, and individual congregations would hold fund-raising services to assist the bishop with his travel expenses, and organise large services on his arrival for acceptance of new members, local ordinations, and other important church business needing the attention of the bishop.

The spread of the more distant congregations of churches with headquarters in Soweto has been shown in chapter 3. The concentration of congregations decreases fairly uniformly with distance from Soweto, but it is interesting to note that international boundaries are apparently not a limiting factor — thus Swaziland, which is closer to Soweto than many parts of the Cape, had a higher representation of Soweto churches despite its being a foreign territory. Many of the congregations claimed to exist may in fact consist of very few people but, taking this into account, it is clear that individual churches in Soweto have contacts stretching into various parts of South Africa and beyond.

INTER-CHURCH INTERACTION

Networks linking groups and individuals in specific independent churches are to be expected, but at the start of this project it was thought that there would be not very much contact between separate independent churches, possibly because of the fission and leadership disputes within the movement which had been emphasised in much of the literature. During fieldwork, however, it became clear that leadership disputes and the continuing fission within the movement did not in fact preclude inter-church contact. Disputes and splits usually occur within the one church and result in two new churches. While there might be some hostility between the two churches thus created, this in no way precludes them from having amicable contact with other independent churches in the area — and in Soweto there are many to choose from. There is in fact a great deal of inter-church contact in Soweto on different levels and for different purposes, and we shall deal first with contact on an individual level and then on a group level.

We see from the results of survey C that nearly every church member interviewed had friends or relatives in his or her own church (99 per cent), and that a majority had both. As far as contact with other churches was concerned three-quarters had some contact with other independent churches through friends or relatives (75 per cent), and rather fewer had the same contact with mission churches (61 per cent). In chapter 5 the movement of members from church to church was discussed, and it was shown that most members had come initially from mission churches. It is therefore to be expected that they might retain some links with people in churches from which they came. There is also a fairly free movement between independent churches, and no stigma is attached to a change in church, so a change in denomination does not necessarily mean that friendships formed in a previous church will be severed.

Individual contact between independent churches may thus be seen firstly as a result of individuals involved having been at some stage members of the same church. Contact may be through informal visiting, and it is also not unusual for friends to attend services together at one or other church. On many occasions during fieldwork people in different uniforms were seen at church services, and usually they turned out to be visiting friends of members. This is one way, of course, of gaining new members. Thus, for example, a person may leave church A and join church B, and then invite friends in church A to attend services in the new church with the object of encouraging them to join the church as well.

In some cases people will make contacts with other independent

churches with a view to joining. The most common reason for this
is a wish for healing. A member of one church may hear of a prominent and effective healer in another church and then make contact,
often through consultations in private. If the consultations are a
success the patient may then attend the prophet's church, and if it
turns out to be attractive, may join it. In this way the prophet acts
as a catalyst, drawing together different peoples into the same church.
For when one consults a prophet the object is to be healed, and the
criteria in selecting a prophet concern mainly the prophet's healing
abilities. The prophet's language and background, for example, are
not important. Once healed, the patient may have a desire to remain
well by staying in the prophet's church, and by then considerations
which might have been important in selecting a church (language,
background, home areas, etc., of most of its members) are of less
importance. Perhaps the most important factor now is that the patient
shares a common experience with other church members — that of
being healed — which is sufficient to cut across other ties of kinship,
language, residence, background etc.

In certain cases a patient who has been healed may decide to join
another independent church which also offers healing, but usually —
from the evidence of those interviewed in survey C — people join
the church to which the prophet who healed them is attached: thus
we showed in chapter 5 that no fewer than 83 per cent of the members of both the BBCAC and Full Gospel churches had joined their
church because they had been healed in it. Visits to another church,
or another church's prophet, for healing purposes will usually be
kept secret from members of the patient's own church. Secrecy will
be less important in Zionist-type churches than in Ethiopian-type or
mission churches, where healing rituals and the activities of prophets
are frowned upon. For an Ethiopian-type church member, or one
from a mission church, to consult a Zionist-type prophet could mean
suspension from that church or even expulsion. We have seen in the
analysis of members of the BBCAC and Full Gospel churches that a
majority had left mission churches to join independent churches;
there are certainly some who are reluctant to leave their churches,
but at the same time are attracted by the healing attributes of the
independent churches.

For people in this position, there appear to be two possibilities:
to consult prophets overtly and risk expulsion if found out, or to
join one of the secret healing groups in Soweto. The existence of a
secret prayer movement in Soweto, which was alleged to be ecumenical, was established fairly early in the fieldwork period, but information on it was only obtained right at the end of the period, and then
from a single informant who had been a member of one of the groups.

Since then, Schutte (1972) has suggested that there are numerous secret prayer groups operating in Soweto, but it is not clear from his paper whether or not some of those referred to are acknowledged offshoots of particular churches. In the absence of full information, we can refer only briefly to the phenomenon.

The informant referred to above stated that the *sephiri* (secret) movement, as it is called, consisted of a number of groups of people who met weekly for healing rituals. He stated that their membership was predominantly Sotho-speaking, and drawn mainly from members of the mission churches (he mentioned the Methodist church particularly). He suggested that the reason most members were Sotho-speaking was because those who were Zulu-speaking had no compunction about consulting diviners or prophets. What was more interesting was that he suggested that established church members joined *sephiri* because it gave them the healing benefits of an independent church while allowing them to remain members in good standing of their mission churches. He said that he himself was a good example: he had been a member of the Methodist Church of South Africa, and had in fact held responsible office in it. He had not wanted to lose this, but at the same time he felt the need for healing. Rather than join an independent church, he joined a *sephiri* group, where there was much less chance of his being found out. He mentioned that there were to his knowledge several prominent Methodists in the *sephiri* movement.

The structure of the movement he joined was similar to that reported by Schutte. There were various levels of membership: at the bottom were recruits, sick people, who were invited to come to a healing meeting. The people at the next level, distinguished at meetings by white gowns, did most of the recruiting and knew the initial passwords (two words dealing with physical complaints) which gained admission to meetings. Those at the third stage were fully-fledged members, distinguished by red collars with white crosses, who knew the seven passwords which allowed full participation, and who were permitted to read the 'sacred healing books' − certain passages from the Bible were believed to play a central part in the healing process. At the fourth stage were the ministers who wore gowns and clerical collars and who played the major part in healing. Finally the group had a leader, who was the senior minister.

Schutte's material supports the above. He does not stress the language or church affiliation of members directly, except to say that 'the tendency for a local group to use one of the vernaculars dictates a certain ethnic clustering. Established churches, especially the Anglican, Methodist, Lutheran and Dutch Reformed churches were well represented among the members and ex-members of these groups.' (Schutte 1972: 248.) However, in several places (e.g. pages 252, 258) he suggests that many members are from mission churches and know that their churches would disapprove of their activities. As has already been indicated, only mission churches or Ethiopian-type independent churches would be likely to object to most of the healing practices outlined by Schutte.

This is not to suggest that there are no independent church members involved in the *sephiri* movement. Zionist-type members will consult effective healers if they feel the need to, no matter what their affiliation, and there is no doubt that many will have found their way into the movement. But it may well be that its major *raison d'être* is to minister to members of mission churches who do not wish to consult healers openly.[1] The movement is thus another way in which members of different churches may have contact with one another. There may also be contacts between different *sephiri* groups, as Schutte has suggested (1972: 251).

We see, therefore, that there is considerable movement of individuals between different churches, through informal friendship networks, through attending services together, and in some cases, although these are probably a minority, through secret membership of an extra-church organisation.

Contact between churches as organisations is also very important, and we shall distinguish between formal and informal contacts. Formal contacts will be defined rather rigorously as contacts through formal associations of churches, and this aspect will be dealt with later. In this section I shall deal with the informal contacts, which cover a wide range of activities.

The most practical reason for inter-church contact is for collective fund-raising. With few exceptions independent churches are not at all wealthy, and in many cases they are unable to pay their clergy, let alone find money to build churches. Church leaders are usually employed full-time, and churches can get by on the small Sunday collections, mainly for such items as candles, books and certificates. Special fees are levied for important services and for the church conference, to pay for hire of a classroom or hall and for the food consumed by participants. But on these important occasions, and

1. As we have shown, most independent church members are poor and ill-educated, and consequently do not lose status by consulting prophets and joining the independent churches. It would be very interesting to see whether this fear of loss of status (cf. Vilakazi 1962: 101) is a factor with *sephiri* membership. This of course would require an analysis of *sephiri* members, paying particular attention to level of education, occupation, etc., which could then be compared with data for the independent churches. A difference in this would explain to some extent why, when Schutte's description is so close to the description of ordinary independent churches, secrecy is observed.

on others such as a consecration service, or funeral where the church
has to contribute, or a tour of congregations by the church leader,
the financial resources of the church are often not enough to meet
immediate requirements. It is in these cases that collective fund-raising
is important. These occasions follow a similar basic pattern: church
leaders will agree to combine and a suitable date and venue are chosen
— most usually a Saturday night in a school classroom, if neither
church has large enough accommodation. The service lasts the whole
night and involves prayer, singing and addresses. The highlight of the
occasion is the giving of money. Typically, one church, or one congregation, will come forward singing, and rhythmically place money
(usually in small coins, which draws out the proceedings) on a table.
This will be counted and the total announced. A second group will
then follow and try to better the amount. Leaders of the various
groups encourage their members, and there is a lively competitive
spirit. In the end a grand total is announced amid rejoicing, and
often the recipients of the money will sing a thank-you song to all
the contributors. In this way one church is able to draw on the resources of another to raise a larger sum than it would be able to do
on its own — and the competitive spirit increases donations from
individuals. Later another fund-raising service will be held, and this
time the proceeds will go to the second church.

In some cases these fund-raising ventures will be organised on a
regular basis, in others it will be *ad hoc*. This co-operation may be
between different denominations or between individual congregations
of the same church. There is further important co-operation between
manyano groups — as Brandel-Syrier has pointed out (1962: 70ff),
manyano women often provide the major portion of their church's
income through their fund-raising activities, some of which are interdenominational, and based on the reciprocal obligations described
above.

The second important aspect of informal co-operation between
independent churches concerns special services. Throughout the
fieldwork period it was usual to find visitors from other churches
present on special occasions, and in some cases their presence was
considered obligatory. Thus there would be an obligation for churches
to be represented at funerals and marriages — particularly the former
— if there had been any contact with the church of the person who
had died, or who was being married. Similarly with thanksgiving
services it was customary to invite members of other churches to be
present. In these cases officials of the other churches would be accorded the same standing as 'home' ministers, and would be invited to
take an active part in the proceedings.

It was usual for officials of other churches to be invited to parts of a church conference, and particularly to the closing service. Often the closing service of a church conference is the time for ordinations, and it is the norm for ministers of other churches to be present at those. In the specifically selected churches in survey A 2 (see Appendix 1), all 13 stated that ministers of other churches were present at ordination services. However there was one interesting difference: of the 13 churches, 8 could be classified broadly as Zionist-type and the remaining 5 as Ethiopian-type. Of these *all* Zionist-type leaders, and one Ethiopian-type leader stated that the presence of other ministers was necessary and usual (one leader went so far as to say that he would not hold an ordination service without the presence of other ministers, in case the validity of the ordination was later questioned – their presence as impartial observers was therefore essential). The remaining four Ethiopian-type churches said that other ministers were 'usually' or 'sometimes' present, but that their presence was not important.

One might interpret this in terms of the need of small churches for a wider validation of their activities – all the Zionist-type churches were small, as was the one Ethiopian-type which had the same attitude towards ordinations. The other Ethiopian-type churches were generally larger, and self-validating. This particular aspect, however, is more clearly seen in relation to the consecration of church leaders. There is a fixed rule among Zionist-type churches that no bishop may consecrate himself as leader of the church, and this is an extremely important rule which ensures that each church must at the outset have some contact with other churches. This rule applies uniformly to churches which are led by bishops, because episcopal succession is regarded as being very important, and may be translated only from one bishop to another. In Ethiopian-type churches, which have elected presidents, this is not a factor, and the newly elected president is usually inducted by his predecessor, or by other senior officials. In survey A 2 three churches followed this pattern, and the rest required the presence of at least one other bishop.

In a few cases the presence of one bishop was regarded as sufficient, but in the vast majority more than one bishop was required, and three or more were regularly cited as being the norm. Of these, one would be the senior officiant and would lead the consecration ritual, while all bishops present would join in laying on of hands at the moment of consecration. In survey B all 194 church leaders interviewed gave the name of the leader of another church as the person who had consecrated them. Although these consecrations spanned a period of over 50 years, it was interesting to see that very few names came up regularly as 'consecrating' bishops. The general procedure would be to approach as well-known a bishop as possible in the area, and request him to organise a consecration. One or two bishops in Soweto, however, seem to have gained a reputation for effective organisation of consecrations and are asked more than others, but it appears that most bishops will be met with requests for consecrations at some time or another.

Leaders of associations of churches may be called upon more regularly than others to perform consecrations, but this again would be by virtue of their position and not on the grounds of any special competency in performing consecrations. In only one case during fieldwork was a church encountered where the bishop had been ordained by what appeared to be a syndicate of bishops organised for the purpose. This leader had a certificate issued by a 'Christian Ministers' Association' with a leader based in the Cape Province, and he had no knowledge of services offered by this association other than that it consecrated leaders of other churches for a fee.

The very act of becoming the leader of your own independent church thus usually brings you into contact with at least three other church leaders. These may well then provide the nucleus for interdenominational contact in the future, at special services, inaugurations, fund-raising meetings and so on. Other church leaders may then be met at similar gatherings of other churches, and thus one church leader may get to know a large number of independent church leaders in his area and have contact with them from time to time. This was confirmed by observation during fieldwork and supported by the fact that 90 per cent of the church leaders in survey A stated that they had regular contact with other independent churches.

Interdenominational contact is generally between churches of roughly the same type — thus Zionist bishops will be invited to attend Zionist-type special services, and Ethiopian-type churches will usually invite only church leaders of similar type. This is not a rigid rule, however, and not only because the dividing-line between Ethiopian-type and Zionist-type is not always clear. Cases were observed during fieldwork of co-operation of churches of different types, but these were invariably because the church leaders involved belonged to the same association of churches. The combination was also of one sort only: Zionist-type leaders would sometimes invite Ethiopian-type leaders to services — but at no time was the reverse witnessed.

This type of co-operation ensures a wider sanction for the work of individual churches, and has an importance in securing government recognition for a church. Some church leaders are believed to have greater ability to gain government recognition than others, and are approached by other church leaders to act for them. This appears to be the case particularly with smaller rural churches, whose leaders

have great respect for some 'Johannesburg bishops' (Sundkler 1961:
75–6), and such leaders may enter into a patron–client relationship.
This type of relationship may also be seen in the way that some
church leaders reportedly sign the reference books of other leaders
– an illegal practice which allows those signed for to stay in the
urban area, because the signature is taken as evidence of continuous
legitimate employment.

While individual church leaders may co-operate rather informally
in this way, it is more usual for co-operation to occur through common membership of an association. This I shall deal with later.
Another way of co-operating, taking co-operation to its logical
conclusion, is by amalgamation of churches, and this in fact occurs
from time to time.

The simplest type of case occurs at the death of the leader. In
some cases there may not be a logical successor – particularly where
the church is very small – and the alternative to disbanding the
church is to place it under the protection of another leader. One
such case was encountered in Soweto, where the bishop of a Zionist
church said that he was in fact bishop of two churches. This had
happened when the bishop of a church which had co-operated with
his died, and there was no immediate successor. He had been approached by the lady bishop and church ministers, who asked if
they could amalgamate with his church while retaining their old
name. He agreed to this, and stated that he would attend their church
conference later in the year. He subsequently appointed one of the
church ministers as president of the church under him, and for most
purposes it remains autonomous, although the groups co-operate
from time to time. The same bishop mentioned that another church
in the same position had made overtures to him while he was at a
conference in Durban, but as yet he had heard nothing further, and
the church might have joined another group.

In the situation described, amalgamation takes place to solve a
problem of leadership, but there are other reasons. A rural case,
which appeared to be the result of pressure from a chief, was interesting because it involved more than one church. The organisation
was called the 'Zion Combination Church of South Africa', and its
inception was explained in the following terms by its first president,
in a letter to a district magistrate in Natal under the heading 'Unification of Zionist and Sabbath Bantu Individual Churches':

> Dear Sir, I greet you in the precious name of the Lord. I wish to inform you
> that in July 1969 Chief N. called members of the above churches to his
> kraal, and asked them to unite their churches into one group. He said if
> this happened he would help them and give them a site for a church to be
> built where they could all worship together. He said he was not satisfied

with their holding services in private houses, and said as soon as they amalgamated and chose one leader, he would give a site. At noon on Sunday 28th December 1969, thirteen men who are leaders of these churches came to me to discuss the views of the chief. After I confirmed what the chief had said, and said that we could follow his advice, they agreed to unite our churches so that we shall receive the same privileges obtained by other churches. . . .

The problems of this unification were later described by the same leader, who had assumed the title of Amalgamation Founder, to an adviser at the Christian Institute:

I wish to tell you that this Unification is very hard: to dissolve and amalgamate these separated Churches into one group. The leaders are untrained but some of them have made good progress and they are followed by many converts; some of them are surely saved. . . .

January 17. We had another meeting to repeat our amalgamation views; but we never completed them as we are doing it bit by bit. I can't force them because I may lose some souls . . . they are coming to me daily, these old men, to ask me what is going to happen after this unification? I promise this shall be a very good Church of our Lord Jesus, whom you all preach, but He said we must be One as they are one in heaven.

At the end of the fieldwork period the amalgamation was still proceeding slowly. Other cases of amalgamation of churches in rural areas have been observed,[2] but usually these have concerned only two churches at a time.

During fieldwork in Soweto two further mergings of churches were observed, and others have been reported since then.[3] One particularly interesting case involved the BBCAC, described in chapter 3. The BBCAC was a broadly Zionist-type church, and the church which wished to amalgamate with it, the 'Republic Church', was Ethiopian-type. The reasons the Republic Church had for wishing to merge were twofold. On the one hand their church was weak, with few members and a not very dynamic leadership; and they felt the lack of a healer in their congregation or, as the Lady Bishop of the BBCAC put it, they 'wanted the Spirit'. The BBCAC leader was known to the leader of the Republic Church, and a preliminary series of discussions was held, after which the Republics came to a BBCAC service, where they were conspicuous in their black uniforms compared with the blue and white of the BBCAC members. After the service the Republic leader said that his people had been impressed by the warmth of their reception, but that some of his members had not liked the drums used in the service.

2. Personal communication, Dr H.-J. Becken of Natal.
3. Personal communication, Dr A. G. Schutte of Witwatersrand University.

After the initial service the two groups continued to hold separate services while their leaders discussed unity, but the Republic leaders would attend BBCAC services from time to time, and on one occasion a combined evening fund-raising service was held. Later, after a meeting between the two leaders a statement was drawn up and typed by the secretary of the local association of churches. Some of the more important points in the statement are listed below:

1. It was agreed that the abovementioned two churches should amalgamate and form one big and strong church.

2. It was agreed that each church should ask its Conference to approve of the union and also to approve the new date for the Annual Conference.

3. It was agreed that Union should proceed slowly and that the points of difference between the Churches should only be settled after prayer on both sides.

Points 4 and 5 showed the BBCAC to be definitely the senior partner: point 4 gave the BBCAC as the official name of the church, while point 5 said that the BBCAC leader would be leader of the church with the leader of the Republic Church as his Vice-Bishop.

6. All other church leaders will hold their present positions in the New Church.

7. The colour of the Church Uniform will be decided later. . . .

11. One is not many — One Church is not like many Churches and its duties are not the same.

12. (a) Uniting this Church we have appreciated one good duty done by it. It helps the blind people and Orphans together with aged people. . . .

13. (a) We have asked permission to the Government to grant us to be one and we shall work uniformly.

(b) If the Government grants us permission, I'll inform the World as whole.

The document ended with provisions for objecting to the constitution, the aim of the church ('to do God's work as it is written in the Bible — Matthew 10:11') and then listed branches and ministers, explained that the ministers were married and qualified for their work, and gave the names of the banks the church would use.

This document was interesting in that it stressed a number of important aspects of the amalgamation — point 1, for example, reflected the BBCAC leader's desire for a bigger and stronger church, while point 3 acknowledged that there were differences which would take time to resolve, and point 7 shelved the vexing question of uniform (the BBCAC did not want to give up theirs, and the Republics felt that taking the BBCAC uniform would make them even more junior partners). The two churches were at the same time quick to stress points in common, and point 12 (a) reflects a common activity which was discovered — that both churches used to collect clothes for the elderly and afflicted. Finally, point 13 showed the eagerness for official ratification, and a letter was later sent off to the Bantu Administration Department requesting this, although it was not within the Department's power to provide it.

At the end of the fieldwork period the amalgamation was going ahead slowly — both leaders agreed that there was no need to rush things — and both groups were continuing to meet separately with occasional combined services. There was closer contact between the leaders, however, with the two bishops planning to make an application for a church site in a neighbouring township, and the Republic Church's Vice-Bishop, a 'half-prophet', taking some instruction from the BBCAC Lady Bishop, who, as we have said, was also the senior prophet in the church.

One other, less successful, attempt at amalgamation occurred in Soweto during the fieldwork period. This involved the Full Gospel church. The leader of a church of similar name, in this case, came to Soweto expressly to look for a church with which he might combine. His church was very small (it had only one or two congregations) and was situated in an isolated part of the Northern Cape Province. The leader felt that he would be more effective if he were to combine with an established church of similar type in Soweto. He finally picked the Full Gospel Church, because it had a similar name to his, and started negotiating with its bishop. The Full Gospel leader approved of the idea of merging to form a stronger church, but was wary of some of the details, and said they would have to be thought about, and that he would first have to visit the Northern Cape. This was not rapid enough for the other leader, who said that if a merger did not come about soon he would look for another church with which to combine. He then returned to his home and nothing came of the proposed merger.

We see from the above cases that mergers may occur for a variety of reasons: there may be pressure from someone in authority, there may be a desire to bolster a weak church by joining a stronger one, there may be a desire to have contact with a city church, amalgamation may be the answer to a lack of leadership after a leader's death, or — as in the case of the BBCAC — amalgamation may be seen as a way of gaining some of the attributes of a different type of church.

Many of these aims can, of course, be achieved within an association of churches, and this has the advantage of not threatening the integrity or independence of individual churches belonging to the association. For this reason interdenominational contact through associations is of particular importance.

The discussion so far of contact both within and between independent churches has dealt, at least by implication, with some of

the factors leading to fission as well as fusion within the independent
church movement as a whole, and we shall end this chapter with a
brief discussion of some of these factors.

FISSION AND FUSION

Many reasons have been advanced for the rise of the independent
church movement, with perhaps the most comprehensive list being
contained in the report of the Tomlinson Commission (vol. xv: 66–
71, 1955) where no fewer than 24 'negative causes' and a few 'positive causes' are advanced. Sundkler stressed the political situation
and anti-mission feeling as early causes, but then pointed out (1961:
301) that 'multiplication after 1945 was no longer as a result of racial
tension within the missions, but was rather due to fission within the
Bantu Independent Churches themselves'. Consequently some explanation of fission *within* the movement must also be sought.

Leadership disputes are the overt causes of much secession. As
was suggested in chapter 4, leadership is an important aspect of the
churches: their hierarchies provide outlets for the exercise of leadership abilities and at the same time ascribe status to office-bearers.
Those who do not find immediate scope for advancement within
their church are potential seceders, unless new positions are created
for them (which sometimes happens) with new responsibilities.
Other leaders, as we shall see in the next chapter, may expand their
activities in church associations.

In most cases little is lost through secession — provided a leader
has some following when he leaves. Small independent churches are
in many ways interchangeable structures, offering the same advantages. In fact, as we have seen, a small church has distinct attractions,
providing new members with a small group of fellow-members who
become known personally to one another and who form a close-knit
fellowship, which is very important in an area of the size and impersonal nature of Soweto. Small churches are in many ways rather like
autonomous congregations of a large church, but they are not isolated in their autonomy; Zionist-type churches feel kinship with
one another by virtue of their common attributes, and therefore
co-operate with each other provided such co-operation does not
threaten their individual autonomy.

Autonomy is important, because this appears to be the major
factor giving rise to numbers of small independent churches rather
than numbers of small congregations of a few larger independent
churches. By and large, a small independent church in Soweto
offers the same advantages as a larger one. At the same time, the
existence of numerous small churches allows for 'independence'
(which has been a driving factor in the movement as a whole), as

well as making many more leadership positions available.

We saw in the previous chapter how the search for healing was a vital factor in the movement of people between churches, but the same factor can cause splits within churches. To take one example, a church in survey A was founded when its lady bishop found herself to have healing gifts. These were not welcome in the Ethiopian-type church of which she was a member, and she had to leave and form her own church. In so doing, she drew together members of a number of different churches who had been consulting her privately, and who had now joined her new church.

The mixing of traditional beliefs with Christianity is an attractive factor in many independent churches, and appears to be important in drawing people into Zionist-type churches – both from mission churches and from Ethiopian-type churches (see chapter 9).

We can see that whatever the divisive factors are in the movement, these are also factors that link people together. The very fact that there are so many churches, and that fission continues, prevents rancour, for almost every independent church leader has himself split off from another church at some time, and is therefore not in a position to criticise others who do the same. What ill-feeling exists will be restricted to the two churches immediately involved, but there again splits sometimes occur to *prevent* ill-feeling arising, and one case was encountered in Soweto where both parties were still on friendly terms after the split.

Independent church leaders therefore accept splitting and movement of people between congregations as more or less inevitable. When it occurs it is accepted; as one minister said frankly when mentioning that he had had no secessions whilst he had been leader: 'I'm lucky, myself.' It may even be suggested that churches co-operate in some degree to avoid tensions. Thus other bishops are called to witness consecrations and take part so that they are involved; after such participation, they are not easily able to criticise the existence of the new church. Another example of this co-operation is the acceptance of new members. All leaders interviewed in survey A stated that a prospective member would be required to present a 'remove' from his previous church – a certificate stating that he had been a member in good standing before his departure. Most ministers said that if a remove was not produced they would consult the leader of the person's previous church. There appeared to be two reasons for this: firstly to prevent the church taking on somebody who might be a troublemaker and, secondly, to avoid charges of being 'sheep-stealers'. While some leaders are alleged to take any person who wishes to join their church, it did appear as though most exercised some discretion.

Caution about admitting 'troublemakers' is necessary in view of the small close-knit congregations, which might easily be upset by new members who did not fit in.

We have also seen something of the network of co-operation which exists within and between churches, which includes friendship networks, patron—client relationships, and fund-raising organisations, and at the same time provides in many ways a legitimisation for the activities of individual churches. Thus, while fission of churches continues to occur, there is a considerable degree of co-operation between independent churches. Much of this takes place within the framework of official associations of churches, and it is to this subject that we now turn.

CHAPTER **8** **The Rise and Fall of AICA**

A number of associations of independent churches operate in Soweto, with membership ranging from a few to several hundred churches. It is known that other associations are active in other parts of South Africa, but it is impossible to ascertain how many there are. In the previous chapter it was suggested that associations fulfilled certain needs of churches without threatening their individual integrity, and in this chapter I shall examine some of the functions of these associations, concentrating on the African Independent Churches' Association (AICA).

During the fieldwork period, the largest of these associations in Soweto was AICA, with a membership in the area of over one hundred churches. During this period AICA rose to the height of its prestige as the largest and most successful association in the country. By 1974, however, it had all but collapsed entirely. As fieldwork on AICA was conducted up to the end of 1973, some account can be given of the rise and fall of the association. This is particularly important in view of the dearth of information on independent church associations, and also because the history of AICA throws some light on the dynamics of a black voluntary association in contemporary South Africa.

THE AFRICAN INDEPENDENT CHURCHES' ASSOCIATION (AICA)

According to a presidential address (*circa* 1967) by the first President of AICA, the association had its roots in the first-ever African church association. This was called the Transvaal Interdenominational African Ministers' Association, which he described as 'a body that was formed under the tutelage of white churches in 1915, supervised by African Ministers'. This initial association was open to all African ministers from both mission and independent churches, but there was soon conflict between mission and independent ministers. The independent ministers were disparaged for their lack of training and for not belonging to 'proper' churches (cf. Wilson and Mafeje 1963: 95, 100), and the association was split into two distinct camps. Mission church ministers were in the majority, and informants stated that at no time did an independent church leader hold any office in the association.

The AICA president described the situation as follows:

The membership of this Association had no restrictions on the untrained African Ministers [i.e. those from independent churches]. But divergent views and opinions opened a wide gap between trained and untrained ministers because some trained African Ministers under European churches allowed no facilities to other deserving causes [a reference to discrimination against independent ministers]. Some were disparaged and despised by the learned and were openly said to be destitute of education. A show of education and best Theological Training of these African Ministers under white churches led to the formation of a pure African Independent Churches movement which was established in 1922. It consisted of Ministers determined to have their own, who could not boast of education and best Theological Training. This movement was run under the title of 'Joint Council Representing African Churches'. [1]

Thus the Joint Council was formed by independent ministers who felt that they had been snubbed and made to feel inferior and uneducated by African ministers of the mission churches. Little information is available about the activities of the Joint Council after 1922. One informant said that it had a membership of over 70 independent churches, but that one of its aims — to provide training for its members — was never realised. Some indication that its path was not smooth may be inferred from the report quoted above, which continued that officials 'struggled with this Joint Council of churches fortifying it in every way against splinter Organisations trying to obliterate it from the catalogue of African Independent Churches'.

This organisation appeared to be dormant for a long period until one of the Joint Council officials, the Revd J.R. Mthembu, came into contact with a representative of a foreign ecumenical agency which had money available for theological education. This representative said that money might be made available to a properly constituted association with a viable programme, and suggested that interested independent church leaders should approach the Christian Institute of Southern Africa to assist with the necessary organisation.

Following this, a meeting was organised between representatives of the Christian Institute and a number of independent church

1. There is some evidence that the original title was 'Joint Council Representing Native Churches', which would have still been acceptable at that time, but which was quite unacceptable in the 1960s at the time of the quoted report: hence the use of 'African' in that report.

leaders, and a preliminary meeting of several church leaders took place at Daveyton township near Benoni. This meeting, held in December 1964, requested the Christian Institute to assist in providing theological education through short refresher courses, a correspondence course, and a theological seminary (Van Zyl 1968: 1). In January 1965 a conference was arranged to gauge opinion among a wider group of independent church leaders, and some seventy-five attended the meeting. After discussion, the following resolution was passed by the conference: 'That we . . . this day give full trust in God and His people, that we must love each other as brothers in Christ irrespective of colour, race or creed and to share together those sufferings which He shed on the Cross, with the other nations. . . . We give our fullest confidence to the Christian Institute of South Africa and invite its Director, the Revd C.F.B. Naudé to guide us through every difficulty in the Christian field . . . . We sincerely appeal to the bigger churches, i.e. integrated churches, which we left as early as 1888 that we are their work and we are still looking to their help by all means and kinds . . . .' (Van Zyl 1966: 6.)

This agreement to co-operate with the Christian Institute was an historic step, for up to that moment the churches present had eschewed any contact with mission churches or other white organisations since the Joint Council had been established. The reason for this apparent reversal was that for the first time there appeared the possibility of realising the long-held hope of theological education. It is likely that the Christian Institute was considered an acceptable body with which to co-operate because it was manifestly multiracial and interdenominational. Thus contact with the Christian Institute did not jeopardise the integrity of the individual independent churches.

After this meeting the Christian Institute decided to try to assist the independent churches and to formulate a programme. In June 1965 another conference was held, this time in Queenstown, which formally established the African Independent Churches' Association (AICA). The Christian Institute agreed to advise the association and to assist in drawing up a programme which would be the basis for fund-raising overseas. A Board of Management consisting of a president, vice-president, general secretary, assistant secretary, treasurer, and two ordinary members was elected at the conference, with the Revd J. R. Mthembu as the first AICA President.

The first constitution of the newly formed association gave the following as its aims, objectives and basis:

> 2. Aim. The aim of the Association will be to serve the Church of Christ in every possible way and especially the needs of the African Independent Churches.

3. Objectives. The Association will seek to realise its aim by concerning itself with, although not limiting itself to, the following:
(a) the theological education of ministers of the African Independent Churches — for example, the establishment of a theological training school, Bible correspondence courses, refresher courses;
(b) the establishment of a scholarship fund for theological education;
(c) the problems and needs of members of the Association.
4. Basis. The Association is based upon the Word of God the Father, in Jesus Christ the Son, Redeemer and Lord, and in the Holy Spirit.

The constitution further defined membership as restricted to 'any African-controlled Church' which accepted the aims and objects of the association, and which had at least five ministers, or a congregation of 200 members, or a total membership of 500. It outlined the structure of the association, the powers of the annual conference and central board of management, and the duties and powers of the individual office-bearers.

In the years that followed AICA was unique in that, with the assistance of the Christian Institute, it had access to considerable sums of money which were raised by churches in Europe and America. This money was administered through the Christian Institute, and was audited by them, and meant that AICA was able to run an office in Soweto with a full-time typist, as well as hold theological refresher courses in various parts of the country and organise the annual conference. Funds were also available for a full-time organiser to travel round the country.

AICA membership rose from under 100 churches to over 400 by 1972, and this membership embraced churches of various types — Ethiopian as well as Zionist — which were situated in virtually every part of South Africa. However, the concentration of membership was in the Transvaal, and particularly around Johannesburg, which accounted for at least one-quarter of the total membership. The larger membership brought an increased budget, which ran annually to between R7 000 and R8 000. When the correspondence course and theological seminary were started this budget increased enormously. The AICA Revenue and Expenditure account in 1970 showed expenditure of the association to have been R9 171 for the preceding year (a deficit of nearly R2 000 being made up by the Christian Institute), and in the same year R42 000 was budgeted for the theological education programme, making an overall expenditure of close to R50 000 for the year. At this stage AICA was easily the largest, richest and best-organised association of churches in South Africa, offering greater facilities in terms of meetings and education projects than any other.

In the first five or six years of AICA's existence theological refresher courses were held in Johannesburg, Durban, Bloemfontein, Springs, Cape Town, Port Elizabeth, Umtata and East London. The courses were well organised and usually addressed by a number of local ministers, mainly from mission churches, recruited by the Christian Institute. These were very important because they gave independent church leaders proof that AICA was being effective, and provided opportunities for leaders to meet one another.

This effective image was enhanced by the opening of the AICA Theological College in Alice in the Cape in 1970, with the first fifteen AICA students. An ambitious correspondence course was launched in the same year but owing to staffing problems it sent out its first lesson only in mid-1972. In addition to the education courses, AICA held an annual conference at a different venue each year. Between 80 and 100 churches were represented at the three conferences which I attended during the fieldwork period. During the year the AICA Board of Management met quarterly, but its sub-committees — dealing with such subjects as refresher courses, newsletters, the constitution, church government and the like — met more regularly.

These varied activities are controlled by committees whose convenors are generally elected by the Board of Management. In this way a number of members of AICA churches were able to hold official appointments in AICA which added to their standing within the organisation. Holding office in AICA gave not only status but also some financial advantage, and as a result of this there was intense competition for positions, especially those on the central Board of Management, whose members — as we shall see later — enjoyed considerable power and patronage. This competition reached a climax at the annual conference at which office-bearers were elected.

To understand the complexities of the arguments about leadership in AICA, it is essential to have a perspective over time. We shall therefore look in detail at the leadership of AICA over the period 1965 to 1973, examining the strategies operating and the coalitions which were formed. Competition for office in AICA can be viewed as a zero-sum majority game where the coalition obtaining a plurality of votes wins all at an annual conference at which elections are held. This differs in some ways from a similar situation described by Barth (1959: 15ff) in that there are no *persisting* oppositions, although there were patron—client relationships (with Board members extending patronage to supporters in terms of appointment to sub-committees). AICA therefore experienced a series of shifting, but often predictable, coalitions which were all aimed — despite individual animosities — at securing the prize of election to the Board, or at least the patronage of those who were elected.

In 1965 the first AICA Board was elected with the first President, the Revd J.R. Mthembu, drawn from the leaders of the old Joint Council. In 1966 Mthembu was re-elected, and his Vice-President, Bishop S. Manana, started to vie for the presidency. Mthembu was elected a third time in 1967, and Manana lost his position on the Board. Informants stated that it looked as if a major secession might follow, and the Manana group alleged electoral irregularities and contravention of the constitution. The secession was averted, however, by the intervention of Christian Institute advisers, who suggested to the newly elected Board that to solve some of the immediate problems they should co-opt Bishop Manana and one of his supporters on to the new Board. This was done, and the immediate cause of friction was temporarily removed, although the Mthembu—Manana leadership struggle continued as fiercely as before, with both sides organising for the 1968 conference.

During 1968 the AICA constitution was amended to prevent the co-option of extra Board members. The 1968 conference met in Johannesburg, and the Revd J.R. Mthembu and his strongest supporters were voted off the Board, while Bishop Manana was elected AICA's second President. Informants who were at the conference stated that the rank and file AICA membership were dissatisfied with the leadership disputes that had been going on continuously, and were also annoyed by what they regarded as the autocratic decisions of the Board of Management. There were also allegations that funds had been misappropriated, and as a result a 'new' Board was elected. This was in fact the opposition to Mthembu, most of whom had served on previous Boards.

Following the 1967 precedent, Mthembu and his supporters in turn alleged conference irregularities, and grievances were voiced which they said should have been discussed before the elections. They then hoped that representatives of their group would be co-opted on to the Board, but in terms of the constitutional amendment this was not possible, and did not in fact take place.

AICA was again threatened with a major split and this time there was no immediate attempt to heal it. The Mthembu group stopped taking part in AICA activities, and formed itself into what it called the Interim Committee — and it was clear that this was an 'interim' structure through which to organise and prepare for the 1969 elections, which were to be held in Durban. In the year before the elections, the Interim Committee held one or two inconclusive meetings with the AICA Board — according to an AICA adviser they wanted some admission of incompetence from the Board which would give them an election platform. For the rest of the time they tried to organise support for their cause among a number of AICA members.

As part of his campaign, the Revd J.R. Mthembu sent two circulars to independent church leaders in which the Christian Institute, and specifically their AICA advisers, were severely criticised. It may be assumed that the object of these circulars was to suggest that the AICA Board was manipulated by whites in the Christian Institute, and that a Board consisting of Interim Committee members would be much more independent, and therefore in keeping with the aims of the independent church movement as a whole. The circulars were obtained by the Press, and were publicised widely in certain Afrikaans newspapers which were hostile to the aims of the Christian Institute. The AICA Board of Management issued a statement saying they were not being used by anybody, and that they had confidence in the advice given by the Christian Institute. This statement also gained publicity.

AICA rank and file did not like the attacks on Christian Institute advisers, and they also did not like the adverse publicity in the national Press. It was alleged that the Revd J.R. Mthembu had himself released the circulars to certain newspapers, and informants suggested that the whole incident had served only to lose the Interim Committee some of its supporters and to alienate its opponents further.

Eventually the 1969 conference began at Kwa Mashu township near Durban, and there the dispute between the AICA Board and the Interim Committee came to a head. This conference will be described in some detail as it was fairly typical of other conferences.

The proceedings lasted from 6 to 15 August 1969, with 155 official delegates representing about 90 churches.[2] Delegates came from a number of different areas: Transvaal, centred on Johannesburg (with 56 per cent of the total number of delegates), Natal (12 per cent), the Orange Free State (10 per cent), the Northern Transvaal (8 per cent), the Transkei (7 per cent), Eastern Cape (3 per cent), Western Cape (3 per cent), and Lesotho (1 per cent). The dominance of the Transvaal region can be seen from this, a dominance which was normally reflected in the composition of the Board of Management, although some effort was usually made to have one or two other areas represented on the Board.

The Interim Committee attended the conference, sitting as a

---

2. Each church was allowed two official voting delegates at the conference, provided it had paid its annual subscription. Records were not always accurately kept, and in addition there was considerable coming and going of delegates at various times during the conference. It was therefore impossible to find out exactly how many churches attended the meeting.

group in the hall, and their tactics were immediately apparent: to try to show the AICA Board's general incompetence, and by exposing this to get themselves elected in their place. On the other hand the AICA Board was clearly intent on exposing the Interim Committee as a dissatisfied group who had acted unfairly and who were out to damage AICA. With these conflicting aims, open dispute raged throughout the meeting.

The first day was relatively quiet, with an opening service conducted by the Board of Management. Conference agendas were then distributed and a 5c donation was requested. This was immediately seized upon by the Interim Committee as a popular cause, and the donation was disputed on the grounds that the members could not afford the price. After long argument in which the Interim Committee tried to make it look as if the AICA Board were not interested in ordinary members, the AICA President resolved the dispute by ruling that the agenda should be distributed free.

On the second morning the General Secretary was absent, and the Interim Committee seized upon this to criticise the Board again. The Secretary eventually appeared, and his apology was accepted. The Interim Committee then attacked the presentation of the Minutes of the previous annual general meeting as being incomplete, and finally queried the financial statement for the previous year and the choice of Kwa Mashu as the conference venue, alleging that the previous conference had decided to hold this meeting in another town. The only official business conducted on the second day was the noting of apologies, the election of various conference committees and the appointment of official interpreters. The attempt to pass the Minutes of the previous conference was frustrated by the points raised by the Interim Committee.

Most of the third day, which was a short one as certain other activities had been arranged, was taken up with the complaint of one of the members of the Interim Committee, who had been registered as a delegate and then told that his bishop had said that he was not an official delegate. The attempt to unseat this man caused chaos, and was described as follows in the Minutes: 'He went to the extent of calling the Board liars, misleaders and traitors. There was an uproar in every direction. After the Conference Ushers failed to stop the noise, the President suggested to the Conference that how would it be if police were called to come and give protection.' The police were not called, in fact, and the conference was finally brought to order by the singing of a favourite hymn, which was started off by a few of the delegates and then taken up by the whole congregation, including those who had been shouting. After a few verses the President stopped the hymn and order was restored.

The day ended with a committee being appointed to investigate the complaint by the member whose delegate status was being questioned.

The fourth day of the conference opened with the AICA President appealing to members to stop time-wasting as there was important business to be conducted. However, argument started almost immediately on the Mthembu circulars, and was stopped only after an appeal by an AICA adviser to consider the theological education report. This was done, and the conference approved the founding of a theological seminary and the start of a correspondence course in the following year. Discussion on these matters was conducted amicably and lasted the rest of the morning. In the afternoon there was further argument, with some delegates trying to re-open discussion of the Mthembu circulars and others wanting to go on with the agenda. The conference then approved a new constitution which involved decentralisation of AICA and the founding of several regional Boards. The presidential report was discussed, and again argument started over the Interim Committee. Finally one of the younger delegates, the Revd E. V. M. Maqina, who had been an effective debater against the Interim Committee, suggested the formation of a small committee to meet with the Interim Committee in an attempt to resolve the disputes. The President announced that it was too late to hold the scheduled elections, and that they would be held the following day — Sunday.

On the final day of the conference the President announced that elections would be held and that the eight reports which had still to be considered would not be discussed. The Interim Committee tried to postpone elections and have the reports discussed. It became clear that they were in a minority and that they did not have the support of the delegates; they thus hoped to gain it by exposing inefficiencies in the reports that were still to be read. However, they were outvoted, and it was decided to hold the elections.

As soon as this became clear, the Revd I.P.B. Mokoena, another younger delegate who had acted as a spokesman for the Interim Committee on a number of occasions during the conference, rose and reminded the President that there were irregularities over the 1968 Secretary's and Treasurer's reports and that at the present conference the President's report had been only partly discussed and the Secretary's and Treasurer's reports not at all. He then said that he had an important statement to make which he would read at dictation speed so that nobody would be able to say afterwards that the Board had not heard it. The statement read as follows:

> Owing to our dissatisfaction, we disassociate ourselves from any type of election which may be held now, and we register our dissatisfaction that if

another Board is elected prior to our Circulars number 1 and 2 having been amicably settled between the Interim Committee and the Board of Management, we shall not participate in the deliberations of this election. Lastly, Mr President, please, we enjoy the same status within the organisation and do not want to see other people gloat in borrowed panoply. If this Board does not resolve our dispute, we appeal to the advisers of AICA . . . to take up the task of solving the incipient misunderstanding thus brought about. Not until then will another Board step in.

With this statement, the Interim Committee avoided taking part in an election which they would almost certainly have lost by a large margin. In the subsequent voting, where as usual Christian Institute advisers acted as returning officers at the request of the conference, Bishop Manana was unanimously re-elected President, and then his entire Board was re-elected with one exception – a place was found for the Revd E. V. M. Maqina who had played an important part in the battle against the Interim Committee on the conference floor. He was elected to the powerful position of General Secretary.

Thus the 1969 conference ended with a clear defeat for the Interim Committee, but this at the cost of considerable dissatisfaction among ordinary members of AICA at the ways things had gone. While it appeared as though most delegates were alienated by the tactics of the Interim Committee, there were some country delegates who were annoyed by both sides, and spoke out against the 'men from Johannesburg' who were causing all the trouble with struggles for power. This difference between the ordinary members and those seeking office in the organisation will be mentioned again later.

As the Interim Committee dispute was the most important that AICA had had to face up to that time, I shall continue to relate the sequence of events after the 1969 conference. The Interim Committee left the conference without any general support, and it was arranged that they should meet with the special sub-committee which had been set up to try to resolve their differences. This committee was led by the Revd E. V. M. Maqina, who had suggested its formation to the conference. The committee then met in Soweto; the result was further alienation between the Interim Committee and AICA, as can be seen from part of a letter written by the former president, the Revd J. R. Mthembu, to the AICA president and Board of Management:

re: *My Complaint*

I wish to lodge a very strong complaint against the General Secretary of AICA the Revd E. V. M. Maqina.

He called me to meet his Committee at the AICA Offices on the 6th

November 1969. During this meeting he made some allegations against me, and that I had insulted the whites and that I must apologise.·. . .

At this juncture he (Maqina) became very aggressive and said he had laid five (5) charges against me and that they will recommend to the Board my suspension from AICA with my church. I told him that the information was not acceptable to me and he said before he can say grace I should get out of his office.

I refused to do this and he came up to me and man-handled me, trying to throw me outside. I stood the ground altinately [sic] when he failed, he left me and said the grace.

Now I appeal to you, to institute an immediate enquiry into this matter.

Mr Maqina gave his side of the story to the Board, and no action was taken following this letter, but the incident wrecked any chances of reconciliation between the two groups.

After this things were quiet for some time, with both sides trying to consolidate their positions. At the end of 1969 one of the Interim Committee supporters, who had been unable to gain a position of authority on the committee, formed LAICA, the Life Aid Independent Churches' Association. The aims of this association were to establish a building fund for member churches, instruct ministers how to fill in wedding banns, to instruct ministers how to do welfare work, and to teach ministers about church administration and finance. These aims were all undertaken in one way or another by AICA, and although LAICA tried to organise a refresher course on AICA lines, the organisation was unsuccessful, gaining little support, and it soon became defunct.

Early in 1970 rumours started that the Interim Committee was about to form a separate association and break all ties with AICA. In March 1970 the break was announced through the Afrikaans morning newspaper *Die Transvaler*. A front-page report said that 46 churches had broken away from the Christian Institute and from AICA, and there were allegations that the independent churches in AICA were unwitting pawns in the political ambitions of the Christian Institute. Complaints of mishandling finances and of an inadequate theological education programme were also made.

An informant who attended the meeting at which the break from AICA was organised said that about 46 churches were represented. A white minister of the Dutch Reformed Church had been introduced and had made a long speech, in which he said his church would be prepared to assist the independent churches. According to the informant he promised a car for organising, a theological school in Soweto, railway concession tickets to members and marriage-officer licences. He had prepared a statement in Afrikaans which he read out, and 46 leaders signed it, after they had been told that help would only be forthcoming if they were to break with AICA and form their own association.

After this the AICA Board of Management issued their own statement, part of which read as follows:

It came as a great surprise to read that those churches were breaking away from C. I. [the Christian Institute] because of the simple reason that C. I. is not an Association of churches. Our AICA offices have not received any letter of resignation from any member church this year. These churches we do not know as they have not been mentioned in your paper, and they allege that we are being used to further certain political thinking. We would like to make it quite clear that our object is for the needs and problems of our churches. Up to now we have never had to discuss or be involved in politics. . . .

After saying that AICA was more than satisfied with its theological education programme, the statement concluded:

Lastly, may we add that we are happy with the manner the C. I. has been advising and guiding us these last five years, and we will make use of the help as long as we need it.

The new association was named RICA, the Reformed Independent Churches' Association, and had the Dutch Reformed minister, Ds N. van Loggerenberg, as its adviser. A constitution was published shortly thereafter in Zulu and Afrikaans, with a 'Security' clause in four languages at the end, the English version of which read: 'RICA is a non-political organisation to promote the Church work among the Bantu on separate lines to the honour of the Kingdom of God, and to work in harmony with the State.'[3]

From then on it was uncertain whether any members of RICA would attend the AICA conference, and this became less likely when RICA arranged its own annual conference on the same dates as the AICA conference, AICA's to be held in Port Elizabeth and RICA's in Johannesburg. In the event no RICA members attended the AICA conference, although one or two former Interim Committee members, who had broken with their fellows on the grounds that they did not want to have anything to do with the Dutch Reformed Church, did come to the AICA meeting. The 1970 AICA conference was subsequently very quiet, but the absence of an opposition group allowed individuals more opportunity to vie for position on the Board. In the 1970 elections Bishop Manana was again re-elected President, but whereas he had been elected unopposed in 1969, in 1970 he was elected on a minority vote.[4] The Vice-President was

3. The Afrikaans version read slightly differently: 'RICA is no political organisation but an ecumenical Church organisation which is working for the spiritual upliftment of the Bantu population, and which for the sake of the Kingdom promises its co-operation with the Government of the country.'
4. Until 1971, all AICA elections were held without a majority-vote system.

re-elected also on a minority vote, while the General Secretary (the Revd Maqina) was the only person to be re-elected who increased his 1969 majority. One of the three remaining positions was also filled on a minority vote.

At the RICA conference in Johannesburg, it was announced that 50 to 60 churches had attended, although AICA members said that not all were officially members of RICA but had gone along merely to observe, and a first Board of Management was elected. The former AICA President, the Revd J. R. Mthembu, had expected to be elected the first RICA president, but this position went to the younger Bishop I. Mokoena. Mr Mthembu was given a much less important position on the Board, and subsequently was excluded from much of the inner deliberations of the organisation. This finally led him to break with RICA towards the end of 1970 and to rejoin AICA; he announced that his dispute had been settled, and proceeded to organise his supporters for the 1971 conference, where he clearly hoped to gain the presidency, particularly as there were signs that the AICA President was losing support. He was not successful in the 1971 elections, however, and was not re-elected to the Board, although he gained considerable support for the position of Vice-President.

After RICA had been formed, another group of ministers, led by two early AICA members, one of whom had been a prominent member of the Interim Committee until it started to co-operate with the Dutch Reformed Church, formed yet another alternative organisation to AICA. This was AASIC, the All Africa South Independent Churches. A conference was announced in Natal, but was attended by only a few ministers. Thus in a three-year period AICA gave rise to LAICA, AASIC and RICA, with only the last showing any signs of viability. RICA members were given a motor car, and in 1972 it was reported that a small Bible-study course had been started for RICA members in Soweto.

Although the dispute between the AICA Board of Management and the Interim Committee took up a lot of time while it continued, this did not mean that there was no internal dispute on the Board itself. It has been mentioned briefly that a position on the AICA Board of Management brought with it not only added status to the incumbent and the opportunity to be in on AICA decision-making, but also certain financial advantage. An early decision in AICA was that people on official business would be paid travel expenses (based

---

Thus in 1970 the President was elected with 42 votes against his opponents' 27 and 17, while the Assistant Secretary was elected with 30 votes, his two opponents polling 29 and 28 respectively.

on mileage if they used a car, or else on a second-class rail ticket) and a daily subsistence allowance which was fixed at R2 per day for ordinary work and R3 per day for Board of Management meetings. In addition a number of AICA office-bearers were assisted in buying cars, which had a considerable effect on ordinary members, who saw some of their fellows living in a more affluent style than they had enjoyed before taking office.

It has already been shown that most independent church ministers are poor and not very well educated. Most of them had some employment, which because of their limited education was not well remunerated. Travel expenses for those who were AICA officials were necessary if the work was to be done, and the subsistence allowance was introduced to pay for incidental expenses such as meals, as well as to compensate for any loss of earning. However, during the fieldwork period, there were very few officials of AICA who lost earnings through their official duties, and consequently much of their expenses while on official business was in fact profit. Those members who were paid a mileage allowance for their vehicles also made a profit as the allowance was designed to cover insurance, repairs, etc., but was usually spent only on petrol, with the balance going into family budgets. While these amounts were small, taken in relation to the poverty of the members who received them they were significant, and were one important reason for gaining office, and once there attempting to stay there.

Leadership dispute within AICA was implicit in the nature of the leadership itself. We have seen that AICA had its inception in a feeling of inferiority caused by better-educated mission church ministers, and this was not forgotten. AICA leaders stressed that their organisation was for the poor people with little education, and to some extent members of the association remained suspicious of those who were better-educated than the norm. AICA leaders consequently tended to the norm, with fairly elderly, ill-educated men being in charge. As with individual churches, the one exception was often the position of General Secretary: it was generally agreed that an educated man was essential for conducting the association's correspondence with members.

As a result, many of the AICA Board members were not particularly competent in office — for example AICA had a treasurer for some years who was unable to multiply or divide — and this laid them open to attack by other members. There was also — as with many individual churches — some conflict between the General Secretary, who was often better-educated than his fellow Board members, and the rest of the officials.

To take just one example of internal dissension, an official who was demoted from General Secretary to Assistant Secretary at one of the conferences, not only lost prestige, but also suffered financially as he had been receiving a weekly salary to cover the fairly considerable duties of the General Secretary, and this amount now went to his successor. The demoted secretary was, possibly as consolation, elected convenor of the AICA newsletter committee, and he produced a newsletter reporting the events of the conference at which he had been demoted, and pointed out that his demotion had come without his being able to read his report to the conference. There were also allegations that the new Secretary was not running the AICA office satisfactorily. When the AICA Executive saw the newsletter they tore out the article and distributed the newsletter without consulting its editor. Subsequently an Executive meeting was held at which the editor apologised for his article, and the matter was referred to the Board of Management. A few days later the newsletter committee met, but the editor was informed that he had been suspended pending a decision by the Board. Backed up by other Executive members, the Treasurer refused to pay the normal expenses for the meeting.

One result of this was the following letter, written by the editor to an AICA adviser, which gives some indication of the tensions aroused within the organisation:

> The information from the President, Treasurer and the General-Secretary, that I was instructed not to meet until the next Board meeting, I DO NOT KNOW IT! All I know is that the said three men decided that my article be referred to the coming Board meeting. I was only told on the 10/12/69 at about 10 a.m. verbally by the General-Secretary, that I was suspended, and that the meeting called for 10/12/69 is NULL AND VOID. I was very much upset, even now, but I could not do otherwise, because that was just on the last minute. However, I am not in the mood to argue with the Treasurer....
> It will seem that AICA is now controlled by the President, Treasurer and General-Secretary, who has powers to suspend members unconstitutionally, and refused to pay their claims. I am very much disappointed to receive a letter from the said Secretary, with a word — SUSPENDED — which was never said at the meeting. However, this is a lesson to me, and to our fellow member churches. I shall never and never forget this! Atanyrate, we all know the truth is dangerous and leads to awkward questions. Duties are assigned to members by the Board of Management, only for the President, Treasurer and the General-Secretary, to SUSPEND them unconstitutionally, and expect them not to voice out their dissatisfaction to their fellow member churches who officially elected them. I am afraid that this is going to create a delicate and explosive situation between the Board of Management and the coming Conference. Enclosed please find the copy of unconstitutional SUSPENSION.

This particular incident served to bring up a number of complaints against the Board, including their autocratic handling of AICA affairs, their readiness to contravene their own constitution, and their incompetence to handle the finances of the association. When incidents like this occurred opponents were ever ready to capitalise on them to improve their positions within the organisation. This sort of incident occurred fairly regularly through acts or omissions of Board members. Many AICA leaders were drawn from men who had rather small or weak churches — in other words men who for one reason or another had not been particularly successful church leaders. It did seem during fieldwork as though many of the more competent leaders in AICA were sufficiently busy with their own churches, and did not therefore stand for election to the AICA Board.

By 1970 a new factor had emerged in AICA internal politics, largely as a result of their theological education programme. The AICA Theological College was opened in early 1970 with fifteen students, a number of whom were mature men who had already been ordained in their churches. These students were put into an academic situation in Alice, and exposed to students from the near-by Federal Theological Seminary (which trained African students for the ministry of the Anglican, Congregational, Methodist and Presbyterian Churches) as well as the adjacent University of Fort Hare. The new AICA students, assisted by some of their lecturers, showed signs of developing into a new force in AICA during the 1970 conference, and their role was even more important in 1971. Their plea was for better-educated and more competent men to run AICA, and in particular they spoke out against the President and Treasurer of the organisation.

This coincided with the rising influence of the AICA General Secretary, the Revd E. V. M. Maqina, a former school principal, and the best-educated member of the AICA Board. His standing had risen in the association through his actions against the Interim Committee, and in 1970 he had been the only sitting member of the Board to be re-elected with an increased majority. Other Board members saw him as a threat to their positions, and in any case opposed some of his ideas and actions: for example in suggesting smaller expenses for officials, and in his handling of his office, which some thought was too autocratic. He, on the other hand, realised that his position was by no means secure, and that jealousies were often directed towards the person in the General Secretary's position if he was too efficient, but that he could lose his position if he were inefficient. Despite this, relationships between the General Secretary and the rest of the Board worsened during the year, and were near breaking-point by the time of the 1971 conference.

In contrast to the 1970 conference which was relatively quiet, the 1971 conference again saw disputes come into the open, with attacks against the General Secretary on the one hand, and attempts to show the incompetence of the rest of the AICA Board on the other. As in 1969, few of the official reports were read, and most of the time was taken up with the disputes. One particular issue was that a new constitution had been accepted the previous year, which made provision for a three-year term of office for the Board. Board members argued that they had been elected to a three-year term, and that there would therefore be no election. This was disputed by one faction which wanted to hold elections, and maintained that the 1971 elections would be the first under the three-year rule. Largely as a result of the suspension controversy described above, there was also heated debate on a suspension clause for the constitution.

Eventually elections were held, and as usual AICA advisers were asked to act as returning officers. Three issues were voted on: the suspension clauses, whether to hold elections, and whether the term of office of any new Board of Management should be three years. Largely because of the extreme opposition of some members to the suspension clauses, which gave certain powers to the Board to suspend churches or individuals, both clauses were easily defeated. A motion was then put regarding elections in 1971, and it was made clear that those voting in favour of elections would by implication be agreeing that the 1970 Board had not been elected for a three-year period. The voting was 67 in favour of having elections in 1971, 43 against and 6 abstentions. The next motion was on the term of office of the new Board which was to be elected, and the voting was 120 in favour of a three-year term with one against and no abstentions.

Before the voting for the Board of Management took place, the senior AICA adviser, C. F. Beyers Naudé of the Christian Institute, addressed the delegates and pointed out that under the old voting system people could get elected to office who did not have majority support: the point was illustrated using 12 men who voted in the ratio 5, 4, 3 for three candidates. It was shown that the person polling 5 votes would win the election although there were 7 people who did not vote for him. It was suggested to the delegates that a new voting system should be adopted where if one candidate did not get an overall majority over the other candidates, the candidate polling least should be discarded and a further vote held for the remaining candidates. The delegates agreed to the new system, and voting began.

In the voting for President, Bishop Manana received more votes

than any other candidate, and under the old system would have been
re-elected for a record fourth year, but his total was not an overall
majority. The bottom candidate dropped out, and in a straight con-
test between Bishop Manana and Revd E. V. M. Maqina, the latter
won by a margin of 62 votes to 57, to be elected the new President.
Likewise in the vote for Vice-President, one candidate – the Revd
J. R. Mthembu, who had entered an alliance with Mr Maqina –
gained most votes but did not get an overall majority. On the second
ballot Mr Mthembu lost to the sitting Vice-President by 53 votes
to 55.

The positions of General Secretary and Assistant Secretary were
voted on next, the General Secretary winning by a simple majority
on the first ballot, and the Assistant Secretary on the second ballot
following a tie. The Treasurer was also elected by simple majority,
while the Assistant Treasurer converted a simple majority on the
first ballot to an overall one on the second.

This result produced the biggest upheaval of Board members since
the 1966 elections, with only two of the six members retaining their
seats, and only one – the Vice-President – retaining the same position. But it should be noted that the election would probably have
been very different had the new voting system not been in operation.
Under the old system Bishop Manana would have been re-elected,
and it is likely that his supporters would have filled many of the
lower positions. His fall in the first election of the series had a ripple
effect in those that followed; at the same time it can also be seen
that it was only in the first two elections that the new rule produced
a winner other than the one who would have been elected under the
old system.

The voting also shows that the association was split fairly evenly
between the two opposing groups: President 62/57, Vice-President
55/53, General Secretary 58/32, Assistant Secretary 60/45, Treasurer
56/33 and Assistant Treasurer 50/49. This split was to have considerable consequences after the conference.

What followed was in some ways similar to the dispute that had
led to the creation of the Interim Committee, which subsequently
became RICA. Bishop Manana and his defeated supporters claimed
after the conference that the election had been invalid, and that
Manana had in fact been legitimately elected on the first ballot.
They therefore refused to recognise the conference or its elections
and claimed that Bishop Manana was still the President of AICA.
Bishop Manana died during this dispute, and his supporters elected
Bishop C. J. Bhengeza as the new President. Thus in 1972 two
groups, each claiming to be the legitimate AICA, held conferences
on the same dates in different places, and both groups wrote over-

seas soliciting funds.

However, the AICA group under the Revd Maqina retained control over AICA's physical assets, and it eventually became clear to the other group that — particularly as the Christian Institute refused to recognise them — there was no point in continuing as an alternative AICA. Finally in 1973 a conference was held at which the group became officially the African Independent Churches' Movement (AICM) with Bishop Bhengeza as the new President. At this meeting the Vice-President Revd Mthembu was unsuccessful and did not gain a position on the new Board. AICM continued as a new association, but modelled itself closely on AICA, and in 1973 was attempting to raise money for theological education projects.

With AICM out of the way the uneasy coalition presided over by the AICA President began to crack. The structure which allowed this was a Theological Education Committee (TEC) that was appointed by the AICA conference to oversee all education projects (which in 1973 meant that it had some jurisdiction over about R90 000 of a total budget of about R113 000). The TEC thus became a second important power base in AICA in addition to the Board. It initially comprised AICA Board members, Christian Institute advisers and outside experts, but following the election of the Revd Maqina in 1971 the TEC shed all non-AICA members, and became a stronghold of Maqina's supporters on the Board.

What developed, then, was a protracted struggle between opposing Board and TEC members on a variety of fronts. At the same time the AICA College was drawn into the dispute. The college had itself been plagued by troubles almost since its inception, mainly over staff, and had resulted in the temporary closing of the college in 1972, when agreement could not be reached over the appointment of a principal. Following the Revd Maqina's election as AICA President and his consequent membership of the TEC, one of the college students (a supporter of Maqina) was appointed to the TEC, and was subsequently appointed as a lecturer. This situation caused a great deal of dissension within AICA, and between members of the TEC and the newly elected principal.

The election of the Revd Maqina also brought a new mood to the AICA Board regarding its relationship with the Christian Institute, particularly in terms of finance. The Christian Institute until that time had handled AICA's finances from its own office. As overseas donors required accurate accounts and AICA did not have the necessary expertise in this field, the Christian Institute kept AICA's books, drew up budgets and presented balance sheets. Although all this was done with the full knowledge of AICA Board members, and all accounts, budgets etc., were approved by either the Board or the

conference, in fact AICA had very little control over this area because of their lack of expertise. This situation was regarded as un-
satisfactory by both sides, and in 1972 it was decided by the Christian Institute that full control of the finances would be handed over
to AICA in January 1973. They recommended that AICA employ
a full-time book-keeper, and said that AICA would raise its own
funds and administer them.

The handing over of finances took place as planned. AICA did
not appoint a qualified accountant, and following mismanagement
of funds (including the purchasing of motor cars and the increasing
of the salaries of all officials) it used up its resources in nine months.
By the end of 1973 AICA had virtually collapsed, the college and
correspondence courses had been closed down, and the Revd Maqina
had been deposed as President. After supporting AICA financially
for six years and making good regular deficits, the Christian Institute
finally withdrew support entirely, and there did not appear to be
any hope that AICA could be revived.

It might be useful now to try to put AICA's 'political history' into
some overall perspective. Leadership disputes followed a fairly clear
pattern, as opponents struggled to win the presidency (and at the
same time get their supporters into the lesser positions). In this it is
interesting to see the coalitions that formed. In 1969, for example,
the basic opposition was as follows:

1. Manana/Maqina versus Mthembu/Mokoena. (Manana/Maqina
achieved office.) When the Mthcmbu/Mokoena coalition lost heavily
they formed RICA, as wc have seen. This left the field open in each
association for the former colleagues to fight each other for the respective presidencies in 1970:

2. AICA: Manana versus Maqina. RICA: Mthembu versus Mokoena.
(Manana/Mokoena won.) Maqina had been unable to topple Manana
in 1970, and so looked around for extra support. Mthembu, having
lost the RICA presidency, was prepared to try again in AICA, and
was offered the position of Vice-President if he supported Maqina
for President. Thus the 1971 coalition was:

3. Manana versus Maqina/Mthembu. (Maqina won.) As described,
Maqina deposed Manana, but Mthembu did not get sufficient support. In the dispute that followed before the founding of AICM,
Manana and Mthembu brought the wheel full circle by uniting to
try to depose Maqina. Thus in 1971/2 the coalition was:

4. Maqina versus Manana/Mthembu. (Maqina retained his position.)

So over a five-year period the three major contenders for the AICA
presidency formed all possible coalitions (Manana/Maqina in 1969;
Maqina/Mthembu in 1971 and Manana/Mthembu in 1971-2). This
cycle was broken for two main reasons — the death of Bishop Manana,

and the fact that the rules of the game had been changed. As Bailey (1969: 121) has suggested of political competition: 'Orderliness depends on anticipation, upon expectations being fulfilled. Yet the paradox of political competition is that the prize goes to the team which can act in a way unforeseen by its opponents, and perhaps unanticipated by the rules of the game. This element of self-destruction is built into any political structure from the moment it defines prizes which not everyone can win.'

The rules of the game in AICA were that elections were held annually. Although only one side could win any one encounter, the next was always close enough to make continuing the game worthwhile. However, when the constitution was changed in 1971 to allow a three-year term of office for the Board, this proved to be too long for the opposition group to retain their support, and allowed too much time — in their view — for the Board to entrench its position. This is basically what led to the split which gave rise to AICM.

But the departure of AICM members did not solve AICA's leadership problems. As in the case of the RICA split, the departure of the opposition merely gave former colleagues freedom to develop incipient cleavages within their ranks. It may be useful also to see this in terms of the 'size principle' in the theory of political coalitions: 'In social situations similar to n-person, zero-sum games with side-payments, participants create coalitions just as large as they believe will ensure winning and no larger.' (Riker, 1962: 32-3.) Faced with a large dissident group, the AICA Board would present a unified front in order to win. In the absence of this threat their coalition was larger than was necessary, and members would be shed.

All this has been recounted in some detail, not only because it is important as a case history, but also because it gives some indication of some of the forces at work within the association, and some of the factors which made for both cohesion and division within its ranks. Following this, it will be useful to consider in a little more detail the nature of AICA's composition and the importance of several factors in maintaining its viability.

I have mentioned that although AICA's membership was centred on the Johannesburg and Reef areas, it was represented in most parts of South Africa. After the Transvaal, the next most important areas of representation were the Orange Free State, Natal and the Transkei, with fewer members from the far Northern Transvaal and the Western and Northern Cape Province. This spread of membership meant firstly that AICA members spoke a variety of languages and had a number of different backgrounds, both urban and rural. Although numerous languages were spoken, AICA's official business was normally conducted in an Nguni and a Sotho language – generally Southern Sotho and Zulu or Xhosa. As with individual churches in Soweto, there was always simultaneous translation.

AICA members not only spoke different languages and came from a variety of backgrounds, they also represented a wide spectrum of types of independent church, from conservative Ethiopian-type to Zionist-type. While the latter appeared to be in the majority, one or two fairly large Ethiopian-type churches were members of the association – notably the Presbyterian Church of Africa and the Gardner Mvuyana African Congregational Church. AICA had a number of smaller Ethiopian-type groups, and a whole range of Zionist-type churches, including Zionists, Apostolics, Baptists and Sabbatarians. Member of both types of church served regularly on successive Boards of Management, where theological differences were generally unimportant either for co-operation or for strife.[5]

We see, therefore, that AICA membership was similar to the composition of some independent churches, in that it included people of different languages, backgrounds and geographical areas. Where it was different is that it encompassed a very wide range of beliefs and types of church. Perhaps the only notable absences in its membership were the largest independent churches – particularly the Zion Christian Church (generally regarded to be the biggest independent church in South Africa), Shembe's Nazareth Baptist Church, and some of the biggest Ethiopian-type churches, such as the Zulu Congregational Church, and the African Congregational Church. Reasons for this stemmed from both sides – on the one hand AICA was reluctant to approach the larger churches for fear of being swamped, and on the other some of these churches were put off by the evident leadership struggles that had taken place.

While there was much divergence in AICA's composition, as outlined above, there was also some uniformity. This was largely reflected in age, education and occupational status of its members, and was comparable to the situation described for individual churches in previous chapters. AICA's membership was predominantly elderly, poor and with little education; as far as could be ascertained no members had any university training, and none were in any of the professions. Except for a few theological students youth played no significant part in the organisation, and certainly nobody under the age of 35 to 40 was ever elected to any office, high or low.

The great importance of women in the independent churches has already been stressed, and in 1967 the AICA conference established

5. To take one example, an AICA Executive Committee which was asked by a foreign visitor to classify itself showed the following composition: Zionist, Catholic, Spiritualist and Ethiopian.

a parallel organisation for women, known as WAAIC — the Women's Association of the African Independent Churches. In 1969 a Christian Institute adviser was appointed, and WAAIC started several practical programmes including literacy classes, and classes in sewing, cooking, hygiene, biblical knowledge and child-care. Successful fund-raising drives were also held to provide for widows and orphans and to support the various WAAIC programmes.

The position of WAAIC in relation to AICA was anomalous. Constitutionally, the two organisations were distinct and autonomous, but in practice the affairs of WAAIC were closely linked, and in some ways were subservient to those of AICA. WAAIC elections followed those of AICA fairly closely and, for example, when the Interim Committee left AICA, wives of members left WAAIC also although there was evidence that they were reluctant to do so. The general attitude of AICA was that WAAIC was a daughter organisation and not independent of AICA, a standpoint which was accepted by some but not all of the WAAIC members.

The question of the independent status of WAAIC came to a head at the 1972 conference in Cape Town, when the WAAIC conference decided to suspend its constitution and not hold elections, on the grounds that attendance at the conference was not representative of WAAIC membership. The AICA President wished elections to be held, and summoned the WAAIC Board of Management. When he told the women that as AICA President he had authority over WAAIC, they walked out of his presence, and defied him by confirming the conference decision not to hold elections. The AICA conference confirmed their authority over WAAIC in a special resolution, but this had little or no effect.[6]

The composition of WAAIC was similar to that of AICA, showing the same diversity in language and background and similarity in age and education. But there were certain important differences in the two organisations. From its inception, for example, WAAIC concentrated on practical projects. Most of these were successful, and in late 1973 WAAIC was still a viable organisation running successful

6. The AICA General Secretary's report to the 1972 conference dealt with the WAAIC matter as follows: 'WAAIC. This wing of AICA has been met thrice this year by the Board and Executive for the purpose of a dialogue. The crucial issue being the aims and objects of bringing mutual understanding between the two Boards. WAAIC denies the official resolution taken at the last conference of the three-year period of the office-bearers. It also denies the official induction ceremony executed on them. Thirdly, they claim to be totally independent of AICA. May this Conference assembled here rescue this grave and dangerous detrimental state of affairs. WAAIC and AICA is and should be a well run Family, with mutual and Spiritual co-operation. Brothers in Christ, is WAAIC not married to AICA? Surely it is. The marriage was solemnised by a marriage officer. AICA, Watch!! WAAIC, Be Subject!! Please!!'

programmes and expanding. WAAIC also suffered leadership problems, but never on the same scale as AICA, and people who lost their positions on the WAAIC Board tended to remain within the organisation. As mentioned, WAAIC lost members only when wives of AICA dissidents were compelled by their husbands to leave WAAIC, at the same time as they left AICA. But there was no overt dissatisfaction with WAAIC, even though they left, and in fact a number of former WAAIC members expressed the desire to return to the organisation, if only their husbands would solve their disputes. It was probably significant that although AICA gave rise to both RICA and AICM as relatively viable organisations, no parallel women's associations emerged.

Examining AICA and WAAIC over the fieldwork period, it was quite clear that WAAIC coped better with its situation. Part of its success may have been due to a different approach by its Christian Institute advisers which led to the WAAIC women having more direct control over the finances and a stricter system of travel and subsistence allowances. Consequently the disputes over money which were frequent in AICA were not important in WAAIC. By the end of 1973 the WAAIC leaders were becoming openly critical of AICA, its disputes and its financial mismanagement. While AICA was dying rapidly, WAAIC appeared to be stable and successful.

Having looked at the history of AICA, we now turn to an analysis of why AICA was originally successful in attracting members and how this very success led to its ultimate downfall. To do this we must start with an examination of some of the important cohesive factors within AICA. We have already seen that a lack of theological education had caused a feeling of inferiority in relation to mission churches, and how this was a major reason for founding AICA. The theological education programmes of AICA and the increased standing they gave to member churches as well as the advantages of the education itself, constituted perhaps the single most important cohesive factor within AICA. The college and correspondence course, for example, were cited regularly by informants as evidence of the effectiveness of their organisation and the excellence of its aims.

These educational projects would have been impossible without the practical assistance and financial support of the Christian Institute and various European church agencies. The availability of money for the various AICA projects was another extremely important cohesive factor — not only because it made the education projects possible but also because it enabled AICA members to meet together in various parts of the country. Without the subsidisation of AICA conferences and refresher courses, it would not have been possible to draw together the variety of people who constituted AICA.

AICA's financial status was sufficient attraction to transcend differences of language, background and theology.

The money available to AICA allowed the AICA leaders to profit to some extent, and this was another important factor. In addition, of course, the AICA hierarchy provided new opportunities for individual church leaders to exercise their abilities in a much wider field, and to gain new standing both in their churches and in the organisation. Leadership brought with it new opportunities for status, exercise of power, travel and financial advantage.

At the same time, the organisation had the advantage of providing an avenue for wider recognition of independent churches. Small individual churches gained prestige through belonging to a large and relatively wealthy organisation which could boast similar facilities to those of many mission churches. Membership of AICA therefore involved wider recognition not only inside South Africa but also internationally, as AICA was supported by church agencies in various parts of Europe, and was visited by their representatives from time to time.

In addition to the theological education opportunities, AICA provided a number of practical advantages. The most important of these stemmed from the advice and assistance offered by the Christian Institute's full-time adviser, who was particularly effective in dealings with those in authority.[7] The adviser was able to assist church leaders, for example, in gaining special permits to visit members in hospital outside normal visiting hours, and in liaising with the various authorities over travel concessions, the granting of church sites, the requirements for candidates for marriage-officer licences, the formalities for banns of marriage certificates, and so on. The adviser assisted in drafting letters to authorities, such as magistrates, and on some occasions was able to mediate in disputes. He was also called upon on occasion to assist with problems arising from legislation affecting Africans in urban areas — such as troubles over passes, the right to remain in certain areas, and even housing.

Apart from the Christian Institute adviser, the AICA office offered other secretarial facilities for members, including typing and duplicating services, while the Christian Institute would occasionally undertake other secretarial work and sometimes small printing jobs.

We see from the above that a number of factors were important

7. This was an important factor in the rejection by AICA of a Christian Institute proposal that their adviser be an African, the reasons advanced being that in the specific South African situation a white man had far more advantages and privileges in dealing with most authorities than did an African. WAAIC, on the other hand, had both white and black advisers from the Christian Institute.

in drawing diverse peoples and churches into AICA in the first place, and then ensuring that they remained within the organisation despite tensions and leadership disputes. But cohesive factors can also be divisive. We have seen that theological education programmes in AICA — in this case mainly the theological college — to a lesser extent caused tensions, and in the case of the college these culminated in its temporary closing down. From the start of the programme, however, the AICA leaders and Christian Institute advisers realised that the programmes could cause a split between those who were educated and those who had not attended any course. They foresaw a particular problem with graduates of the AICA college returning to their churches and being dissatisfied with elderly, relatively uneducated leadership: in fact, one aim of the parallel correspondence course was to help the more elderly AICA members to approach the standard of the college students, and thus reduce the possibility of tensions between them. However, the internal dissension within the college forestalled this other problem.

As I have indicated, the financial standing of AICA was at once its biggest asset and its greatest problem. Individual members became involved in damaging leadership disputes in their efforts to gain office, and thereby to profit to some degree. The lack of financial training of AICA leaders also made them the easy targets of other AICA members when called upon to explain income and expenditure, and from its inception AICA leaders were accused regularly of mishandling, if not misappropriating, funds. It is clear, too, that the very advantages outlined for individuals in terms of status, exercise of authority, and various new opportunities, made the holding of office in AICA a prize worth fighting for, and I have recounted in some detail the lengths to which this could go, and some of the splits that occurred as a direct result.

Finally, even the practical assistance offered by the Christian Institute and the AICA office became on occasion a bone of contention. When frustrated in their efforts to gain office, minority groups regularly turned against the Christian Institute advisers, for example, and campaigned against white co-operation. The right to use facilities offered also became matter for dispute on many occasions — as for example when the General Secretary tried on one occasion to control the use of the typist and duplicating facilities in the AICA office, an attempt which led to vociferous complaints to the Board by ordinary members who felt their privileges threatened.

When leadership disputes arise and become overt, the possible lines of cleavage within the organisation become apparent: thus a member voted out of office blamed this on the fact that he was the only Sotho-speaker on a Zulu-speaking Board; others blame regional partisanship (particularly the Transvaal with its large core of members), whilst others try to create power bases on a regional level. In some cases, too, the type of church has also been raised — for example that the Board was 'controlled by Zionists'. However, at least until 1972, the cohesive factors outweighed those that were divisive, with the one exception of the secession of RICA.

In the RICA secession, however, it is important to note that the final break with AICA took place only when RICA members were offered similar facilities for their own organisation, and were in fact given a car to organise with, and were promised theological education courses. But even with this break, numerous members of the Interim Committee followed the Revd J. R. Mthembu back into AICA when he returned to help form a new coalition to gain power. In this respect, then, there is an important difference between associations of independent churches and the churches themselves. With individual churches, we have seen, fission is relatively easy because little is lost by breaking from one church and forming another, provided one has some followers. Fission within associations, particularly one like AICA, is not nearly so easy, because advantages are obtained through membership that are not easily duplicated without considerable support and funds. Where splits occurred and these were lacking — as with LAICA, for example — the new association was unlikely to survive.

Why then did AICA collapse, if it had the support and the finance? As I have tried to show, AICA's stability was always fragile and it experienced unending leadership struggles. These struggles were partly over the status of leading a large and wealthy organisation and partly over the financial advantages of holding office. A balance was kept between winners and losers so long as there were annual elections, but when the constitution was changed to allow a three-year term of office this upset the balance significantly.

A second important factor was the role of the Christian Institute. Throughout its early years, AICA relied heavily on advice given by its Christian Institute advisers. Although it was in theory at liberty to disregard the advice, in practice it followed advice on certain crucial issues. Thus the suggestion that the Revd Mthembu be co-opted to the Board after his defeat in 1967 saved what would have been a damaging dispute. The Christian Institute's assistance in financial matters was also vital in keeping AICA solvent, as was its help in the formulating of projects for which overseas aid was sought. But in the early 1970s both the Christian Institute and AICA became affected by the growing black consciousness movement in South Africa. As a result some Christian Institute advisers felt that AICA should become completely independent, and this view was shared

by some (but not all) AICA leaders. This feeling came to a head with
the election of the Revd Maqina as President of AICA. He subscribed
to the view that AICA should become independent, and this pushed
matters along.

At the same time, Maqina's election virtually split AICA down
the middle, and long, bitter disputes followed between holders of
different attitudes on a number of subjects. At this time the Christian Institute advisers began to feel that they could no longer whole-
heartedly support AICA in view of its internal situation, and this
hastened the handing over of funds. When AICA became completely
independent in 1973, it was not able to handle its finances successfully, and this more than anything else led to the speedy downfall
of the association. Not all of AICA's leaders approved of the way the
finances were handled, but no action was taken in time to save the
association, despite the deposing of the Revd Maqina.

SOME COMPARISONS

The affairs of AICA have been discussed in detail in view of its
position as the largest and wealthiest of the associations of independent churches, and as a case study of leadership struggles in the
independent churches. AICA was in some respects unique, and for
purposes of comparison we should now look briefly at one or two
other associations.

Perhaps the second largest association operating in Soweto was
the PMCA — the Pentecostal Mission Church Association. This was
an association of some 60 independent churches, the majority of
which were Zionist-type. Unlike most associations it was similar to
AICA in that it had co-operation with a white adviser. This adviser,
an elderly railway employee living in the Transvaal, felt a call fairly
early in life to leave the Dutch Reformed Church and start mission
work as an Apostolic among African people. He started by holding
church services in various places, but eventually he received a vision
instructing him to form an association of churches and work in the
African townships.

The PMCA was formed as a result of this, and the adviser took
the titles Archbishop and White Superintendent Adviser. The role
of the association was to assist member churches to become better
organised by drawing up a constitution to be used by all members,
to assist them in their relationships with various authorities, and to
give advice. In this regard the PMCA issued regular newsletters,
which included short Bible-studies as well as practical advice, for
example on building churches and handling church funds. Like
AICA, the PMCA had an Executive Committee to control the affairs
of the association between the annual conferences.

The major difference between AICA and the PMCA was financial: the PMCA had no external source of revenue, and was dependent on annual subscriptions from member churches. Most of this money appeared to be used on circulars, and office bearers were not paid expenses. It is interesting to note that the PMCA did not experience the sort of leadership dispute usual in AICA, and the absence of any external revenue was a possible reason for this.

From a brief study of the PMCA it appears as though it gained its members through the services it offered. Thus the president of the association said that when he was having difficulty in registering his church with the authorities in Pretoria he heard of the PMCA adviser, and approached him. He joined the association, was given a church constitution, and was then registered. The concern for official recognition is an important reason for joining associations, and the importance of registration is stressed by the PMCA — for example, in a circular advertising a meeting, the following appeared, despite the fact that the South African Government no longer registers churches: 'The government has expressed their concern about malpractices among ministers of separatist Bantu churches. You will be well advised to come and listen to avoid unnecessary trouble and your church being scratched off the roll.'

Another fairly well-known association based in Soweto has as the major service it offers the registering of churches with the South African Government. The leader of the association charges a fee for this, which involves writing a letter to the Bantu Administration Department which then makes out a file for the church concerned; the file number is quoted on the reply, and this is taken as an official registration. It is alleged by both AICA and PMCA leaders that the president of this organisation uses it to make money. However it is also known that the association acts as mediator in disputes between member churches, and between member churches and non-members.

Other smaller associations may exist for more specific purposes, for example to act as burial societies or fund-raising organisations. But in all cases encountered during fieldwork, the reason for the existence of any association appeared specifically to be the provision of services to members that could not easily be met by individual churches.

CHAPTER 9 The Old and the New

It has been generally accepted, at least since Sundkler's statements
on the subject (1961: 238ff), that African Zionist-type independent
churches are a blend of Christianity and traditional religion. This is,
of course, to be expected: independent churches are no more likely
to stem from only one tradition than are the mission churches from
which they came. As Ringgren points out (1969: 8) in a much wider
perspective, '. . . few religions are totally "pure" or homogeneous
and free from elements of syncretism or traces of encounter with
other religions.'

The independent churches which have been described in the fore-
going chapters have been, with the exception of some Ethiopian-type
churches, neither similar to the mission churches from which they
originally came nor similar to what we know of traditional African
religious organisation. But at the same time, as we shall see, they
contain elements of both, and in the final chapter I shall suggest
that this is one of their important attractions in gaining converts
from both Christian and pagan communities.

The Zionist-type churches, then, were different from other forms
of religion in South Africa in both form and content — but not too
different. Discussing religious change, O'Dea suggests that 'new
doctrines . . . are in fact a complex mixture of the new and old.
Unless they found people's minds in some measure prepared they
would not gather converts. But at the same time they proclaim
something new, or something old in a new way. In this way they
are able to appeal to those who are seeking new values.' (O'Dea 1966:
60.) We might say of the Zionist-type churches that they fulfilled
both these functions, and thereby attracted two sorts of people:
their Christianity was 'new' to pagan converts, who at the same time
were encouraged by the familiarity of certain 'traditional' aspects.
On the other hand their Christianity was 'old' and familiar for
Christian converts from the mission churches whilst the African
elements, particularly in healing, were in a sense 'new' to them, and
were part of the new values being sought by those who were unhappy

with the strictly western nature of most of the mission churches.

The presence in the Zionist-type independent churches of these elements is relatively easy to suggest, but not as easy to prove or quantify. In addition the whole subject has been the victim of considerable speculation as well as value-judgement. Sundkler's chapter (1961: 238) referred to 'deals with syncretistic tendencies arising out of the Zionist prophet's and the Zionist Church's interpretation of the Christian message in terms of the Zulu religious heritage'. Syncretism, a word which has derogatory connotations for many, is a concept often applied to the independent church movement, particularly by Christian theologians and missionaries. Thus Martin, to take just one example, shows her evaluation of the concept by concluding an address to a conference on independent churches by saying, '. . . but the real witness is God himself, . . . He alone will break through all syncretism, and all other walls which men erect against the Gospel of Jesus. . . .' (Martin 1965: 24.) Thus although syncretism can be used in a neutral sense 'to denote any mixture of two or more religions' (Ringgren 1969: 7), it will not be used in this work because of the value-judgement which would be inferred by many readers.

For Sundkler, when he completed his first study of independent churches in Zululand, their 'syncretistic tendencies' were originally seen as a negative factor. Thus he says towards the end of his book: *'The syncretistic sect becomes the bridge over which Africans are brought back to heathenism* – a viewpoint which stresses the seriousness of the whole situation.' (Sundkler 1961: 297 – author's own italics.) This view has been shared by many missionaries and theologians to varying degree. Some, for example some officials of the Christian Institute, are worried that the movement *might* revert to 'heathenism', whilst for others independent churches are mostly not Christian at all. This viewpoint is shown most clearly perhaps by Oosthuizen, who says of independent churches (1968: xi): 'Many form easy bridges back to nativism. They are neither Christian nor traditional, but a syncretism of both, and thus a new religion.' This religion he dubs 'post-Christian'.

It is interesting to note that Sundkler's viewpoint as quoted above was modified by later research. In the second edition of his *Bantu Prophets in South Africa* (1961: 302ff) he suggested that a simple view of the independent churches providing a bridge from Christianity to paganism might be an inaccurate assessment. Later, in personal communication, he suggested that the whole movement should be seen more in terms of a positive synthesis.

For the anthropologist, certain problems of analysis are raised. Sundkler was dealing mainly with rural Zululand, but this study deals with urban Soweto. In Zululand people could be assumed to share a fairly homogeneous cultural background, but not so in Soweto, which as we have seen is populated by people speaking many different languages, and coming from various parts of South Africa. Some of this diversity is reflected in the membership of independent churches, and this creates further problems of interpretation. In many cases it is not possible to refer to some aspect of urban independent church ritual as being rooted in some particular tribal tradition, and in any case we accept Epstein's caveat about attempting to explain urban phenomena by comparing them with a traditional tribal model (Epstein 1964: 99).

A further problem arises from the diversity of the urban situation, where members of Soweto independent churches may be either migrants or established townspeople. One may observe an offering, for example, which is attended by a number of members of the same congregation. This event may in fact be interpreted in various ways by different participants: for some it may be a thanksgiving, for others a sacrifice to God as found in the Old Testament, and for yet others it may be taken as an offering to the shades. We shall argue that one of the strengths of many independent churches is their flexibility in allowing differing points of view, but this very flexibility makes accurate analysis extremely difficult. As Hellmann (1971: 173) suggests in another context, 'the extent to which the performance of ancestral rites by Christians is what has been called a "folklorist survival", comparable to the white community's Easter practices, or the incorporation of the ancestral spirits in Christian worship as mediators between man and the remote Christian God, or a protest against a Christian Church which has failed to match practice with precept, is not known. All three responses are evident.'

The subject of traditional elements in the ritual of the independent churches is a particularly difficult one because of the value-judgements which have been made, particularly by those in the mission churches. Thus, for example, a belief in the power of ancestral spirits is 'bad' or 'primitive' in mission church terms, and independent church members are aware of this and are reluctant to admit anything which will lay themselves open to criticism or ridicule. This, more than any other aspect of the churches, is one which required the building up of relationships of trust with informants, and demanded competence in at least two African languages. The rigid conditions under which field-work had to be done in terms of official regulations made it difficult to achieve this, and analysis of attitudes towards traditional beliefs was the least satisfactory aspect of the research.

The section which follows is by no means an exhaustive study in depth, but I shall try to indicate the possible significance of certain practices. Unless otherwise mentioned, the churches referred to are Zionist-type.

One of the first things which should be noted is that although much of the ritual of the independent churches might seem familiar to one brought up in a mission church using Anglo-Catholic ritual, it is not familiar to most of the church members. Taking individual church leaders in survey A and the members in survey C, we see that only 25 per cent of the total had any experience of direct member-ship in a mission church of this type, and yet we find a number of attributes of these churches to be the norm in most independent churches.

In support of this I give as examples first the church hierarchies. As we have seen, most churches are led by bishops, who are conse-crated by other bishops through laying on of hands in apostolic succession. Laying on of hands, which takes place in consecrations, ordinations, admitting new members, healing, and blessing, is another factor, as is the use of holy oil in certain rituals. Most church leaders wear rich vestments, and for bishops mitres, copes and stoles are usual, while most have staffs of office also. The use of candles during services is widespread, as is solemn procession with banners. It should be stressed that most of these features were not attributes of the churches from which independent church members have broken. The Roman Catholic church is the mission church which has most of these attributes, and it is interesting to note that it appears to have lost fewer members to the independent churches than most other mission churches (v. graph, Van Zyl 1968: 2); one explanation which has been advanced is that its ritual fulfils some of the needs which are other-wise met by the independent churches.[1]

Other aspects of the independent churches would be familiar to members of most mission churches. Much of the liturgy, for example, is based on mission church experience. Most of the churches in Soweto whose leaders were interviewed in survey A in fact used a Methodist prayer book, which was the one most freely available in a number of different African languages. From it were taken some forms of service, such as ordinations, marriage and communion, as well as some prayers: notably the Lord's Prayer and the Creed. Prayers in most cases were said kneeling with eyes shut, the only difference in some churches being that all doors were closed while the congregation was praying.

The emphasis on the Bible is particularly important, and most

---

1. Another very important factor in preserving numbers of converts is of course the discipline of the Roman Catholic Church. Independent church informants agreed that it was more difficult to break away from the Catholic church than from any other, and only a few ex-Catholics were found in the churches studied.

independent churches are fundamentalist. To give just a few examples, the Last Supper is taken to be an injunction to hold communion services only at night, whilst most Zionists remove their shoes before services, taking Exodus 3:5 as their authority: 'Then he said, "Do not come near; put off your shoes from your feet, for the place on which you are standing is holy ground." ' Different individual churches will take their own special texts to be instructions to behave in a certain way — for example two churches encountered during fieldwork wore white sun-helmets as part of their uniform, citing Ephesians 6:17 as their authority: 'And take the helmet of salvation and the sword of the Spirit which is the word of God.'

Some leaders are more fundamentalist than others — for example one who took Revelation 2:27, 'and he shall rule them with a rod of iron . . .', to be an injunction for the bishop to have a metal rod of office — but all place great emphasis on knowing and reading the Bible. Most services will have more than one reading of the Bible and texts form the basis of nearly all sermons (no church leaders interviewed made use of any other aids in composing sermons). Short Bible-study correspondence courses are very popular, and most leaders have their own lists of texts for various occasions, the Old and New Testaments being used regularly. The BBCAC leader, for example, when asked to give a list of the most important texts for his church, cited Exodus, Matthew, Mark, Luke, John, and various Epistles as being important for various aspects of the church's work.[2] The leader of the Holy United Methodist Church gave Genesis, Exodus, Isaiah and Matthew, Mark, Luke and John, as his most important books. One Zionist-type leader, when asked the same question, took out his Bible and painstakingly went through it giving various marked texts — these eventually numbered no fewer than 66, with 50 from the New Testament and 16 from the Old.

Also to be found in most churches including the independent churches were special services on special days: thus the independent churches celebrate Christmas, Good Friday and Easter as major festivals of the church. Communion services, while not as frequent as in Anglican or Catholic churches, are conducted regularly, usually four times a year and on major festivals, while 'normal' marriage and funeral services are also held — as mentioned, these services usually

2. These tests were for baptism, communion, prayer and ordination, and were as follows: Baptism: Gal. 3:27–29; Mark 16:15–20; Matt. 28:18–20; 1 Cor. 10: 1–6; Exod. 13:21. The texts used during communion were: Luke 22: 14; John 6: 36–60; Mark 14: 16–25; Matt. 26: 20–37; Exod. 20: 26–27 and parts of Exodus chapters 12, 16 and 18. Texts for use during ordination services were: Eph. 4:11–13; Titus 1:7–10; Titus 2:2–5; 1 Tim. 3; 2 Tim. 4:2–4; 2 Tim. 4:5. The text for prayer and speaking in tongues was Mark 16:17–18.

follow those in a mission church prayer book.

Much of the structure of the independent churches is also similar to that in the mission churches. There is the same dichotomy between clergy and laity, with the former having special status and duties. And as we have seen the churches have constitutions, governing bodies, and often a number of committees which have various functions. Many of the churches also have the usual sub-groups: church choirs, prayer groups, etc., and, as we have seen, women's groups, the *man-yano*, are universal.

I have concentrated briefly above on some aspects of the independent churches which I believe to be held in common, apart from minor differences, with most mission churches. At the same level, of course, there are also a number of differences, not stemming directly from traditional sources, which should be mentioned.

A mission church member attending an independent church service for the first time would notice a number of differences at once. The first would probably be the uniforms, all full members wearing the distinctive colours of the church, and with many probably wearing protective healing-cords as well. If it were a 'true' Zionist church, members would be carrying sticks and be without shoes. In most services men and women would be separated, and the altar would be an ordinary table spread with a cloth on which typically there might be candles, a prayer book, Bibles and an alarm clock. And the independent church would be meeting in a home, garage, or class-room, and seldom in a church building.

When the service started other differences would become apparent. Independent church services do not normally follow a fixed liturgy, and considerable flexibility is allowed with opportunities for the congregation to take part. In Zionist-type churches singing is rhythmic and often accompanied by drums, bells and clapping. Much greater use is made of dancing in services — not only for healing, as I have described, but also to express joy (for example at the admission of new church members) or thanksgiving. Dancing may in fact occur in many different parts of church services, from offertories to healing sessions.

Healing ceremonies — as described in chapter 6 — would also be new to a convert from a mission church, as would the prophets and prayer-women. Spirit possession, according to various informants, occurs in most churches in Soweto, both independent and mission, but is treated in different ways. Many mission church leaders frown upon it, and members may face expulsion, whilst Ethiopian-type leaders tend to try to play it down. Thus a minister of the Presbyterian Church of Africa said that possession occurred occasionally in his congregation, particularly during a 'strong service', and that he accepted the manifestation as genuine, but that to avoid upsetting other members of the congregation he would go and try to calm the person who was possessed, usually by praying, and sometimes with laying on of hands. This approach is very different from that in the Zionist-type independent churches where spirit possession is strongly approved of, and taken to be evidence of the working of the Holy Spirit among the congregation. Members who become possessed are watched by others to see that they do not come to harm – on no occasion was a possessed person seen to be injured, or even in danger of being injured.

Much of the symbolism of the independent churches, as we have to some extent seen, is different from the mission churches. To take one example, the identification with the Old Testament Israelites wandering through the desert, which was shown in the Full Gospel Church (chapter 3) with its symbolic tent, is common to other churches. The Holy Places, flags, and symbols of stars, moons, suns, hearts, and crosses are widespread among Zionist-type churches, as is the significance of colours: white for purity, yellow for the Holy Spirit, green for fertility, and so on. The usual black of the mission churches, as we have seen, is eschewed by the Zionist-type churches, being equated with death and disease.[3]

Vilakazi, writing about Christianity in South Africa and the role of the mission and independent churches, provides the following analysis:

> It is true that the Africans, among whom are the Zulus, are very much disappointed in the Christian Churches in South Africa . . . but the people have not given up the Church. On the contrary, they have declared the mission or white churches apostate, and have decided that they would found their own churches. . . . It is not, then, that the African has tried Christianity and found it wanting. He has found it eminently useful as a new basis for integration. What he criticises and rejects is 'white' Christianity with its arrogance and colour attitudes. To put it differently, the African has learned to distinguish between the message and the messenger in his attitude towards Christianity. (Vilakazi 1962: 101.)

This analysis can be taken in two ways, both political and cultural. The political motivation for the emergence of independent churches has been stressed by various writers (see, for example, Sundkler 1961: 32ff) and, while this was important in that it enabled African Christians to control their own churches with their own leaders, the cultural aspect should not be ignored. Taken in its simplest form, we may use the phrase given by Vilakazi – there was no reason why

3. A notable exception to this is the leader of the Nazarite Church of Zululand, the Shembe church, who is the only member of the church to wear black – all the others wear white (Sundkler 1961, plate facing page 111).

the messengers should be accepted with the message: why, for example, African Christians necessarily had to wear black clothes, sing western hymn tunes, and meet in western churches. The Christianity of the mission churches was western in trappings; the Christianity of the independent churches is both western and African. We have discussed briefly some of the western aspects of these churches, and we should now turn to some of the African elements that have been incorporated into many independent churches.

Most traditional African religious systems have focused on a cult of the shades, with usually a secondary belief in a supreme being. Much has been written and discussed about African concepts of God and how they correspond to western concepts (Smith 1950; Mbiti 1970). This is the preserve of the theologian and not strictly the anthropologist, but the anthropologist can ask what is the role, if any, of ancestors within the independent churches (see also West 1975b).

This subject is frequently misrepresented; the term 'ancestor worship' is often used, implying that the shades[4] were worshipped as gods. But normally the shades are not seen as gods and are not worshipped: they are revered, and possibly feared, for the power they are believed to have in bringing fortune or misfortune to their descendants. As Makhathini says (1965: 155), 'The early missionaries looked at the Amadlozi (ancestors)–man relationship as worship; however, it was a near fellowship. . . . The Ancestors are not an end but are there only as witness to the strong belief in the continuity of life and human relationships. They are not objects of worship, but of fellowship and very mutual relationship.'

Despite ethnographic descriptions which support this, many people still see the traditional cult of the shades as 'ancestor worship' and suspect that the independent churches have replaced the Trinity by the shades, or at least brought them to the fore in their beliefs. In no instance during fieldwork was this ever found to be the case.

The traditional cult of the shades was in any case the concern of a group of kinsmen, and it would be unlikely that church congregations, with their variety of members, would honour the shades as a group, and again this was found to be an accurate assessment in most cases. Some exceptions are given below. But we should also ask to what extent individuals within the independent churches retained a cult of the shades. This in itself raises a number of problems: we have already suggested that performance of ancestral rites may be interpreted in a number of ways, and performance may in many

---

4. The term 'ancestor' is a general one, and need not refer to spirits of the dead who may still affect the living. The term 'shades' is used here to refer to this more specific category.

cases be situational — for example only at some crisis of life. Investigation was further complicated by the fact that mission church opposition to belief in the shades has made independent church members wary of admitting any such belief to outsiders for fear of being scorned.

It is important to refer again to a case that was described in chapter 3, because it illustrates some of the points made. The occasion was an interview with the leader of a fairly large Ethiopian-type church. When asked whether his shades had any power to help or harm him his answer was immediate and negative — belief in the shades was not Christian. Likewise there was never any honouring of the shades in church. At the time this answer seemed a little too rapid, and too much in the form of the reply that might be expected by someone who was not a member of the independent churches. We then discussed the subject of ancestors, and agreed that the traditional cult of the shades had been misunderstood as worship.

At this point the church leader said suddenly, 'I'd better tell you the truth', and proceeded to recount the following story. He and his wife had been away from Johannesburg (a few weeks before this interview) attending an AICA conference. While at the conference he had a dream, and in his dream he saw his father, who was hungry. In the dream he gave his father some money and saw him go into a shop to buy food, and then come out, obviously happy and satisfied. When he awoke he told his wife about the dream he had had, and she said that when they returned to Johannesburg they would have to do something about this, as it was clear that the father felt that he had been neglected.

When the couple returned to Soweto, an offering was arranged. A large church service was held at which the animals (two sheep) were slaughtered, but church members were not told of the real significance of the occasion: the church leader and his wife announced that a special service of thanksgiving was being held for the fact that the church was still going strong and that they had returned safely from a long journey. Only close members of the family were informed of the true significance.

This particular case is interesting because it shows that people can in fact attend the same event and interpret it in different ways: thus the church leader and his family saw the service as an offering to propitiate a shade; other church members may or may not have suspected this, whilst others certainly saw it merely as an ordinary thanksgiving where the usual feast was held after the service.

This was an event in an Ethiopian-type church: a similar occurrence in a Zionist-type church would certainly have been more openly dealt with. This raises a further question whether belief in the shades is more prominent among independent church members, or merely more overt than among those belonging to mission churches. No specific data are available for Soweto about the extent of belief in the power of the shades over their descendants – and in any case this may be a matter of degree and situation – or incidence of offerings. However, a number of informants stated that such belief was widespread, and that offerings were common – and as evidence of this they pointed to the large number of live sheep and goats that are sold every Saturday in Soweto. Hellmann, although she produces no evidence, agrees with this (1971: 11):

> Soweto, today, it appears to me, is more conscious of the dead ancestors than it was twenty years ago. The degree of observance varies greatly, ranging from not more than a general awareness of the ancestors and the holding of a feast with meat purchased from a butcher on the occasion of the termination of mourning, to a recurrent and meticulous setting aside of home-brewed beer for the ancestors and sacrifices of goats on all the appropriate occasions. If any generalisation may be attempted, then I would suggest that it has today become more general to regard the ancestors, who represent a limited social universe, as the intermediaries between the Christian God, who holds sway over all people, and the individual.

Here we may give another example to illustrate some further points we have raised. The occasion was again an interview on the subject of ancestors, with a minister who had been a prominent layman in the Methodist Church of South Africa. This man, the Revd L., had reached the highest councils of the Methodist Church as a layman, but at the same time, he said, he had continued to honour his shades and to make offerings to them.

This he knew to be contrary to the teaching of his church, and if he were found out he risked expulsion. Thus, he said, he constantly experienced conflict: his firm belief in the need to honour his shades against the guilt of flouting his church. On many occasions, as with the Ethiopian-type leader already mentioned, he would try to hide from people the real purpose – thus a live animal was not slaughtered because any crisis had occurred in the family, but because visitors had arrived and 'the butcher was closed'. Eventually he decided that the deception was dishonest both to himself and his church; he honestly did not believe that what he was doing was wrong or unchristian. In fact it had close parallels in some of the mission churches. His view of this is shown diagrammatically in Fig. iv opposite.

In this diagram we see the behaviour of an African contrasted with that of a mission church Roman Catholic, anywhere in the world. According to the Revd. L., if he as an African takes a goat and slaughters it and requests a guiding shade to intercede on his behalf with God, this is wrong and condemned by the mission chur-

FIG. iv

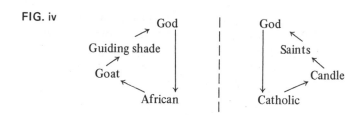

ches. However, he saw a parallel in a Roman Catholic's entering a cathedral and lighting a candle and praying to a saint to intercede on his behalf with God. This, he pointed out, was acceptable behaviour, and he wanted to know why one was acceptable and the other not. He was unable to get a satisfactory reply to this problem (essentially a theological one of the position of saints *vis à vis* guiding shades) from clergy within his church, and he then left to form his own independent church where he would not feel guilty about remembering his ancestors.

In this case we see firstly that the move from mission church to independent church has not *changed* beliefs about the shades, but merely brought them out into the open. In it we also see evidence of Hellmann's suggestion that the shades may have become more important as intermediaries between man and God. I shall examine this more closely when I discuss prophets later in the chapter.

We should now turn to the extent of belief in the shades to be found in some independent churches. In survey A2, the leaders of thirteen churches were asked the following questions:

1. Do you believe your ancestors have power to help or harm you?

2. Do you believe that departed members of your church have any power to help or harm your church?

3. Do you communicate with your ancestors?

4. Does your church communicate?

Of the thirteen churches included in this particular survey, seven could be classified broadly as Ethiopian-type and six as Zionist-type. All seven Ethiopian-type churches answered no to all four questions, although one or two leaders said that it was legitimate to remember one's ancestors, even if they had no powers over the living. A number of the others said that they preached strongly against cults of the shades, and would take action against any members of their congregations who went against this.

The six Zionist-type churches showed a very different attitude. Only one church leader did not answer yes to all four questions, and he stated that belief in the shades was a personal matter for individuals and was not the business of a church. He himself believed in the powers of his shades and communicated with them. The other five leaders, who answered yes to the questions, had slightly differing views on some details, and it is worth examining these briefly.

Leader 1 said that the shades were remembered in church by the lighting of candles, when members of the congregation would 'talk' to them. He was emphatic in his distinction between 'talking' and 'praying'; the shades were concerned and had powers, but they were not prayed to. As he said of them, 'They are still interested in the church, but you pray to God.'

Leader 2 said that his church communicated through offerings of animals and prayer. Another important role of the church was to assist in memorial services for past members.

Leader 3 said that communication was by offerings of meat and beer. Some members of the congregation were able to communicate with certain ancestors, and they were occasionally able to receive instructions. He gave as a recent example a message received from a former member, who had instructed her son to return to the church which he had left after her death.

Leader 4 said that communication was through offerings and prayer, and that occasional church services were held to commemorate the dead.

Leader 5 said that communication was through offerings, and through dreams. Only five members of the church were able to communicate with their shades, and the church relied on them.

This last church was particularly interesting for the form of its offerings, which was as much based on a traditional sacrifice as on parts of the Old Testament. I shall examine one such service.

In this church, offerings are usually made in thanksgiving for the healing gifts of their Senior Prophet, and often for specific cases of healing. The service to be described was held at the home of a young girl whom the Prophet had healed, and was a thanksgiving to the Prophet's shades and also to God for the work of the Prophet and the church. Approximately 40 church members took part, and the Prophet played the major role in what followed.

After opening prayers and hymns, the congregation was addressed by the Bishop on the significance of the occasion, and then the Prophet took over and explained the form of service. On a table in front of the church officials, who included three visiting ministers from other churches, there were candles and dishes of scones. The scones accorded with the instructions in Leviticus 2:4–11, which describes 'cereal offerings' which are to be taken by the priest and burned upon the altar. After the preliminaries two sheep were brought in. They were blessed by prayer and laying on of hands. While the service continued the sheep were led out. One was taken aside and slaughtered by having its throat cut (the second was reserved for another offering). As the throat was cut a prayer-woman standing by caught the first blood in a basin and took it back to the service. The Prophet took the bowl and blessed the blood.

Leviticus 3:6–11 was then read, a passage which instructs how an offering 'from the flock' is to be taken, must have hands laid upon it, and then be killed. The passage also prescribes what parts of the animal are to be taken — fat, tail, kidneys, liver, etc. — and burned as an offering. After this there was more singing and prayer, then the service stopped and the invited guests and senior officials were given supper. While they were eating, the sheep was skinned and dismembered and the prescribed parts were set aside for the offering.

At about 10.30 p.m. the congregation returned to the tent in which the service was being held (the house was too small to hold everybody). The service resumed and after a hymn a basin of holy water was blessed. There was a short sermon by the Bishop followed by testimonies by the girl who had been healed and by her parents — they confirmed that their daughter had been unable to speak until treated by the Prophet, after which she had been able to speak normally again. The Bishop and the Prophet went off to change their robes while the congregation sang, and when they returned candles were handed out to all members and lit. The parts of the sheep were brought in on plates and these and the plates of scones were blessed by the Prophet.

After the blessing the whole congregation moved out into an open yard behind the house, in the centre of which was an upturned bin on which was laid a fire. (The Prophet said later in an interview that the form of the fire had been taken directly from a picture she had seen of an Old Testament sacrifice which had appeared in a book of children's Bible stories.) The Bishop and the Prophet came forward carrying the parts of the sheep and the scones, while the rest of the congregation stood in a large circle around them with their candles, singing hymns. The two then lit the fire. When the flames were high enough they started placing the meat and scones on the fire and continued until all were burned up. While this was happening the rest of the congregation continued singing, and danced in a circle about the fire, and the officiants gave thanks to God and the shades for helping the church and its work. After this, the holy water was brought out and each member of the congregation was given a small glass to drink. There was more dancing in a circle. A few people became possessed at different points of the service, but it reached a peak with the dancing. Thereafter the congregation returned to the tent where the ordinary service was resumed, to finish in the early hours of the following morning.

So we can see that there is still a strong belief in the shades and their powers in Soweto, and that the independent churches are flexible enough to allow this to be overt, whilst the mission churches are not. Belief in the shades in the independent churches does not supplant Christian beliefs, but in many cases the shades are seen as intermediaries, and are propitiated by offerings and prayer.

Hellmann (1971: 11) has suggested that the increase in belief in the shades is partly attributable to the influence of diviners: 'The diviner is frequently the agency whereby people are brought back to a consciousness of the influence of the ancestors, for when they consult him in a time of difficulty, he may well diagnose it as arising from neglect of one or more ancestral spirits, and prescribe sacrifices to appease them.' To this analysis we may add the role of the prophet. We have also mentioned that a number of prophets believe their powers to come from the Holy Spirit through their shades. It is thus important to examine at this stage the precise relationship between prophets and diviners.

The prophets whom I interviewed during fieldwork all shared a common background. They were people who had usually had a long history of illness which could not be cured by western means. Eventually they had been taken to a prophet who was able to help them. After their cure they became apprenticed to the prophet, and underwent certain rituals, including purification by vomiting and bathing in a river. They made offerings, usually to their shades, asking them to assist them in their work. Training usually takes some time and involves regular offerings, purification and interpretation of dreams. At the end the prophet emerges as a fully fledged practitioner who is able to predict, divine and heal.

It is instructive to compare this with the typical history of the diviner. The diviner, usually, is also a person with a long history of illness which has been cured only after consulting another diviner. This diviner diagnoses that the patient's shades are calling him to be a diviner, too, and that the trouble will not stop until he agrees. There follows a fairly lengthy apprenticeship under a senior diviner, where the novice undergoes training which again includes regular offerings and purification. After a final purification and offering, the new diviner emerges and is able to practise on his own.

From this the parallels in training and experience of diviner and prophet are quite clear. There are further parallels in the complaints they treat: thus a number of prophets interviewed during fieldwork stated that their work was essentially 'the same' as that of the diviner, except for the fact that their power came from the Holy Spirit. Another important factor in the link between the two types is that all prophets who were interviewed were found to have at least one relative who was a diviner.

There is evidence, too, of some co-operation between prophets and diviners — for example in the exchange of information and patients. In chapter 6 a prophet was referred to — Mrs A. N. — who had close contact with a diviner with whom she exchanged information. It is also clear that some prophets were originally called as diviners, but preferred to become Christian prophets by undergoing their training period with a prophet and not a diviner, provided their shades were agreeable — again Mrs A. N. was an example of this.

One prominent Transvaal diviner wrote in a private communication: 'Strictly speaking most Zionist/Apostolic healers are originally sangomas (diviners) . . . some will tell you that they did not have the means to promote their powers as sangomas as it entails too much (expense) — so they performed certain ceremonies asking their guidances to accept the Christian type which is less expensive. Others even undergo certain treatment by sangomas before their Christian powers can function, but the latter they generally hide.' While it would be an oversimplification to suggest that the extra expense involved in becoming a diviner (which is not necessarily true) is what makes people become prophets, rather than a desire to remain Christian, there is considerable evidence to suggest that many prophets could also in fact have become diviners. There is also some evidence to support the contention that some independent church members will make use of both prophets and diviners in times of personal crisis.

We see therefore that there are considerable parallels between the tribal diviners and the independent church prophets. While prophets are by definition members in good standing of churches, diviners may practise without the knowledge of churches to which they may belong, and there are cases where diviners belong to both mission and independent churches. If found out in a mission church, diviners would almost certainly be expelled unless, possibly, they promised to stop practising. A diviner discovered in an independent church is treated in an entirely different manner, one which attempts to draw the diviner into the church community rather than expel him.

This is done by attempting to convert the diviner into a Christian prophet, and cases of this sort were reported by all the prophets interviewed. Once a diviner is discovered in an independent church congregation, usually by a prophet who is able to 'see' the other's powers, an attempt is made to discuss the matter. The reasoning which follows is that if the diviner comes to church it must mean that he believes in God and in the power of the Holy Spirit. It is then suggested to the diviner that a diviner who works with the powers of the shades only is not, so to speak, working at full potential. If he were to accept the power of the Holy Spirit, which can be channelled through the shades, his power will be greater — in fact all he will need to be able to heal is prayer and holy water; the herbs and potions of the diviner will not be necessary.

If the diviner is prepared to accept this argument, he undergoes a second initiation. But before this an offering is made to his guiding shades to ask their approval for the change. When this is given the second initiation begins, and follows the normal pattern, with purification, offerings and sessions of dream analysis. Finally the former diviner returns to the river and ritually throws away into it the skins, beads, bones, etc. which he used as a diviner, and then enters the water for a final purification. On emerging he is clothed in a gown with a cross, and after a final feast is accepted as a prophet.

The belief in the shades remains, similar complaints are treated, and divination and prediction continue — but a different source of power is admitted, and healing methods are changed, with prayer and holy water becoming as important as herbs, potions and sometimes bone-throwing once were. As I have mentioned, cases where diviners were converted into prophets were reported by all the prophets who were interviewed, and in only one case was it said that the power of the shades had been too strong for an individual: they had not wanted him to be a prophet and he had had to return to practise as an ordinary diviner.

Sundkler also referred to parallels between prophets and diviners in rural Zululand (1961: 350–3) but reported no conversions of the sort that we have observed in Soweto. The conversion from diviner to prophet may be interpreted as another example of the integrative effect of the independent churches. Where the healer or diviner has two separate roles in the mission churches, they are integrated in the independent churches. Healers hold an honoured place in the ranks of church members, and may in fact reach positions of authority within their churches.

Where prophets reach positions of authority in their churches, the role of their guiding shades may become important to all. As the shades guide the prophet to divine and predict, so their effect encompasses the church. When the prophet propitiates his shades, as we have seen in the case of Mrs A. N., the church is drawn in to take part. Thus we can see how the prophet can be an agent through which church members are brought to increasing interest in the shades and their role in society.

Healing has been shown to be a very important part of a prophet's activities, and the discussion of healing techniques in chapter 6 referred to their variety. While most prophets did not use the traditional medicines of the diviners, there were some who did, and the use of ash — a traditional symbol of the shades — was widespread. In the prophet's consultations we see a synthesis of old and new:

divination and prayer, ash and holy water, purification and western medicines, and so on. One important factor in this is purification, which takes place in consultations through use of emetics and enemas, but which also takes place in a river. This latter type of purification has been confused with baptism because both activities often occur at the same time.

In his study of Zulu independent churches, Sundkler (1961: 201–2) stated categorically that 'the propensity of the Zulu Zionist to total immersion is intimately linked up with traditional Zulu ritual practices in streams and pools. . . . The Zionist Church is a syncretistic movement of baptizers. Baptism and purification are their main rites, of which other activities are more or less dependent corollaries. . . .' He continued, 'They have made baptism into a purification rite which cleanses from magical pollution, and thus it can and should be repeated in order to accumulate its healing and redeeming power.'

While this may indeed have been the case in Zululand, it does not appear to be so in Soweto. In the churches investigated there was always a clear distinction made between baptism – usually by triune immersion (which could only occur once provided it was by total immersion) – and purification, which took place more regularly, for example at the start of each new year, after death or illness within the congregation, or at the instruction of a prophet, to name a few possible instances. In Soweto, the *form* of the two types of immersion was different: baptism was by triune immersion and laying on of hands, whilst purification usually involved repeated immersions, shaking, driving out of evil spirits, and so on.

Ritual purification is well known among Nguni peoples (see, for example, Hunter 1936: 228 for the Pondo, and Krige 1936: 135 for the Zulu). However, as Pauw pointed out, while Sundkler's interpretation might hold for the Zulu, it did not for the Tswana. He says (1960: 194–5):

> Baptism by immersion, then, has no close morphological parallel in traditional Tswana rites. Moreover, some of the churches have rites of purification which are definitely connected with traditional notions of 'impurity' . . . for which the traditional rites of purification were performed, but the church rites performed to remove the impurity often resemble the rite of baptism by immersion, and not the traditional rites. The propensity for baptism by immersion and rites of purification in rivers or pools must therefore have a different explanation in the Taung churches.

His explanation is in terms of the magical value which the Tswana attached to baptism, but suggests also that the purification practices he observed might owe something to Nguni contact.

In view of the heterogeneous nature of Soweto's population which is reflected in the composition of the independent church

congregations, we should beware of explaining purification rites
purely in terms of traditional Nguni practices — in Soweto they are
indulged in by Nguni and Sotho alike, and Pauw's explanation for
the Tswana might be more acceptable for the Soweto situation.
There is probably no doubt as to the influence of Nguni traditional
purification rites, but we should also note that purification has a
magical connotation for those who take part, and has an important
role in the healing and cleansing activities of the churches, which as
we have seen are so important for people, of whatever background,
who live in Soweto. Purification may be attractive for its links with
tradition, but it is also attractive for its immediate, alleviating role
in the urban situation; in other words this is another aspect of the
independent churches which is a blend of old and new, and which
cannot be analysed simply in terms of one or the other.

The same view may be held of other aspects of independent
church ritual. Spirit possession may also be seen in terms of traditional possession cults. For Sundkler, Zulu Zionist possession has
'the finger of traditional Zulu religion' (1961: 200), while Lee
(1969: 152) has traced the Zulu *ukuthwasa* possession among women
into the independent churches in Zululand. At the same time, we
may see possession in Soweto's independent churches (as distinct
from spirit mediumship — see Beattie and Middleton 1969: x) as a
means of release of the tension and frustration brought about by
life in the townships. In this it has clear parallels with religious
movements in other parts of the world where possession is encountered (I. Lewis 1971). In these terms possession may be just as much
part of a wider phenomenon, seen from a sociological perspective,
because it may have roots in certain traditional practices.

The same point may be made about dancing in church, or about
the drums and Holy Places which are used by prophets and traditional diviners alike. One of the central problems in all these cases
is to be able to distinguish *form* from *content*: although a modern
rite may look substantially the same as a traditional rite, it is not
necessarily seen in the same light by participants. This has already
been indicated in the discussion on offerings — the slaughter of an
animal may have different meanings for different participants.

We contend, therefore, that while much of the independent church
ritual may have links with traditional practices, any analysis must
take into account both the specific urban situation and the wider
significance of certain symbols. By and large the participants in independent church ritual in Soweto are townsmen, living in an urban
environment and reacting to its pressures. In this they resemble
black Americans in storefront churches (Fauset 1944) and West
Indians in pentecostal movements in London (Calley 1965) who

react to the pressures of the societies in which they live.

The independent churches draw on both Christianity and tradition; the movement started from a Christian and not a pagan base, but it drew on African as well as western tradition. The resulting synthesis has succeeded — where the mission churches have not — in meeting the needs of many of the people of Soweto.

CHAPTER **10** The Attraction of the Churches

I should like to attempt now to put the movement of African independent churches as a whole into some perspective. In the first chapter I suggested that any explanation of the independent churches would need to be on two levels – general and specific – to give a balanced perspective. We shall, therefore, look first at the wider context of these movements in general, and then at the specific situation in South Africa and Soweto.

The explanations that have been offered for the proliferation of independent churches in South Africa have tended to be specifically situational. While these are important, and we shall deal with some of them later in this chapter, we should start with a broader look and attempt some explanation which might hold in a variety of situations. This would be what Burridge (1969: 136–40) would call the 'Hegelian' type of explanation, which is open-ended and tries to take into account the total situation.

Evans-Pritchard (1965) provided a good starting-point to the problem of explanation with his analysis of the intellectualist, emotionalist and sociological approaches to the theory of religion in primitive society. Later both Peel (1968) and Burridge (1969) provided critiques of the various approaches to the problem of explanation, and stressed the importance of explanations which take account of beliefs for their own sake. This has become known as the 'neo-Tylorian' or 'intellectualist' approach, and has been sharply criticised (for example, by Leach 1967) and defended (Horton 1968) by various protagonists.

I do not intend to revive this debate here, and what will be taken as the intellectualist type of approach is simply what Ross has defined as the 'literalist thesis', which suggests that one of the functions of religion is the explanation and control of events (Ross 1971: 105). This approach is clearly set out in Peel (1968) and summarised by Horton in a review article (1971: 94), in which he designates the approach as one 'which takes systems of traditional belief at their face value — i.e. as theoretical systems intended for the explanation, prediction, and control of space–time events'. Both Horton and Peel see traditional African religious systems, to use Peel's terminology, as 'this-worldly' as opposed to the 'other-worldly' nature of, for example, Christianity as conveyed by some missionaries (Peel 1968: 6).

Peel's terminology is not entirely satisfactory, as 'this-worldly' and 'other-worldly' may be interpreted too simplistically. The dichotomy is obviously not clear-cut. Horton (1971) has made a commendable attempt to clarify these terms by using 'explanation-prediction-control' in place of 'this-worldly', and 'communion' in place of 'other-worldly', but although these terms might be more accurate, they are clumsy. In the absence, then, of completely suitable terms, and in the attempt to avoid unnecessary duplication of terminology for the same concepts, we shall use Peel's terms. But the point should be stressed that the terms are not mutually exclusive. They are used to indicate an *emphasis*. 'This-worldly', then, does in no way imply the absence of the 'other world', but merely denotes an emphasis, as Horton says, on the explanation, prediction and control of space–time events.

The this-worldly/other-worldly distinction must also be seen in terms of the question of power.[1] As Burridge suggests (1969: 5), 'Religions . . . are concerned with the systematic ordering of different kinds of power, particularly those seen as significantly beneficial or dangerous.' The understanding of power is at the same time also directly related to the function of religion as answering 'the problem of meaning' (O'Dea 1966: 6) by providing adequate explanation.

With this background we can offer some analysis of the movement from mission church to independent church, but stress again that this is only a part explanation. Traditional African religious systems provided an answer to the problem of meaning and identified sources of power: a supreme being, ancestral shades, and spirits of various sorts. These powers were used to explain, just as in any other religion, the human condition. Importantly, however, the orientation was 'this-worldly', in that they were not primarily concerned with an after-life, but with space–time events, and with their explanation, prediction, and control. To take one example, the role of the ancestors was seen in terms of the effect they could have — either to help or hinder — on their living descendants. Ancestors were thus propi-

1. This factor has been brought to prominence in the literature on African religion by Tempels (1959). I am also grateful to the Revd Dr H.-J. Becken for further explanation on this point as being important in Zulu independent churches.

tiated to ensure their benevolence towards the affairs of their descendants.[2]

If we return to the contact situation for a moment, the traditional religious systems were confronted with the bearers of a new religion, Christianity, whose missionaries proclaimed it to be superior to the traditional systems in that it represented a superior power. Wittingly or unwittingly these missionaries brought with them unmistakeable signs of a technologically superior culture, which later was able to dominate politically as well. The power behind these manifestations of superiority was not strictly explicable in traditional terms, but an obvious way of resolving conflict thus aroused was to accept the superior power claimed by the missionaries, as evidenced by their technological superiority, and to accept Christianity.[3]

As Christianity was accepted by those who had an essentially 'this-worldly' approach to religion, Christianity would be judged in these terms. Much of mission Christianity, however, appeared to be more 'other-worldly' oriented, particularly in relation to the specific problems faced by African people in South Africa, and one reaction to this was to form independent churches which could satisfy some of these 'this-worldly' desires.

Now this analysis could be made irrespective of time or place. Thus it may be just as valid for, say, Nigeria as it is for South Africa, and it can also transcend the differences between rural and urban areas. Any observed differences between 'this-worldly' desires in rural and urban areas in South Africa, for example, would in no way detract from the overall explanation.

The explanation outlined above would be sufficient to account for the general phenomenon of independent churches in Africa in a general way. The 'this-worldly' desires, for example, could be political in some cases, social in others, economic in yet others, or some combination of these. Thus the explanation lacks precision. But it is doubtful whether precision can be obtained at this particular level of explanation, and we shall now have to turn to the specific situation of the study and examine the 'this-worldly' emphasis of the independent churches in Soweto.

In support of the general analysis we shall suggest that the whole emphasis of the independent churches in Soweto has been in this

2. This is of course only one solution to the problem. As Burridge has shown for millenarian movements, millenarian activity may result as 'occasioned by the manifestation of a power outside current comprehension' (Burridge 1961: 143).

3. The importance of 'this-worldly' desires in the formation of independent churches has been discussed by Peel in dealing with the Yoruba. In particular, see Peel 1968: 290–2. See also Max Weber's use of the 'this-worldly'/'other-worldly' distinction: Gerth and Mills 1948: 277–8.

direction. For example, let us take — as discussed above — the role
of religion in ordering different kinds of power. The previous chapter
showed how independent churches have been able in some cases to
integrate the shades and their powers into a Christian framework.
The work of the prophet (particularly one who has been converted
from being a traditional diviner) is perhaps the best example of this
integration of power. And as we have shown, the prophet's activities
are exclusively concentrated on the problems of this world: the healing of the sick, the divining of the causes of misfortune, and the
predicting of future events. The role of the prophet is crucial in the
Zionist-type independent churches, it shows a most marked divergence from the mission church pattern, and it is clearly 'this-worldly'.

The 'this-worldly' emphasis of the churches in Soweto is best seen,
however, in the analysis of their role in the urban situation, and this
will be dealt with below. It leads us to a consideration of what

m   obvious attractions of the independent
c   *276.822*   ed most attention
f   se explanations deal
                                          ered by most socio-
W5 2   these independent
                                          s. They are an answer
                                          or social goods, and
                                          and authority which
                                          ge.' (Peel 1968: 6.)
                                          re not in themselves
                                          plexity.
                                          ersus functional ex-
                                          we may follow Spiro's
igges   ending on the aspect
rel   isition of religion is
                                          eliefs to be explained
                                          17ff). Relating this to
                                          tellectualist' analysis
                                          n, and as such the argu-
                                          be offered must in
                                          the attractions of the
                                          same time we must be
                                          ctors and later functions

                                          ore manifest general
                                          ve been outlined without
                                          adership opportunities,
                                          bility, mixture of western
and African   explained both causally

and functionally, they are also relevant in both rural and urban areas. We should therefore look more specifically at the urban situation and the role of the independent churches in it.

THE URBAN SITUATION

Nearly twenty-five years ago Sundkler suggested that a study of the independent churches and urbanisation would be worthwhile if it were 'treated in all its implications and in its sociological setting'. (Sundkler 1961: 80.) He himself stated that the churches were 'adaptive structures' in city life in South Africa (1961: 302), but offered no evidence.

It has been surprising that since then very little has appeared on this subject — and indeed on the wider subject of the role of religious organisations of any sort in the urban situation. Some have referred to the matter in passing, as does Sundkler, without producing evidence. An example of this is Kiev, who states (1959: 172) that in the urbanising and industrialising areas of Africa 'sects patterned along traditional lines have developed to meet the psychological needs of detribalised Africans'.

In a more recent example Thomas has pointed to the functions of religious institutions in assisting women in adjusting to the pressures of urban life (Thomas 1970) and his is one of the few studies which attempts to deal systematically with the subject in a limited area, and to produce evidence to back conclusions. For the rest, the literature on urbanisation in Africa is disappointing for its failure to deal with the subject except peripherally. Even when the subject is raised, the approach is often to view urban situations only in relation to rural situations left behind, without trying to analyse the movements specifically in terms of their urban environment.

We shall therefore examine the role of Soweto's churches in the urban situation in which they are placed, a description of which was given at the beginning of chapter 2. As we saw there, Soweto is the largest African urban area in South Africa, comprising twenty-one townships to the south-west of Johannesburg. Its population is in the region of one million people who speak many different languages and come from a variety of backgrounds. Soweto, then, is South Africa's largest and most cosmopolitan township complex, and its citizens face a variety of difficulties. These range from insecurity of tenure (created by legislation) to problems of transport, crime and poverty. The latter are common to modern cities, but the citizen of Soweto faces them in addition to numerous restrictions imposed without his consent by an external government. The facilities in Soweto are probably better than in many other African cities, but we may agree with Mayer (1971: 178) that African townships in South Africa have 'less physical hardship . . . [but] more hardship in terms of unjust family separation and restrictions of movement . . . insecurity (through denial of freehold) and restriction of social mobility'. In addition, Soweto is larger than any other African township in South Africa, and its scale magnifies many of its problems.

It is in this situation that independent churches flourish, and an estimated number of 900 separate churches makes Soweto the area with the greatest concentration of independent churches in South Africa. These churches are voluntary associations, and in this there is an important difference between the independent churches which recruit mainly on a voluntary basis, and the mission churches which recruit largely from children of members who grow up and become members in turn.[4] As voluntary associations, there is considerable mobility of members between churches, based on preference. What Brandel-Syrier has said of the women is true of the whole movement: 'One "joins" a church as one "joins" any other organisation, by paying the required fees and by attending the meetings, and when dissatisfied or forced by circumstances one "resigns" and becomes a member of another church which seems to offer greater advantages.' (Brandel-Syrier 1962: 136.) We shall try to see below what these advantages are, and to whom they apply.

The second point to be taken into account when dealing with the Soweto independent churches is the composition of their congregations. This was discussed in chapter 5, and we saw that most members were elderly with little education, and that most of them had been born in areas other than Johannesburg, and had moved to town as young adults in search of work. Most had stayed in Johannesburg permanently, and the average length of stay of those members who could remember the year that they had come to Johannesburg was 24 years. From this we can see that these members are not migrants but townspeople, by and large of the first generation.

People coming to the city have to adjust to a new situation which is radically different from the old. One of the most important differences is in increase of scale (Wilson and Wilson 1945: 24ff); the city has much larger numbers of people closer together, its population in the case of Soweto is markedly heterogeneous, there are many more contacts with western society particularly in the sphere of economics. The system of social organisation in the rural areas, based largely on

4. Calley uses this distinction to define 'sect' (voluntary recruitment) from 'church' (natural recruitment) (Calley 1965: 2). The distinction is useful, but sect has a derogatory connotation for many, and consequently is not used here. It should be pointed out that a few of the older independent churches also recruit naturally.

co-operation between kith and kin, is no longer viable in Soweto, as kin are usually far apart, and administrative decrees determine where you shall live. What is required in order to adapt to this new and changing situation are new bases for social organisation, and we should examine the churches in this light.

In his study of urbanisation in West Africa, Little suggests (1965: 1) that new roles are created which require co-operation between people on the basis of common interest rather than descent, and that a new system of relationships is required:

> Before, however, the new forms of association can be fully institutionalized there is required a new system of relationships which will link the old with the new structure. This is needed because, the gap in terms of social values being very wide, traditional roles have to be adapted and the fresh social institutions integrated within a wider social system than previously prevailed. My suggestion is that the system of relationships referred to is provided largely by voluntary associations. . . .

In the preceding chapter we have seen something of how the independent churches in Soweto combine traditional African and western elements in their ritual and organisation. We have seen that they have, for example, a place for the shades within their cosmologies, and believe them still to be potent. We have also examined the role of purification, and the close links between prophets and tribal diviners. The churches stress many of the traditional values — respect for age, obligation towards kin, marriage-payments — and at the same time have created certain new forms. We suggest that this blend of old and new in the churches is an important factor in attracting members into their congregations because it facilitates adaptation to the urban environment by providing an important link between it and the environment from which they came (cf. Little 1965: 87).

Thomas has shown that religious institutions in a Rhodesian township have certain functions in fulfilling needs for 'sociability, status, security and approval' among members (Thomas 1970: 284), and these were discussed in some detail in chapter 5. Little (1965: 88–102) has an expanded list of what he shows to be relevant factors for voluntary associations in general in the urban situation he was interested in. Expanding on the material already given, we may look at some of these factors and try to show how they are important for the independent churches in Soweto, and how they may meet many of the needs of townspeople which were formerly met by kin groups on a smaller scale in rural areas.

The first of Little's factors is what he calls *fraternity*, where individuals within the voluntary association are encouraged to regard one another in some senses as siblings. This can be seen very clearly

in the independent churches where the terms 'brother' and 'sister'
are regularly and widely used between members who are in no way
related. Independent church congregations are encouraged to act as
a family, and to support and if necessary sympathise with fellow
members. A good example of this, of course, is the emphasis on
visiting the sick and assisting any members who may be in need.
This impinges on the second factor, also used by Thomas, of *sociability*.

Sociability is particularly important in the independent churches,
and we have seen that members make friends within their churches,
and that visiting and other contacts are widespread. In the impersonal, sprawling townships of Soweto, independent church congregations are small groups of friends — important as reference and
supportive groups in the wider society. In them members are able
to feel at home, and are secure in their standing. The problem of
insecurity is a very real one in Soweto, not only in terms of people
having to face the variety of new problems of an urban environment,
but also because of the variety of laws and regulations enforced by
the South African Government which affect most aspects of the
lives of urban Africans, and which make security of residence doubtful for most, and arrest under the 'pass laws' a reality for many.

As Monica Wilson has pointed out (1971: 66), 'The basic insecurity
of men comes, not from poverty, but the feeling that no one cares
for them.' Little, too, refers to the problem of insecurity, and shows
how voluntary associations can restore a sense of identity and give
'even the most humble member an opportunity to feel that he
"matters" ' (Little 1965: 88). We have seen in the independent
churches that the church hierarchies are elaborate, and allow many
members to hold office and title, but this is only part of their role.
We have tried to show also that the independent churches are what
we have called caring communities, where individuals 'matter' and
are supported by fellow-members.

Little (1965: 91-2) points out that part of the security offered
to members in voluntary associations is in terms of *protection*. In
many of Soweto's independent churches the leaders are important
for the advice and assistance they can offer their members in their
daily affairs, as are the church prophets. The independent churches
offer supernatural protection to members through ordinary church
membership and attendance at services, but also through the activities
of the prophets. In the discussion on healing we saw how prophets
offered cures and also protection — for example for those trying to
find employment, and those having difficulty in obtaining passes.

The independent churches and their leaders are also important in
terms of *social control*. Mayer has referred to the problem of social

control in urban African areas in South Africa, and of the role that 'sects' may have in the maintenance of social control in these areas, taking a case from East London as an example (Mayer 1971), using Dubb's (1961) material on the Bhengu church. While Soweto churches do not appear to be as 'totalitarian' as Mayer suggests of Bhengu's church, they are nevertheless active in various ways.

I have mentioned that the churches emphasise certain norms such as proper marriage ceremonies, one wife, no smoking, drinking or dancing, and no dissension between members of the church. In many cases these rules are strictly enforced both by general opinion within the church, and if necessary by disciplinary action by the leader or church council. One example was given in an earlier chapter of a church leader dealing with a married couple in his congregation, who had been drinking and fighting, in a manner which stopped this, and which was accepted even though the leader had no legal authority over them. In general, church leaders wield considerable authority over their members and are important in ensuring normative behaviour within their congregation and also in the ordinary daily lives of members.

Little (1965: 90) speaks of the function of associations with 'tribally mixed membership' as enabling members to learn to co-operate with strangers. One of the most interesting aspects of the membership of the independent churches in Soweto was the fact that it was drawn from people of different languages, and that for most purposes 'tribalism' did not appear to be an important factor within churches, and this despite the efforts of the South African authorities to segregate Soweto on ethnic lines. We may therefore see the independent churches in Soweto as being important institutions for interethnic contact, and consequently for aiding individuals in adjusting to their new society: for example improving their grasp of languages other than their own, and learning to interact with people of different languages and backgrounds. This is done on a small scale, and can be seen to be in some ways a preparation for interacting in the wider, more impersonal society.

Independent church congregations can also assist their members in more practical ways in dealing with the urban situation. For example, new members may be assisted simply by getting information – either formally or informally – about the city and its ways. We have seen that small congregations meeting in the suburbs of Johannesburg often help fellow-members to obtain employment in the area by looking out for vacancies and reporting these, and then introducing their candidates for the job.

Mutual aid is important. We have mentioned this already in a non-material sense, but it is also important in a material way. Members

of churches who are in need are usually helped by fellow congregation members, and the churches always respond in times of crisis.
In the discussion of the Holy United Methodist Church, for example,
we saw that assistance was given to members who were in need
through illness or bereavement, and that a number of people had in
fact joined that church because of the material support it was known
to give to members. This is true of most other independent churches
in Soweto, where members in need are always assisted even if only
in a small way.

We have already suggested that the churches offer opportunities
for leadership within a system where there are few such opportunities in other spheres, and we have also noted that the churches allow
release of tension and frustration through dancing and possession.
These last are attractions peculiar to the independent churches, and
opportunities for leadership are greater than in the mission churches.

To summarise so far, Soweto's independent churches provide a
blend of old and new which is particularly attractive to the people
who join them. These people are mostly elderly, poorly-educated,
and first-generation townspeople. For them Soweto has few voluntary associations, other than sporting clubs, and few opportunities.
Against this background the independent churches are very important as their congregations provide small reference groups in relation
to the wider society. In them individuals are secure as part of a small
community: they have their assigned places, each has an identity as
a church member, and a ready-made group of friends. The group is
able to give both moral and material assistance in time of need, and
assists individuals in their adjustment to city life.

Thus the churches can be seen to provide, for at least some people,
new bases for social organisation. They provide members with personal networks in a city where most relationships for the newcomer,
as well as for the resident without friends, are of the more impersonal
structural or categorical type (Mitchell 1966: 51–56). These personal
networks may be very important in helping people to come to terms
with their urban environment.

The independent churches are particularly well suited to do this
because members meet in small groups and religious sanctions operate.
They are able to draw people together across divisions of language
and social background, and part of their success may also lie in the
fact that there are few competing voluntary associations for the sort
of people who join the independent churches (cf. Thomas 1970: 284).

Explanation has now been attempted on two levels, and in conclusion we should draw some of the threads together before considering
the future of the movement. On a broad level we have tried to advance an explanation for the existence of independent churches

which would transcend boundaries of time and space, at least in Africa. In the Introduction, some parallels between the independent church movement as described here and other enthusiastic movements, historical and contemporary, have been suggested. The conclusion is that from one perspective the movement is specifically an African one, but from another it has links with similar movements in other times, cultures and places.

In the specific context, independent churches have flourished in Soweto, and the reasons for this are complex. Their 'this-worldly' nature, in terms of the general theory, can be divided into a number of aspects some of which would be valid for the whole of South Africa, and others specifically for Soweto and other towns. Thus a number of factors would be of general importance. The evident cleavages based on race, with differences in power and privilege between white and black, and the association of some mission churches with these inequalities, would be important to all independent churches. Problems of poverty and general insecurity which lead to consultations with healers, and the search for emotional outlets for frustrations, are also universal. Inadequate political opportunities and the frustration of the leadership abilities of the less educated are factors in the success of any independent church. And the need for small groups of people in a supportive role is felt by the disadvantaged everywhere.

But what of Soweto itself? The various factors just mentioned are all important in the formation of independent churches in Soweto, and some are accentuated by the conditions under which people live in Soweto. African people living in an urban area are, for example, more insecure than those in rural areas in terms of tenure. They are more insecure in view of the very high crime rate compared with rural areas. They lack even the limited political opportunities afforded in the Government-designated homelands. These reasons alone would emphasise the importance of independent churches in Soweto.

Soweto and its particular conditions therefore demonstrably give rise to the very large number of independent churches that are found there. But the people of Soweto also play a part in the sort of churches that are found in the area. The evidence presented has been that members of independent churches in Soweto are poor, mainly middle-aged and ill-educated. This they share with members in other parts of South Africa, but in addition they are *townsmen*. They are part of a large population which is in close touch with a sophisticated western economy, and live in a polyglot and stratified community. This has had some effect on independent churches in Soweto.

To understand this effect, we should look at the differing attitudes

of Soweto's citizens towards the independent churches. Broadly
speaking, a large proportion of Soweto's population will hold a
neutral to negative attitude towards these churches. Some are opposed to churches in general, and others opposed to the independent churches in particular. Opposition will be rooted in an assessment of the churches as 'uneducated' and 'primitive' and therefore
an embarrassment to educated people. Typically, educated Africans
laugh when referring to Zionist-type churches, and their attitude is
often formed without direct contact with the churches themselves.

Independent church members are aware of this sort of attitude,
and their awareness is reflected in their churches. This would explain
in some measure the distinction some make between Zionist and
Apostolic churches, the latter being more educated and interested
in education. It would also explain the observed tendency towards
a bureaucratic form of hierarchy which has resulted in the separation
of the roles of bishop and prophet, as discussed in chapter 4. It would
also explain to some extent the great eagerness of individual church
leaders to enrol in correspondence courses, and of course the major
educational aim of the African Independent Churches' Association,
as outlined in chapter 8.

The movement in Soweto, then, is towards 'respectable' churches
which satisfy the needs of a section of the community. As shown,
only certain people join these independent churches in Soweto —
those who fall into the particular category outlined who are in
addition not against religion in general and to whom the African
independent churches are acceptable voluntary associations. Those
who find religion and/or the independent churches unacceptable
may find similar outlets in other ways: for example in secular voluntary associations such as sports clubs (cf. Scotch 1970; Wilson and
Mafeje 1963) and fund-raising clubs, in such anomic directions as
crime and drinking, or in other spheres, including the social and
political.

In conclusion, we should look at the independent churches in
Soweto in terms of the future. Succeeding censuses have shown
that the independent church movement in South Africa has been
growing at a rapid rate, and that Soweto has the largest concentration of churches in the country. We should ask, firstly, whether
this growth is likely to continue and, secondly, whether the nature
of the independent churches in Soweto is likely to change. '

Both questions can be answered in part by the analysis already
given of how the churches satisfy a variety of needs within the urban
community. Whilst the same social situation obtains in South Africa,
the same needs will remain in large measure, and as more people
come to the cities it can reasonably be expected that the number of

independent churches will grow. Our analysis has stressed the importance of small groups in meeting these needs, and it is consequently likely that there will be a proliferation of churches rather than an increase in membership of a few, and this will continue as long as the churches are interchangeable structures that can be easily reproduced. It is likely, however, that there is a saturation point for the number of independent churches in South Africa.

More interesting perhaps is the question of the nature of the churches themselves. There has been a suggestion that there might have been a change in Zionist-type churches in Rhodesia towards Ethiopian-type churches (Aquina 1969), based largely on the improved economic situation of Zionist members. However, a previous article by the same author (1966) showed a reverse procedure — Ethiopian to Zionist — based on the Ethiopian-type churches' recruitment of people of low economic standing and education and a higher degree of insecurity. In Soweto the importance of insecurity in the move towards Zionist-type churches has been shown, but it should be pointed out that in this case insecurity is tied not only to economic condition but to a range of what Mitchell (1966: 50) calls 'administrative and political limitations' which are externally imposed.

We have seen that the independent churches, particularly the Zionist-type churches, play their part in accommodating those who are affected by these external determinants, and in aiding them to come to terms with them at least to some extent. This 'comforting the uncomfortable' is done through caring communities, and particularly through the work of prophets and the belief in the power of the Holy Spirit. I contend, therefore, that there is not only a growth in the number of independent churches, but also a movement *within* some churches towards Zionism. Some evidence of this has already been given — for example the case of the Ethiopian-type church wishing to join the BBCAC because of the latter's faith-healing and emphasis on the Holy Spirit, or the example of the leader of the Holy United Methodist Church looking for a prophet to join his church to provide similar advantages.

While the social conditions in Soweto remain as they are, this trend is likely to continue, but it may be that second-generation townspeople will no longer feel the need for what is provided by independent churches. A number of observers in Soweto suggested, for example, that the independent churches were fewer in number in those areas that had been longest settled. If true, this would tend to confirm our hypothesis that the churches play an important adaptive role in the process of urbanisation. Also, should at any time some of the administratively determined insecurity be lessened and greater opportunities in various fields be opened to

Africans in South Africa, one might expect the number of independent churches to decrease.

I would contend, however, that the movement would not disappear, even though it might shrink. For the independent churches in Soweto should not be seen only as a negative 'reaction to conquest'; I have tried also to show their positive, dynamic aspect — in Vilakazi's phrase, their separating of the message from the messengers, and their creating of a new religious organisation of African orientation, which has seemed to be more relevant to many than the Christianity of the mission churches.

APPENDIX 1 Method of Fieldwork

The importance of a section on methodology has been stressed by a number of writers, including some of the early fieldworkers (e.g. Malinowski 1922: 2–25; Rivers 1906: v), but this advice is not always followed. All field projects have faults and inadequacies, and it is important that fieldworkers show that they are aware of them so that readers may judge their work more accurately. Fieldwork in South Africa, particularly, is often subject to severe restrictions, and it is as well that these should be made clear. With this in mind this section gives an account of the project, its origins, problems and procedures.

In 1968 the Christian Institute of Southern Africa, which had been working with African independent churches for some time, made it known that they would welcome an academic project aimed at increasing knowledge of the movement, and that they would try to find suitable sponsorship for such a project. Their fairly broad requirement, therefore, set an initial limitation to the fieldwork, because some general information was required, and not merely an in-depth study of one or two churches.

About two years was available for intensive research, and it was decided that the geographical area studied would have to be limited, as it would have weakened the project severely to have attempted any general survey of the approximately 3 000 African independent churches in existence all over the country. As Sundkler's excellent study of rural churches was freely available, it was decided to concentrate on urban churches, and the area with the greatest concentration of these was Soweto. Soweto was thus selected as the area of study, but this also presented problems. Available estimates suggested that there were about 900 African independent churches in Soweto, spread over twenty-one townships and something like one million people. Again the size of the area precluded any sort of random sampling with available resources.

It was therefore decided to start by trying to gain an overview of the African independent churches, and this was done by accepting a six-month appointment at the start of the fieldwork period as an adviser to the African Independent Churches' Association (AICA) on the staff of the Christian Institute. In July 1969 I attended my first AICA Conference at Kwa Mashu near Durban, and made contact with a number of independent church leaders. Thereafter, between July and December 1969 I was based in Johannesburg, and as AICA adviser was involved in a variety of AICA meetings and conferences, which enabled me to extend my contacts. The AICA adviser's office was also a meeting-place for church leaders with a variety of problems, particularly concerning leadership disputes and relations with various authorities, and this increased my understanding of the movement.

The initial six-month period was spent in making contacts with church leaders, attending AICA gatherings, dealing with various problems raised by church leaders, and in making some acquaintance with Soweto. Part of the time was spent learning my way about Soweto, visiting church leaders, and attending some services.

In January 1970 intensive fieldwork began, and I started visiting church leaders in Soweto and administering Questionnaire 1 (see Appendix 2 for all questionnaires used), which dealt with non-contentious material. I started in the Central Western Jabavu area, which had two particularly good informants, and continued with other leaders I had met at AICA meetings. The survey included a number of opponents of AICA who subsequently joined the Reformed Independent Churches' Association (RICA), some Pentecostal Mission Church Association (PMCA) churches and some churches that were not affiliated to any association. In the end 58 churches were covered by this survey, and a number of similarities became apparent. It was not felt worthwhile to continue with the survey beyond this point. This material is referred to in the text as survey A. In survey A, churches were visited in 14 of Soweto's townships: Central Western Jabavu, Chiawelo, Dlamini, Dube, White City Jabavu, Mofolo, Moletsane, Moroka, Orlando, Phiri, Pimville, Senaoane, Zola and Zondi.

Of the 58 churches investigated, 13 were covered for the purposes of Questionnaire 2, which dealt with ritual and beliefs and which was potentially more contentious than the first questionnaire. This questionnaire was administered to 13 leaders who had been good informants in the first survey, and whose churches covered a reasonably wide range from Zionist- to Ethiopian-type. Again a number of similarities between the churches became apparent as this second survey progressed.

As it was also felt to be important to investigate some of the ordinary followers in the churches, a third questionnaire was drawn up for them. Questionnaire 3 was administered to most of the main congregations of the three selected churches which are described in chapter 3. This proved fairly difficult to do because church members worked during the week and were busy during weekends after church services, and were unwilling to wait for lengthy periods after church to be interviewed. Despite this, over 60 people in the three congregations were eventually interviewed. They comprised most of the adult members of the three congregations who attended services regularly. The data are referred to in the text as being from survey C.

As the focus of my work proceeded from the general to the more specific, I decided to try to get more general information about as large a number of churches as possible in the Soweto area. To this end a research assistant was employed for the last six months of the project. A list of some 100 churches with their addresses was on file at the Christian

Institute, and the research assistant visited these churches and administered a simple questionnaire. He collected information from these churches, and then interviewed other church leaders with whom he was able to make contact. In this survey, which we called survey B, 194 churches were finally interviewed in all parts of Soweto. This represented a considerable effort on the part of the research assistant, Archbishop M. P. Radebe, bearing in mind that the survey was conducted within the space of 6 months and under difficult conditions including much evening work.

In addition to the administering of questionnaires the normal anthropological techniques of participant observation and informal interviews were used. Various services were attended in 18 different churches, as well as a number of combined services, and the three selected churches were attended regularly throughout most of the fieldwork period, and most of the major occasions observed. These included consecrations, ordinations, accepting of new members, healing rituals, offerings, baptisms, communion services, weddings and funerals, in addition to numerous ordinary services.

During fieldwork it became increasingly clear how important healing was to many of the churches, and the latter part of the project was spent mainly on this subject. A number of church prophets were interviewed informally several times and some of their activities observed, and for comparative purposes two diviners were also interviewed. I was very fortunate in getting three prophets to keep diaries of their patients for me, the results of which were presented in chapter 6.

In view of the independent nature of many of these churches it was expected that there might be some hostility towards a white South African investigating their churches, but this was not the case. This was probably partly because I never visited a church or church leader without an introduction from somebody he would know and trust, and partly because of *bona fides* built up during the period spent as an AICA adviser. I found also that what hostility there was was directed at denominations, and not at individuals who did not specifically or officially represent any mission churches.

The most obvious of the problems that any study of Soweto involves are those caused by the sheer size, heterogeneity and complexity of the township. Unless one is studying something on a small scale, such as a neighbourhood, the size of the area makes for numerous complications. Thus the churches included in this study were in some cases miles apart, and much time was spent in travelling about Soweto. Communication is poor, with very few telephones, and a great deal of time was wasted in making appointments, which in many cases were not kept for reasons that could not be communicated in time.

These problems were minor compared with those caused directly by regulations imposed by the South African Government. In a normal anthropological project I would have lived inside Soweto for the duration of the fieldwork period, but this was impossible in terms of the law. My entry to Soweto was governed by a permit issued under Section 9 (9) (b) of the Bantu (Urban Areas) Consolidation Act No. 25 of 1945 as amended.

This permit was granted by the Non-European Affairs Department, and was initially valid for six months at a time on all days of the week between the hours of 7 a.m. and 10 p.m. This was withdrawn fairly early in the fieldwork period following a new regulation, and I was given a permit from 9 a.m. to 4 p.m. on week-days and from 9 a.m. to 12.30 p.m. on Saturdays. As this would have crippled the whole project, I appealed and was given a special permit valid between 9 a.m. and 5 p.m. seven days a week. In order to enter Soweto at any other time a special permit had to be applied for, and in fact was always granted. In terms of the permit I was permitted to visit Soweto, but not the Resettlement areas of Diepkloof and Meadowlands, which are controlled by the Bantu Administration Department. My permit was also liable to be withdrawn at any time without reason, and its final sentences read: 'This permit is not transferable and is only valid for the permit holder and must be produced on demand. This permit expires on . . . but may be withdrawn at any time without any reason given.' I was required to produce my permit by officials on only two occasions during the two years spent in Soweto.

This restriction of mobility had severe consequences for the quality of fieldwork. Instead of living with the people whom I was studying, learning the language properly and observing various aspects of daily life, I was forced to live outside the area and commute daily (during fieldwork I was travelling up to 2 000 miles per month). This precluded learning an African language properly, particularly as informants visited in various parts of Soweto spoke a variety of different home languages. Fortunately all informants interviewed spoke either English or Afrikaans, and an interpreter was seldom necessary. Interviews were conducted in either English or Afrikaans with a small amount of Sotho and a few words of Zulu.

The 5 p.m. time limit on my permit also made it very difficult to interview people who were employed full-time, except at weekends, and the high crime rate makes it inadvisable for either fieldworker or Soweto resident to travel much at night. So with the exception of occasions on which I applied for a special permit (usually for a dawn baptism, a midnight offering, night vigil, communion, or consecration) most fieldwork was conducted within daylight hours on a commuter basis. For the reasons outlined there had to be less emphasis on personal and continuous observation (although this was obviously important on many occasions) and a greater reliance on informal interviews and the use of questionnaires.

APPENDIX 2 Questionnaires

Questionnaire 1 (administered to 58 churches) *survey A*
1. Name of church.
2. Name of leader; title; age; languages spoken.
3. Address.
4. Schooling; theological education.
5. Birthplace; employment history.
6. Church history.
7. Marital status; children; position of leader's wife; wife's occupation.
8. Church history of wife; church history of children.
9. Size of church; no. of full members; residential areas of Soweto members.
10. Membership of church associations.
11. History of church.
12. Congregations in other parts of the country.
13. Church hierarchy; how they are appointed.
14. Conferences and other meetings of the church.
15. Church services, regular and special.
16. Languages used in church.
17. Church vestments: leaders, men, women, children.
18. Finances: income and expenditure; control of finance.
19. Church property owned.
20. Church groups: women's, children's, prayer, choir, etc.
21. Method of enrolling members.
22. Leader's knowledge of other churches in area; degree of co-operation with other churches.
23. General remarks.

Questionnaire 2 (administered to 13 churches) *survey A 2*
1. Name of church.
2. Name of leader.
3. Books used in church: hymnbook, Bible, service-books, other.
4. Hymns often sung.
5. Bible texts which are important in the church.
6. Sacraments:
   Communion. Who administers, who receives, when, elements used, form of service?
   Baptism. Who baptises, who is baptised and at what age, where, when,

form of baptism, can a person be baptised more than once?

Confirmation. Who hears confession, who confesses, when, where?

Marriage. Marriage rules in the church.

Ordination. Who ordains, who is ordained, when, where, are other ministers of other churches present? Who ordained the church leader?

Unction. Who receives unction, who administers it?

7. Does your church follow a confessional statement?

8. Who saves you?

9. Healing services. Who can heal, when do you have services, where, form of service? How are people healed, and with what?

10. Are there prophets in the church? Definition of a prophet.

11. What are the important rules in the church?

12. Ancestors. Do the ancestors have power to help or harm you, your church? Do you, your church, communicate with the ancestors?

13. Does your church use drums, bells, candles, other musical instruments?

14. Do church members use sticks? Who uses them; why?

15. Is there dancing in your church? When, why?

16. Do you use any books to help with sermons?

17. Does the Holy Spirit come to church members during services? How? Feelings about possession.

18. What sorts of independent churches are there?

Questionnaire 3 (administered to over 60 church members) *survey C*

1. Name of church.

2. Name of member, age, languages spoken.

3. Address.

4. Marital status, children, birthplace, education.

5. Occupation.

6. Employment history.

7. Church history: self, spouse, children, parents.

8. Position in the church: self, spouse.

9. Contribution to church funds.

10. Services attended. Meetings attended.

11. Church affiliation of friends and relatives (same, other independent, mission).

Questionnaire 4 (administered by an assistant to 194 churches not covered in survey A) *survey B*

1. Name of church. Church stamp.

2. Years established.

3. Name of leader, whether founder or not.

4. Age of leader, language, education.

5. Leader's previous church.

6. Who consecrated leader: name, church, year.

7. Languages used in church.

8. Number of full members.

9. Areas of South Africa where church is represented.

10. Do you hold healing services?

11. Do you have prophets?
12. Do you use drums?
13. Is there dancing in your church?
14. Do you have the Sacrament at night?
15. Do you baptise in the river?
16. Church association membership, AICA or other.

APPENDIX **3** **Churches Interviewed**

Survey A (* indicates Churches interviewed in survey A 2)

Africa United Church of Christ in
    Zion
African Church of Christ, Republic
    of South Africa*
African Congregational Church —
    Gardner Mvuyana*
Apostolic First-Born Church of Christ
    in Zion
African Free New Church*
Apostolic Full Gospel Mission of S.A.*
Apostolic Jerusalem O.F.S. Church in
    Zion
Bantu Bethlehem Christian Apostolic
    Church of S.A.*
Bantu Church of God in Zion
Bantu Full Gospel Church of God in
    Republic of South Africa
Bantu Full Gospel Church of God in
    South Africa
Bethlehem Apostolic Church in Zion
Bethsaid Healing Faith Mission
Christian Brethren Assembly*
Christian Christ Church in Zion
Christian Gospel Apostolic New
    Jerusalem Church O.F.S.
Christian New Salem Church
Christian National Apostolic Church
    in Zion of S.A.
Church of Christ Faith Healing
Church of Jesus Christ All Over The
    World
Church of the First Born
Damascus Church of God in S.A.
Damaseku Apostolic Church in Zion
Damaseku Congregation Apostolic
    Church in Zion
First Apostolic Church of Christ in
    Zion of S.A.*
First Catholic Apostolic Jerusalem
    Church in Zion of S.A.*

First Christian Apostolic Church in
    Zion
Foursquare Healing Church in Christ
General Faith Assembly in Zion
    Church in S.A.
Hebrew Jerusalem Church of God
Holy Apostolic Jerusalem Church in
    Zion of S.A.
Holy Apostolic Reform Salathiel
    Church in Zion
Holy Bantu Church in Zion
Holy Bros Prophets Church in Zion
    of S.A.
Holy Free Corner-Stone Apostolic
    Church in Zion*
Holy Spirit Apostolic Church
Holy Stars of God Apostolic Church
    in Zion of S.A.
Holy United Methodist Church in
    S.A.*
Independent Bantu Methodist Church
    of Africa
Lights of Bethesaid
National Church of Ethiopia in S.A.
National Church of Ethiopia of S.A.
New Apostolic Covenant Church of
    Christ
New St Matthew Apostolic Church
New St Peter Apostolic Church
    Morning Star
Old No. 1 Holy Apostolic Jerusalem
    Church of South Africa in Zion
Presbyterian Church of Africa*
Reformed Covenant Church of Christ
St Eli Apostolic Faith Mission of S.A.
St Francis Apostolic Church*
St Paul Apostolic Church of S.A.
St Paul Native Apostolic Faith Mor-
    ning Star Church of S.A.
St Peter Apostolic Gospel Church of
    S.A.
S.A. Eleventh Apostolic Church in
    Zion Edamaseku

Spiritualist Church of Africa
Third General Apostolic Church
United Christian Church of Africa
United Congregational Church of
   Christ in S.A.
United National Church in South
   Africa*
Zion Independent Church, R.S.A.

Survey B (This list is not strictly in
alphabetical order. It is given to emphasise the number and variety of
the independent churches.)

African Bantu Methodist Church
Apostolic Assembly and Church of
   the First Born
Apostolic Strangers Church in Zion
African Free Full Gospel Church of
   S.A.
Antioc Orphans Church in Zion
African Church of Christ Society of
   Republic of S.A.
African Methodist Apostolic Church
   of South Africa
Apostolic Jerusalem Church in Zion
   of S.A.
Apostolic Christian Church in Zion
Apostle Church in Zion of S.A.
Apostolic Jerusalem Christ Church in
   Zion of S.A.
A. M. E. Church of Christ in S.A.
Apostolic Holy Spirit Church in
   Zion of S.A.
African Christian Holy Church in
   Zion
African Zion Holiness Church
Antioch Jerusalem Church
African Congregational Methodist
   Church
African Church For All The Believers
   In The Kingdom of God
Apostolic Nazareth Corinthian Jeru-
   salem Church in Zion
African Independent Apostolic
   Church of S.A. Republic
Apostolic Faith Church Association
   in Zion of Africa
Apostolic Catholic Spirit Church in
   Zion of S.A.
Apostolic Kanana Church Witness of
   Jehova
African Apostolic Mission Church in
   Zion of S.A.
Apostolic Church of Christ in Zion,
   R.S.A.
Apostolic Church of Christ in Zion

Apostolic Jerusalem Africa Church
   in Zion
African The First Apostolic Church
   in Zion of S.A.
Brother Holy Apostolic Prophets
   Christ Church of God in S.A.
Bantu Church of Christ Mission S.A.
Bantu Methodist Apostolic Church
   of S.A.
Bethlehem Holy Spirit Apostolic
   Moonstar Church of S.A.
Bantu Eleven Apostolic Church of
   God in Zion
Bantu Seventh Day Adventist Church
   of God
Bethsaida Zion Apostolic Church of
   God
Bantu Apostolic Strangers Church in
   Zion
Bethlehem Holy Spirit Apostolic
   Church in Zion of S.A.
Bantu Full Gospel Church of S.A.
Bees Church of Christ in Zion of S.A.
Bantu Strong Badelwa Apostolic
   Church in Zion of S.A.
Bantu Christian Apostolic Church of
   S.A.
Church of Christ Mission (1)
Church of Christ Mission (2)
Church of Christ Mission (3)
Catholic Church in Zion of S.A.
Christ Holy Church
Christian Bible Church of God in
   South Africa
Christian Apostolic Faith Assembly
   in Zion of S.A.
Christian Zion Apostolic Church
Church of Christ — The Only Church
   of Christ
Christian Apostolic Faith Assembly
   in Zion of S.A.
Church of Christ Jesus of Africa
Christian Apostolic Church of Zion
   in S.A.
Catholic Apostolic Holiness Church
   in Zion
Church of God
Church of Christ of S.A. (1)
Church of Christ of S.A. (2)
Congregation Church of Christ in
   Zion of S.A.
Catholic Apostolic East Church Holy
   Spirit Stone in Zion of S.A.
Christian Apostolic Church in Zion
Christian Catholic Apostolic Church
   in Zion
Church of Christ

Christian Apostolic Church of Christ
in S.A.
Christian Apostolic Church in Zion
of S.A.
Christian Catholic Apostolic Church
in Zion of S.A.
Christian Gaza Apostolic Church in
Zion
Church of Christ Apostolic in Zion
Christian Catholic Impumalanga
Church in Zion
Church of Christ in Zion
Damascus Church of God in S.A.
Damaseku Congregation Apostolic
Church in Zion
Damaseku Apostolic Church in Zion
Ethiopian Church of Christ By
Religion
Evangelist Galilee Apostolic Church
in Zion of S.A.
Ethiopian Holy Baptist Church in
Zion
East African Orphanage Church in
Zion
Ethiopian Catholic Church in Zion
Ethiopian Catholic Church of S.A.
Ethiopian Church of S.A.
Ethuthukweni Apostolic Church in
Zion
Expect Bantu Holy Christian Apos-
tolic Church of God in Zion of
S.A.
Enoni Apostolic Church of Christ
Ethiopian Salvation Light Church of
Christ of S.A.
Ethiopian Baptist Church of S.A.
Free Ganah Church Mission of God of
S.A. (1)
Free Independent Bechuana Church
of S.A.
Free United Apostolic Church of
Zion in S.A.
First Sanai Apostolic Church in Zion
Free Ganah Church Mission of God
of S.A. (2)
Faith Assembly of S.A.
First Jerusalem Church of Christ and
Apostolic in Bethesda
First Public Apostolic Church
Free Apostolic Church of God in
Zion
Free African Bantu Apostolic Church
Faith Church of Christ
Free Methodist Church of S.A.
Gospel of the Kingdom Spirit of God
Gentiles Root Apostolic Church of
S.A.

Gospel Bethsaid Church in Zion S.A.
Galatians Apostolic Church of Zion
of S.A.
General Universal Zion Church of
God of S.A.
Galilee Bantu Zion Apostolic Church
of S.A.
Holy Jerusalem Apostolic Church in
Zion
Holy Spirit Jerusalem Church in Zion
Holy Spirit Makhwela Ntaba
Holy Catholic Apostolic Impuma-
langa Church in Zion
Holiness Church of Christ
Holy Bethlehem Apostolic Church
in Zion of S.A.
Holy International Apostolic Church
of S.A.
Holy Church in Zion All South Africa
Holy Apostolic Church in Zion
Holy Apostolic Church in Zion
Holy Spirit Jerusalem Church in
Zion of S.A.
Holiness Apostolic Church of Christ
Independent Methodist Church of
S.A.
Israel Christian Apostolic Church of
God
Israel Apostolic Sons of Zion
Judia Apostolic Church in Zion of
Africa
Jericho Holy Spirit Apostolic Church
in Zion of S.A.
Jerusalem Christ Twelve Apostolic
Church in Zion of S.A.
Jerusalem Christian Apostolic Mission
of God
Jerusalem Mission Church in R.S.A.
and Botswana
Kanana Apostolic Church of Jeru-
salem
Kingdom Apostolic Church in Zion
Light of the World Apostolic Church
in Zion
Light of Damascus Church Leseding
of S.A.
Morians Episcopal Apostolic Church
in Zion
Messenger Holy Apostolic Church in
Zion
Mount General Faith Assembly Zion
Church
New Church of South Africa
New Assembly Church of Christ in
Zion of S.A.
New Apostolic Covenant Church of
Christ in Africa

New Swaziland Apostolic Church in Zion of R.S.A.

New Messenger Lost Sheep Swaziland Church in Zion

Nazareth Sabbath Apostolic Church of S.A.

New World Apostolic Church in Zion

New Congregational Church of S.A.

New St Peter's Healing Church of S.A.

New National Church of Christ

New Apostolic Full Gospel Church in S.A.

New Jericho Apostolic Church in Zion of S.A.

New Jerusalem Church in Zion of S.A.

New Apostolic Christian Church in Zion of S.A.

New Holiness Christian Apostolic Church in Zion of S.A.

New Chrysolite Apostolic Church in Zion of S.A.

New Church of Christ Apostolic in R.S.A.

New Jerusalem Church in Zion of S.A. — Ekuthuleni

New Apostolic Messenger in Zion

New Bethlehem Spirit Church in Zion

New in Zion Apostolic Church of S.A.

Nazareth Apostolic Church of Africa

New Jerusalem Church in Zion

New African Church of Christ in Zion

New Christian Catholic Apostolic Church in Zion of S.A.

New East Church Holy Spirit in Zion of S.A.

New Christian Apostolic Church in Zion of S.A.

Puthani Congregation Church in Zion

Primitive Church of Africa

Remnant Church of Christ

Reformed Church of God

Rock of Ages Spiritual Church of S.A.

Roman Apostolic Church of S.A.

Revelation St Paul Apostolic Church of S.A.

St Thomas Apostolic Church of S.A.

Sons of Christian Catholic Apostolic Church

St Paul's Apostolic Faith Mission of S.A.

S.A. Christian Jerusalem Apostolic Church in Zion

St Peter Apostolic Church of S.A.

St Petros Temple of God in Damascus

St John Apostolic Faith Mission of S.A.

St Apostolic Synai Church of Christ of S.A.

St Luke Apostolic Faith Mission of S.A.

St Noah Ark Apostolic Church of S.A.

S.A. Apostolic Nature Church in Zion

Twelve Apostolic Church in New Jerusalem

Twelve Apostle Church of S.A. In Zion

The Twelve Stones Apostolic Church in Zion

Twelve Apostolic Church in Zion, R.S.A.

Truth of Zion Kingdom of God in S.A.

United African Catholic Church of S.A.

United Church of Christ in Republic

United Apostolic Church in Zion

United African Federation Apostolic Church in Zion of S.A.

United Apostolic Jerusalem Church in Zion

Zulu Christian Catholic Apostolic Church in Zion

Zion Swaziland Apostolic Church of God

Zion Damaseku Apostle Church of S.A.

Zion Jerusalem Apostolic Church of S.A.

Zion Apostolic Faith Mission Church of God in S.A.

Zion Apostolic Church of Christ in S.A.

Zion Congregational Church of S.A.

Bibliography

Aquina, Sr M., (1966) 'Christianity in a Rhodesian Tribal Trust Land', *Af. Soc. Research*, 1;
(1967) 'People of the Spirit: An Independent Church in Rhodesia', *Africa* 37: 2;
(1969) 'Zionists in Rhodesia', *Africa* 39: 2.
Baêta, C. G., (ed.), (1968) *Christianity in Tropical Africa,* London.
Bailey, F. G., (1969) *Stratagems and Spoils,* Oxford.
Barrett, D. B., (1968) *Schism and Renewal in Africa,* Nairobi.
Barth, F., (1959) 'Segmentary Opposition and the Theory of Games', *J. Roy. Anthrop. Inst.,* vol. 89.
Beattie, J., and J. Middleton, (1969) *Spirit Mediumship and Society in Africa,* London.
Blau, P., (1964) *Exchange and Power in Social Life,* New York.
Brandel-Syrier, M., (1962) *Black Woman in Search of God,* London.
Buchler, I., and H. Nutini, (1969) *Games Theory in the Behavioural Sciences,* Pittsburgh.
Burridge, K., (1969) *New Heaven New Earth,* Oxford.
Calley, M. J. C., (1965) *God's People,* London.
Clark, E. T., (1949) *The Small Sects in America,* New York.
Daneel, M. L., (1970) *Zionism and Faith-Healing in Rhodesia,* The Hague;
(1971) *Old and New in Southern Shona Independent Churches,* vol. 1, The Hague.
De Jouvenel, B., (1957) *Sovereignty,* Cambridge.
Dewey, A. G., (1970) 'Ritual as a Mechanism for Urban Adaptation', *Man* (N.S.) 5:3.
Dubb, A. A., (1961) 'The Role of the Church in an Urban African Society'. Unpublished M.A. thesis, Rhodes University, Grahamstown.
Edelstein, M. L., (1971) 'Attitude Survey of Urban Bantu Matric Pupils in Soweto with Special Reference to Stereotyping and Social Distance: A Sociological Study'. Unpublished M.A. thesis, University of Pretoria.
Edgerton, R. B., (1971) 'A Traditional African Psychiatrist', *Southwestern J. Anthrop.,* 27: 3.
Epstein, A. L., (1964) 'Urban Communities in Africa'. In M. Gluckman (ed.), *Closed Systems and Open Minds,* Edinburgh.
Evans-Pritchard, E. E., (1965) *Theories of Primitive Religion,* Oxford.
Fauset, A. H., (1944) *Black Gods of the Metropolis – Negro Religious Cults*

of the Urban North, reprinted 1971, Pennsylvania.

Fernandez, J. W., (1964) 'African Religious Movements, Types and Dynamics', *J. Mod. Af. Studies* 2: 4.

Field, M. J., (1960) *Search for Security: An Ethnopsychiatric Study of Rural Ghana,* London.

Firth, R., (1970) *Rank and Religion in Tikopia,* London.

Gerth, H. H., and C. W. Mills, (1948) *From Max Weber: Essays in Sociology,* London.

Goody, J., (ed.), (1966) *Succession to High Office* (Cambridge Papers in Soc. Anthrop. no. 4), Cambridge.

Hammond-Tooke, W. D., 'Urbanization and the Interpretation of Misfortune: A Quantitative Analysis', *Africa* 40: 2.

Hartmann, S. S., (ed.), (1969) *Syncretism* (Scripta Instituti Donneriani Aboensis III), Stockholm.

Hayward, V. E. W., (ed.), (1963) *African Independent Church Movements,* Edinburgh.

Hellmann, E., (1940) *Problems of Urban Bantu Youth,* S.A.I.R.R. Johannesburg;
(1948) *Rooiyard – A Sociological Survey of an Urban Native Slum-yard,* Rhodes–Livingstone Papers no. 13, Cape Town;
(1967) *The Impact of City Life on Africans,* Johannesburg;
(1971) *Soweto – Johannesburg's African City,* S.A.I.R.R., Johannesburg.

Hollenweger, W. J., (1972) *The Pentecostals,* London.

Horrell, M. (1964) *A Decade of Bantu Education,* Johannesburg;
(1970–5) (pub. annually) *A Survey of Race Relations in South Africa,* S.A.I.R.R., Johannesburg;
(1973) *South Africa: Basic Facts and Figures,* S.A.I.R.R., Johannesburg.

Horton, R., (1968) 'Neo-Tylorianism: Sound Sense or Sinister Prejudice?' *Man* (N. S.) vol. 3;
(1971) 'African Conversion', *Africa* 41: 2.

Hunter, M., (1936) *Reaction to Conquest,* London.

Jarrett-Kerr, M., (1960) *African Pulse,* London.

Kiernan, J. P., (1974) 'Where Zionists Draw the Line: A Study of Religious Exclusiveness in an African Township', *African Studies* 33: 2.

Kiev, A., (1959) 'Prescientific Psychiatry', *American Handbook of Psychiatry* vol. 3, New York;
(1964) *Magic, Faith and Healing – Studies in Primitive Psychiatry,* Glencoe.

Knox, R. A., (1950) *Enthusiasm,* Oxford.

Krige, E. J., (1936) *The Social System of the Zulu,* London.

Kuper, H., (1947) *An African Aristocracy – Rank among the Swazi,* London.

Lea, A., (1926 ?) *The Native Separatist Church Movement in South Africa,* Cape Town.

Leach, E. R., (1961) *Rethinking Anthropology,* London;
(1967) 'Virgin Birth', *Proceedings of the Roy. Anthrop. Inst.*

Lee, S. G., (1969) 'Spirit Possession Among the Zulu,' in Beattie and Middleton (eds.), *Spirit Mediumship and Society in Africa,* London.

Lévi-Strauss, C., (1968) *Structural Anthropology,* London.

Lewis, I., (1971) *Ecstatic Religion,* London.

Lewis, P., (1966) *The Creation of Soweto,* Johannesburg City Council (mim.), Johannesburg.

Linton, R., (1943) 'Natavistic Movements', *American Anthropologist* vol. 65.

Little, K., (1965) *West African Urbanization – A Study of Voluntary Associations in Social Change,* Cambridge.

Longmore, L., (1959) *The Dispossessed,* London.

Loram, C. T., (1926) 'The Separatist Church Movement', *International Review of Missions.*

Makhatini, D. L., (1965) 'Ancestor, Umoya, Angels', in *Our Approach to the Independent Church Movement in South Africa,* Missiological Institute, Mapumulo.

Malinowski, B. M., (1922) *Argonauts of the Western Pacific,* London.

Market Research Africa, (1968) *An African Day – A Second Study of Life in the Townships,* Johannesburg.

Marks, S., (1970) *Reluctant Rebellion,* Oxford.

Martin, M. L., (1964) *The Biblical Content of Messianism and Messianism in Southern Africa,* Morija;
(1965) 'Syncretism in Biblical Perspective', in *Our Approach to the Independent Church Movement in South Africa,* Missiological Institute, Mapumulo.

Maud, J. P. R., (1938) *City Government – the Johannesburg Experiment,* Oxford.

Mayer, P., (1971) 'Religion and Social Control in a South African Township', in H. Adam, *South Africa: Sociological Perspectives,* London.

Mbiti, J. S., (1969) *African Religions and Philosophy,* London;
(1970) *Concepts of God in Africa,* London.

Middleton, J., (ed.), (1970) *Black Africa: Its Peoples and Their Cultures Today,* London.

Mitchell, J. C., (1966) 'Theoretical Orientations in African Urban Studies', in Banton (ed.), *The Social Anthropology of Complex Societies* (ASA Monographs no. 4), London;
(1969) *Social Networks in Urban Situations,* Manchester.

Missiological Institute, (1965) *Our Approach to the Independent Church Movement in South Africa,* Lutheran Theological College, Mapumulo.

Mqotsi, L., and N. Mkele, (1946) 'A Separatist Church: Ibandla lika-Krestu', *African Studies* 5: 2.

Murphree, M., (1969) *Christianity and the Shona* (L.S.E. Monographs in Soc. Anthrop. no. 36), London.

Norris, D. L., (1967) 'Psychiatry and Religion', *S.A. Med. J.* 41: 2.

O'Dea, T. F., (1966) *The Sociology of Religion,* New Jersey.

Oosthuizen, G. C., (1968) *Post-Christianity in Africa – A Theological and Anthropological Study,* London.

Park, G. K., (1963) 'Divination and its Social Contexts', *J. Roy. Anthrop. Inst.* 93: 2.

Pauw, B. A., (1960) *Religion in a Tswana Chiefdom,* Cape Town.

Peel, J. D. Y., (1968) *Aladura: A Religious Movement Among the Yoruba,* Oxford.

Randall, P., (1971) *Some Implications of Inequality* (Spro-Cas Occasional

Paper no. 4), Johannesburg.

Read, M., (1966) *Culture, Health and Disease,* London.

Riker, W. H., (1962) *The Theory of Political Coalitions,* New Haven.

Ringgren, H., (1961) 'The Problems of Syncretism', in S. S. Hartman, *Syncretism,* Stockholm.

Rivers, W. H. R., (1906) *The Todas,* London.

Ross, G., (1971) 'Neo-Tylorianism: A Reassessment', *Man* (N.S.) 6: 1.

Saunders, C. C., (1970) 'Tile and the Thembu Church: Politics and Independency on the Cape Eastern Frontier in the Late Nineteenth Century', *J. Af. Hist.* 11: 4.

Schlosser, K., (1949) *Propheten in Afrika,* Limbach; (1958) *Eingeborenenkirchen in Süd- und Süd-westafrika,* Kiel.

Schutte, A. G., (1972) 'Thapelo Ya Sephiri − A Study of Secret Prayer Groups in Soweto', *African Studies* 31: 4.

Scotch, N. A., (1970) 'Magic, Sorcery and Football among Urban Zulu: A Case of Reinterpretation under Acculturation', in J. Middleton, (ed.), *Black Africa,* Toronto.

Shepherd, R. H. W., (1942) *Lovedale South Africa,* Lovedale.

Shepperson, G., and T. Price, (1958) *Independent African,* Edinburgh.

Smith, E. W., (ed.), (1950) *African Ideas of God,* London.

Southall, A., (ed.), (1961) *Social Change in Modern Africa,* London.

Spiro, M. E., (1966) 'Religion: Problems of Definition and Explanation', in M. Banton, (ed.), *Anthropological Approaches to the Study of Religion* (ASA Monographs no. 3), London.

Spro-Cas (1971) *Education beyond Apartheid,* Johannesburg.

Sundkler, B. G. M., (1958) *The Concept of Christianity in the African Independent Churches,* University of Natal Inst. for Soc. Research (mim.), Durban; (1960) *The Christian Ministry in Africa,* London; (1961) *Bantu Prophets in South Africa* (2nd ed.) London. (First published 1948, London.)

Taylor, J. D., (1928) *Christianity and the Natives of South Africa,* Lovedale.

Taylor, J. V., (1961) *Christians of the Copper Belt,* London.

Tempels, P., (1959) *Bantu Philosophy,* Paris.

Thomas, N. E., (1970) 'Functions of Religious Institutions in the Adjustment of African Women to Life in a Rhodesian Township', in H. L. Watts, (ed.), *Focus on Cities,* University of Natal Inst. for Soc. Research, Durban.

Turner, H. W., (1967a) 'Typology of African Religious Movements', in *J. Religion in Af.* 1; (1967b) *African Independent Church* (2 vols.), Oxford.

Van Zyl, D., (1966) *Bantu Prophets or Christ's Evangels?* Christian Institute of Southern Africa, Johannesburg; (1968) *God's Earthenware Pots,* Christ. Inst. of S. A., Johannesburg.

Vandervort, E., (1968) *A Leopard Tamed,* London.

Vilakazi, A., (1962) *Zulu Transformations,* Pietermaritzburg.

Welbourn, F. B., (1961) *East African Rebels,* London.

Welbourn, F. B., and B. A. Ogot, (1966) *A Place to Feel at Home,* London.

Wells, J., (1908) *Stewart of Lovedale,* London.

West, M. E., (1971) *Divided Community – A Study of Social Groups and Racial Attitudes in a South African Town,* Cape Town;
(1972) 'Thérapie et Changement Sociale dans les Eglises Urbaines d'Afrique du Sud', *Social Compass* 19: 1;
(1974) 'Independence and Unity – Problems of Co-operation between African Independent Church Leaders in Soweto', *African Studies* 33: 2;
(1975a) 'African Churches in Soweto', in W. Pendleton and C. Kileff (eds.), *Urban Man in Southern Africa,* Gwelo;
(1975b) 'The Shades Come to Town: Ancestors and Urban Independent Churches', in M. G. Whisson and M. E. West (eds.), *Religion and Social Change in Southern Africa – Anthropological Essays in Honour of Monica Wilson,* Cape Town.

West, M. E., and D. van Zyl, (1970) *Breaking Heads,* Christ. Inst. of Southern Africa, Johannesburg.

Whisson, M. G., (1964) 'Some Functional Disorders Among the Luo', in A. Kiev (ed.), *Magic, Faith and Healing,* Glencoe.

Wilson, B. R., (1961) *Sects and Society,* London;
(1967) *Patterns of Sectarianism,* London.

Wilson, G. and M., (1945) *The Analysis of Social Change,* Cambridge.

Wilson, M., (1957) *Rituals of Kinship among the Nyakyusa,* London;
(1971) *Religion and the Transformation of Society,* Cambridge.

Wilson, M., and A. Mafeje, (1963) *Langa,* Cape Town.

Wilson, M., and L. Thompson (eds.), (1971) *The Oxford History of South Africa* (2 vols.), Oxford.

Wishlade, R., (1965) *Sectarianism in Southern Nyasaland,* London.

Young, R., (1902) *African Wastes Reclaimed,* London.

REPORTS

Report on the Native Churches Commission, Government Printer, Cape Town, UG 39–1925.

Interim and Final Reports of the Native Affairs Commission relative to Israelites at Bulhoek and Occurrences in May 1921, Government Printer, Cape Town, A 4–1921.

Index